Panzer Divisions of the Waffen-SS

ROLF MICHAELIS

Schiffer Publishing Ltd
4880 Lower Valley Road Atglen, Pennsylvania 19310

Book translation by Omicron Language Solutions, LLC

Library of Congress Control Number: 2013951220

Printed in China
ISBN: 978-0-7643-4477-0

This book was originally published in German under the title *Die Panzer-Divisionen Der Waffen-SS* by Michaelis Verlag, Berlin. ISBN: 978-3-930849-41-3

We are interested in hearing from authors with book ideas on related topics.

Published by Schiffer Publishing, Ltd.
4880 Lower Valley Road
Atglen, PA 19310
Phone: (610) 593-1777
FAX: (610) 593-2002
E-mail: Info@schifferbooks.com

Visit our web site at:
www.schifferbooks.com
Please write for a free catalog.
This book may be purchased from the publisher.
Try your bookstore first.

CONTENTS

FOREWORD

In the wake of the dramatic fixed-position battles of World War I, such as at Verdun, strategy was again changed in the European war theater, as military leaders realized that it was necessary to return to mobile warfare. The result was the first large-scale deployment of tanks in the history of warfare, launched on November 20, 1917, during the battle of Cambrai.

In 1935, the *Deutsches Heer* had three armored divisions; by 1939, it already had six *Panzer-Verbände*. These formations, motorized and with heavy firepower, were to be deployed to rapidly conquer large areas. They demonstrated this advantage and these tactics in the rapid *Blitzkrieg* in Poland and France.

In keeping with the elite, militant nature of the *Waffen-SS*, in 1942, the first *SS* formations were reinforced with *Panzer Regimenter*. Ultimately, of the first 12 *SS-Divisionen*, which were manned almost exclusively with *Reich* Germans and *Volksdeutsche*, seven were organized as *Panzer-Divsionen*. They were primarily deployed in such battlefields as Kharkov, Belgorod-Prokhorovka, Tarnopol, Cherkassy, Caen, Falaise, Arnhem, and Székesfehérvár [German name: Stuhlweißenburg].

The purpose of this work is to trace the history of these formations–but I will not explicitly delve into the horrors of war! The reader should keep in mind all the millions of personal fates, in which many people–soldiers and civilians–came to grief. In Europe alone millions lost their health and lives!

I thank everyone who selflessly supported me in creating this work–in particular I wish to thank Messrs. Fabisiak and Kwasny.

Berlin, October 2007
Rolf Michaelis

1

SS-PANZER DIVISION LEIBSTANDARTE SS ADOLF HITLER

The Leibstandarte SS Adolf Hitler

In March 1933, Adolf Hitler ordered the formation of a so-called *Stabswache* [staff guard], some 120 men strong, which in October of that year was renamed the Adolf Hitler *Standarte*, and was expanded to two *Bataillone*. A month later, the group was renamed the *Leibstandarte Adolf Hitler*. Just one year later three *Bataillon* had been established, and these were consolidated in Berlin into a *Regimentsverband* [regimental formation] in the following organization:

***Stab SS-Standarte (mot.)* [SS Regimental Staff] (motorized)**
***Nachrichten-Zug* [Signal and Communications platoon]**
***Musik-Zug* [Marching band]**
I. *SS-Sturmbann* [SS Battalion]
(*1.-3. Schützen-Sturm, 4. MG-Sturm*) [1st-3rd Assault Gun SS Companies, 4th Machine Gun Company]
II. *SS-Sturmbann*
(4.-7. Schützen-Sturm, 8. MG-Sturm
III. *SS-Sturmbann*
***(9.-11. Schützen-Sturm, 12. MG-Sturm*)**
1 *Minenwerfer-Sturm* (Mortar Company
1 *Kradschützen Sturm* [Motorcycle Company]

As of December 14, 1934, the *Standarte* and the formerly so-called *Politischen Bereitschaften* [political alert units] combined to form the *SS-Verfügungstruppe* [Special Disposal, or Special Purpose Troops]. On March 1, 1935, the *I.* and *II. Sturmbann* took part in the advance into the Saarland. They marched into Austria in March 1938, and into the Sudentland in October 1938. Former *SS-Mann* Herbert Kühl remembers the prewar period:

> After finishing my labor service in the summer of 1936, I was mustered in Schwerin for the Leibstandarte. The doctors found me qualified. There was some concern about my height, at just 177.5 cm [5' 9"]. One doctor dismissed this by saying: "We'll send him to the Panzerspäh [armored reconnaissance vehichle unit]." So I was one of the few candidates who was taken. At the same time, I also got conscription call-up of October 1, 1936.
>
> I proudly went home as a prospective Panzerspäh-man of the LAH [Leibstandarte Adolf Hitler]. On the morning of October 15, we were some 150 men in civilian clothes, including short pants, in the Kasernenhof [barracks yard] in Berlin-Lichterfelde. The first Führer [SS officer] we saw was an SS-Obersturmführer Kurt Meyer. He approached from the front, talking with one and another, and had some of us step forward. He also spoke to me: "Where are you from?" "From Güstrow in Mecklenburg, Obersturmführer," I answered. "Step forward!" He had selected 15 men and told us that we would join the 14. Panzerabwehr Kompanie as recruits. I raised my hand and pointed out that I had been mustered for the Panzerspähzug [armored reconaissance platoon]. He retorted: "Here, you only have a say if you're asked." My dream of being a Panzerspähmann was over. I became a Panzerabwehrschütze [anti-tank gunner]. Years later I was promoted a bit, to Panzerjäger.
>
> In September 1937 the 14. Kompanie, like the entire LAH, was encamped for the Nuremberg Reichsparteitag [Nazi Party day, or Nuremberg Rally]. Before the big parade of the SA and SS in front of the Führer, the Reichsführer [Heinrich Himmler] had his various formations perform a parade rehearsal before him and his staff. The LAH always came at the end. We had to march several miles beforehand, carrying our weapons raised to the left side of our chests as we had learned as soldiers. Other pathetic figures carried their weapons on a long strap over the right shoulder.
>
> For physical relief on longer marches, the command "Change arms–arms right!" was executed in four steps. The Kompanie leader gave the command. We approached the leaders' parade reviewing

> stand. The whole Regiment was carrying their arms on the right. For the companies ahead, we could hear the commands "Change arms–arms left!" With us, nothing happened. For the first and only time, we carried out a parade with our weapons on the right shoulder. We could not figure out what the Reichsführer's reaction was. His expression never changed, anyway. We marched a good stretch further. We were still carrying our weapons on the right. Our leaders halted us. We were given the command "Order arms!" and did not react. We had learned that wrong commands will not be executed. SS-Obersturmführer Kurt Meyer looked puzzled and realized his mistake. Then came: "Change arms–arms left," "Order arms," and "Parade rest!" Then he said, "Boys, I thank you!"
>
> On March 13, 1938, in the late afternoon, the LAH–placed under command of the 2. Panzer-Division–marched into Vienna as the population cheered. We kept having to halt. Then our vehicles were "stormed." Girls crowded into our jeeps. As a mixed unit, we went to Hietzing. Here our 14. Kompanie was quartered in a school. During the next few days, the neighbors supplied us with delicious apple strudel and, with all the many invitations, we got to know the specialties of Viennese cuisine. Our Sarge couldn't get rid of our pea soup, and ended up driving to the poorer parts of the city and handing it out there.
>
> For the March 15, 1938, Wehrmacht parade on the Vienna Ring, we cleaned up our dusty uniforms and brought our leather gear to a high polish after our 1,000-km trip. The 14. Kompanie cordoned off the Führer's reviewing stand. Infanterie, Artillerie, and Panzer units, as well as the Austrian Bundesheer [National Army] marched past, and at the end came the LAH in 12 Kompanien. An elderly but lively woman who had entertained us well was standing behind me, and said when she saw our Regiment, "Just look at those dashing guys."

In mid-March 1939, the regiment-strong *Leibstandarte* took part in the occupation of the remaining part of Czechoslovakia (later the *Protektorat Böhmen und Mähren* [Protectorate of Bohemia and Moravia]). Back in Berlin, the unit left its garrison on August 25, 1939, and was redeployed to Upper Silesia, in the sector of the *XIII. Armee-Korps*. Placed under command of the *17. Division*, the Regiment, moving from the area northwest of Kreuzburg, crossed the border river Prosna at Golja, and on September 1, 1939, pushed forward northwards through Boleslaw to Wieruszow. Turing eastwards, the units crossed the Warta and reached Pabianice on September 7, 1939. After heavy street fighting, the *Leibstandarte* reached the Nadarzyn region (about 20 km southwest of Warsaw) on September 9, 1939, and here was placed under command of the *4. Panzer-Division* in the *XVI. Armee-Korps.*

There was more heavy fighting near Oltarzew (about 15 km west of Warsaw), as Polish units tried to break through to the east. With the *4. Panzer Division*, the *Leibstandarte* moved to the Bzura river sector, where it was able to prevent the Polish units from crossing the river to the east. When the Battle of the Bzura ended on September 18, 1939, the *Standarte* was sent to attack the fortress of Modlin in the nearby southern forests. On September 21, 1939, it was placed under command of the *XV. Armee-Korps.*

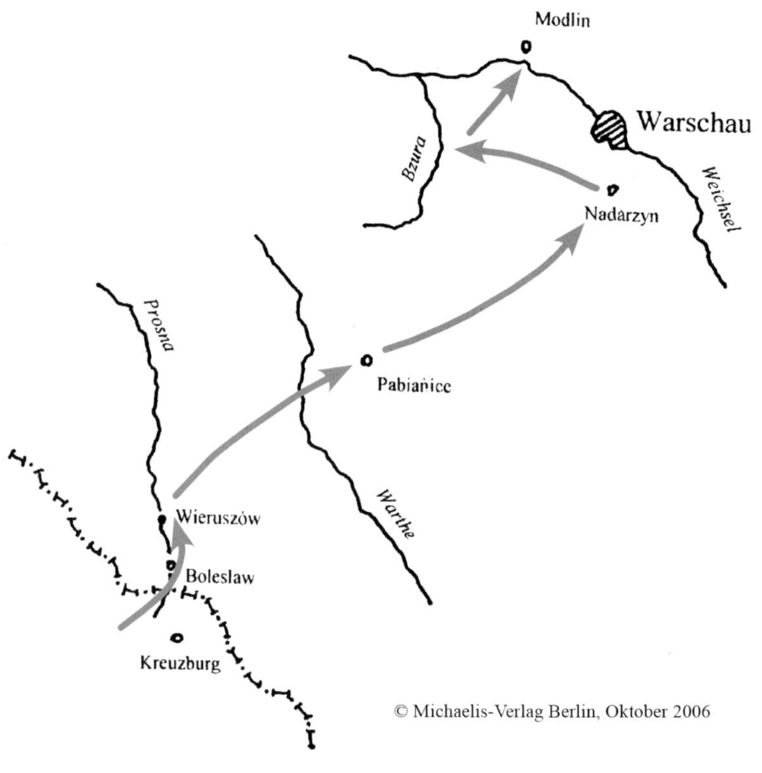

Members of the Leibstandarte SS Adolf Hitler at the Nuremberg Rally.

Leibstandarte barracks in Berlin-Lichterfelde.

Sepp Dietrich at the celebrations for the fourth anniversary of the formation of the *Leibstandarte-SS Adolf Hilter.*

From left to right: *SS-Obergruppenführer* [SS Lieutenant General] Dietrich, Dr. Ley, Adolf Hitler, *Reichsführer-SS* Himmler.

The Leibstandarte Führer-Schutz-Kommando [Führer Protection Detail].

Fred Zura (center) with a comrade on the Lüneburger Heide [Lüneburg Heath].

Leibstandarte elements marched into Austria in March 1938, together with a *Heer Panze*r unit.

The units were stationed in the siege ring around Modlin from September 22 to 27, 1939. Even before the Polish campaign ended in late September 1939, it was transferred to the *Protektorat Böhmen und Mähren*. The *Standarte* had to report a total of 108 killed in action and 292 wounded. On November 11, 1939, it started its march to the Koblenz area, where it was placed under the command of the *XIX. Armee-Korps*. Here, in December 1939, the *Standarte* was reinforced by the *IV./SS-Artillery Standarte* (three batteries).

In February 1940, the formation was redeployed to the *VI. Armee-Korps* in the Rheine region, about 250 km away. Placed under command of the *227. Infanterie-Division*, the *Leibstandarte* reported for service in the attack on the Netherlands on May 10, 1940, in the following order:

***Standardenstab* with**
- ***Nachrichten-Zug***
- ***Musik-Zug***
- ***Panzerspäh***
- ***Pionier-Zug* [Engineer platoon]**[1]
- ***Kradmelde-Zug* [Motorcycle messenger platoon]**

I. *Sturmbann (1.-5. Kompanie)*
II. *Sturmbann (6.-10. Kompanie)*
III. *Sturmbann (11.-15. Kompanie)*
12. (*Infanteriegeschütz*) [Infantry gun] *Kompanie*
13. (*Panzerabwehr*) (Anti-tank) *Kompanie*
14. (*Kradschützen*) *Kompanie*
15. (*schwere Infanteriegeschütz*) (Heavy Infantry gun) *Kompanie*[2]

Moving by way of Oldenzaal, some elements reached Zwolle on the same day, while other elements were advancing through Hengerlo to Zutphen, where they crossed the IJssel. From there, they marched by way of s'-Hertogenbosch to Geertruidenberg, where, on May 13, 1940 they were placed under command of the *9. Panzer-Division*. The next day, the units crossed the Meuse river to Rotterdam and pushed into the area of Delft.

After the Dutch capitulation, the *Standarte* was redeployed through Belgium to the area of Valenciennes. On May 24, 1940, they were placed under the command of the 1. *Panzer-Division*, which was stationed in front of Dunkirk, and fierce battles ensued at Watten (about 8 km southwest of Dunkirk). Just three days later, the *Regiment* was placed under command

1 This *Zug* was put under its command in March 1940.
2 This *Kompanie* was put under its command in May 1940.

of the *20. Infanterie-Division (mot.)*, which was positioned on its right. There was heavy fighting at Wormhoudt (about 5 km southeast of Dunkirk). It was there, near Esquelbecq on May 28, 1940, that members of the *7./ Leibstandarte SS Adolf Hitler* herded about 80 British prisoners of war into a barn and then threw in hand grenades. Even after the SS members shot at them with handguns at least 15 soldiers survived, and were taken into custody by other German units.

Finally the *Standarte* was pulled out of the area, and by June 4, 1940, was assembled in the area of Cambrai, about 40 km distant. Under the command of the *XXXXIV. Armee-Korps*, the men crossed the Aisne river near Soissons on June 9, 1940, and, moving by way of Villers Cotterets, reached the Marne near Chateau Thierry (about 22 km south of Soissons) on June 14, 1940.

Again under the command of the *9. Panzer-Division*, the *Standarte* marched over 200 kilometers via Montmirail to Nevers, and crossed the Loire there between June 17-19, 1940, in order to form a bridgehead over the Allier river, about 50 km further south at Moulins. On June 21, 1940, the *Leibstandarte* captured Clermont-Ferrand, and was then ordered to move towards St. Etienne, which they were able to take four days later after minor skirmishes.

Under the ceasefire agreement, the *Standarte* moved out of the area on July 4, 1940. Originally ordered to Paris for the big parade, it was, however, transferred to Metz at the end of the month. In the preceding battles, the *Leibstandarte* had lost 111 men killed in action and 390 wounded.

Only cars and trucks could be successfully attacked using the 3.7 cm Pak [Panzerabwehrkanone: anti-tank gun] during the Western campaign.

The *Leibstandarte* route in the Western campaign

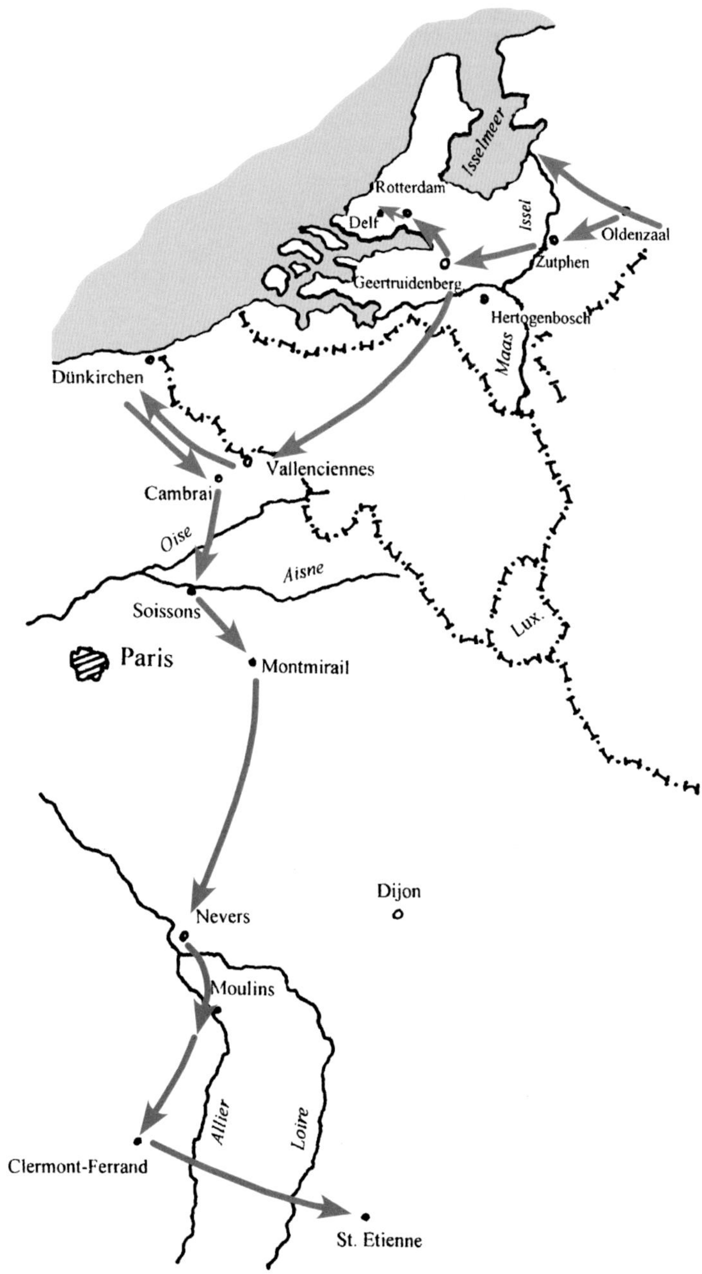

The verstärkt Leibstandarte SS Adolf Hitler

While it was in Metz, the *Leibstandarte SS Adolf Hitler* was ordered by the *SS-FHA* [*Führungshauptamt*: Main Operational Office] on August 13, 1940, to expand to brigade strength as a field formation. To achieve this, the following units were newly formed:

> ***1 SS-Artillerie Regiment***[3]
> ***1 SS-Pionier-Bataillon (mot.)***
> ***1 SS-Aufklärungs-Abteilung* [Reconnaissance battalion]**
> **1 *gemischte SS-Nachrichten-Kompanie* [combined Signal and Communications Company]**
> **IV. *SS-Bataillon*[4] *(17.-20. Kompanie)***

This brought the formation, which was placed under the command of the *XI. Armee-Korps* and designated the ***verstärkt*** [reinforced] ***Leibstandarte SS Adolf Hitler***, up to a strength of about 6,500 men.

In addition to integrating the replacements, and to training as the larger military formation it had now become, the *Leibstandarte* also periodically carried out training exercises for the landings planned as part of Operation *Seelöwe* [Operation Sea Lion]. After this operation was initially postponed and the *Leibstandarte* had to conduct its training under consideration of a deployment to the Balkans, the exercises were moved to the 200-meter-high Mosel mountains.

In mid-January 1941, the formation was transferred to Romania. Here, camouflaged as a so-called *Lehrtruppe* [instruction unit], the *verstärkt Leibstandarte SS Adolf Hitler* was billeted in Câmpulung (about 120 km northwest of Bucharest) on March 6, 1941. The units were redeployed to Bulgaria on March 21, 1941. After a march of over 400 km, the *Brigade* reached the Kyustendil area by April 5, 1941 (about 75 km southwest of Sofia).

Without any major battles, the *verstärkt Leibstandarte SS Adolf Hitler* marched into the *XXXX. Armee-Korps (mot.)* sector, through Skopje and Prilep to Monastir. They encountered heavy fighting with Yugoslav troops there on April 8-9, 1941. The offensive against Greece was launched one day later, on April 10, 1941. The *Brigade* crossed the Klisura Pass to reach Kastoria (about 60 km south of Monastir) on April 14-15, 1941, sometimes facing fierce fighting in the difficult mountain terrain.

3 Along with the existing *Abteilung*, there was a *Regimentsstab* and another *Abteilung*.
4 This *Bataillon* served as *Wach-Bataillon* in Berlin.

On April 21, 1941, after marching some 100 km, the units reached the area of Ioannina and "asked for honorable capitulation" from the Greek Epirus Army. From there, the *Brigade* marched another 150 km to Mesolongion, facing hardly any more hostilities. While the Greek units partially demobilized themselves, the British forces, still defending the Isthmus of Corinth on the Peloponnese peninsula in the east, attempted to make it possible for their troops to embark.

On April 26, 1941, the *Leibstandarte SS Adolf Hitler SS-Aufklärungs-Abteilung* was the first military unit to leave the Nafpaktos area, crossing over the Gulf of Patras; it then cleared the region to the east and southwest. Together with the *III. Batallion*, the *SS-Aufklärungs-Abteilung* pushed forward through Pyrgos-Tripoli and reached Kalamata on April 29, 1941.

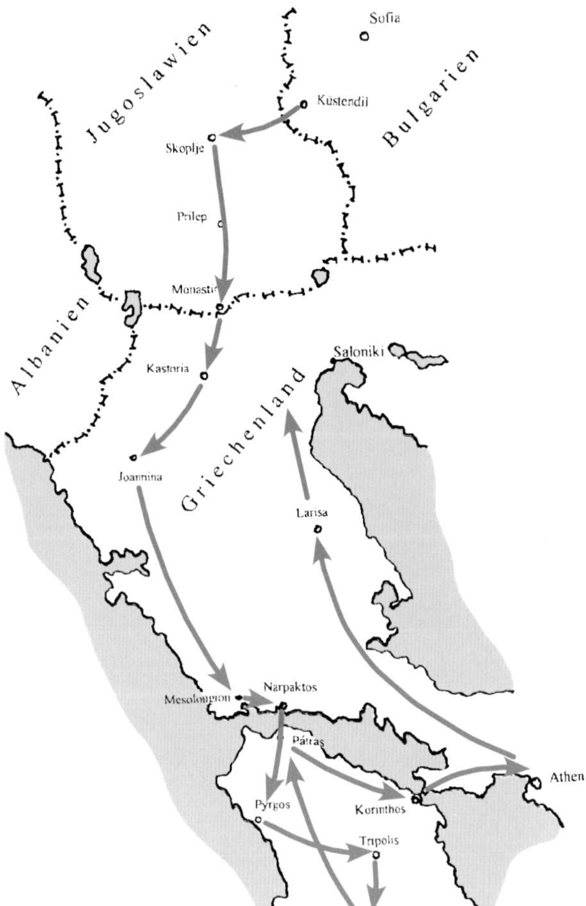

Josef "Sepp" Dietrich commanded the *Leibstandarte SS Adolf Hitler* from April 1934. In July 1943, he was appointed the commanding *General* of the *I. SS-Panzer-Korps LSSAH*. Made leader of the *5. Panzer-Armee* in August 1944, in September 1944 he was given command of the *6. (SS-) Panzer-Armee*.

Sepp Dietrich in Greece in 1941.

After the surrender of Greece, the units marched through Patras-Corinthos-Athens-Larissa to northern Greece; on May 17, 1941, they left the country. The troops had relatively few losses during the Balkans campaign. By the end of the month, they had secured Serbia and Croatia. Redeployed to Vienna, the *verstärkt Leibstandarte SS Adolf Hitler* was concentrated in Gaya (about 100 km northeast of Vienna); there the formation was refitted and reorganized, and brought to almost *Division* strength.

A new *IV. Batallion* was formed, and the former *IV. (Wach-) Bataillon* was renamed the *V. Batallion* in Berlin. The combined *Nachrichten-Kompanie* was expanded into a *Nachrichten-Abteilung* and a *Pionier-Bataillon*, a *Flak-Abteilung*, and some heavy units were newly organized. With a strength of 10,796 men the formation, already being referred to as a *Division*, was organized as follows:

Staff Leibststandarte SS Adolf Hitler
I.-IV. Batallion (1.-20. Kompanie)
V. ***Battalion (Wach-Bataillon*** **in Berlin)**
Abteilung Schönberger
  1. (Sturmgeschütz) Batterie **[Assault gun battery]**
  2. **(4.7 cm** ***Pak) Kompanie schweres Bataillon***
  1. (leichte Infanteriegeschütz) **[Infantry gun]** ***Kompanie***[5]
  2. (schwere Infanteriegeschütz) Kompanie [6]
  3. (5 **cm Pak*****) Kompanie***[7]
SS-Aufklärungs-Abteilung
  1. /2. Kradschützen-Kompanie
  3. Panzer-Spähwagen-Kompanie
  4. schwere Kompanie
SS-Artillerie-Regiment with:
  I. ***(leichte) Abteilung (1.-3. Batterie)***
  II. ***(schwere) Abteilung***
    4.-5. Batterie (schwere FH)
    6.-7. Batterie (**8.8 cm*****)***
    8. Batterie (**10 cm** ***Kanonen)***
SS-Flak-Abteilung[8]
  1. ***/2. Batterie (*****3.7 cm*****)***
  3. ***Batterie (*****2 cm*****)***
SS-Pionier-Bataillon (**3** ***Kompanien)***
SS-Nachrichten-Abteilung
SS-Nachschubtruppen **[SS-Supply troops]**[9]

5 Former *13. Kompanie.* **6** Former *16. Kompanie.* **7** Former *14. Kompanie.*
8 Formation of the *lt SS-FHA* on May 30, 1941, in Brno [German: Brünn]. **9** Formed on June 20, 1941

Although they had been sufficiently reinforced for a renewed deployment, the troop units were surprised by the sudden attack against the Soviet Union; on June 27, 1941, they began marching, by way of Olomouc-Ratibor-Bytom-Annopol (about 70 km southwest of Lublin), to Lutsk (about 125 km northeast of Lviv). There, the *Leibstandarte* was put at the disposal of *Panzergruppe 1* on July 1, 1941.

The very next day came the order to go into action; the *Leibstandarte* was to reach Rivne, about 70 km away, by way of Klevan, and there relieve thc *III. Armee-Korps (mot.)*, which was engaged in heavy fighting. On July 8, 1941, the formation was deployed at Sokolow-Miropol, on the northern flank of the *Korps*, which was pushing forward to Zhitomir.

The *Leibstandarte* had hardly experienced any heavy fighting in the previous action, and was primarily deployed to pursue the fleeing enemy forces; they already had to witness the true face of war in the first days of Operation *Barbarossa*. In two days of fighting, the units lost more soldiers than in all the previous campaigns combined.

Following the *III. Armee-Korps (mot.)*, they encountered heavy fighting in the area of Belgorodka during July 17-24, 1941. On July 31, 1941, placed under command of the *XXXXVIII. Armee-Korps (mot.)*, the *Leibstandarte* moved south to the Novo Arkhangelsk region, and there closed off the Uman pocket. By mid-August 1941, the units had reached the region east of Voznesensk, and on August 19, 1941, took Kherson, on the Dnieper river. The men had fought their way over a total of 900 km in just seven weeks.

After the battle for Kherson, the *Leibstandarte* got a few days rest in the area of Bobrinetz to overhaul their weapons and equipment, and were sent personnel replacements from Germany. On September 8, 1941, the units crossed the Dnieper, and were initially used to mop up enemy troops on the southern bank of the Dnieper, down to the Black Sea. Pushing on through the Nogai steppe, in late September 1941, the *Leibstandarte* reported for duty as part of the *LIV. Armee-Korps (mot.)* for the breakthrough at Perekop.

During the march on Melitiopol which followed–under command of the *III. Armee-Korps (mot.)*–there was very heavy fighting from September 30 to October 3, 1941; the march continued to Mariupol, which they occupied on October 8, 1941, essentially without a struggle. The units then reached the mostly evacuated villages of the Black Sea Germans.

Almost without fighting, the *Leibstandarte* pursued the enemy troops, breaking away in a headlong fashion, to Tanganrog, which was taken on October 17, 1941, after renewed heavy fighting. Due to supply problems the units initially remained in this area, where they fought off repeated attacks by the Red Army.

On the advance march on Rostov, on the Don: passing a Soviet Stalinez tractor towing a 15.2 cm *Haubitze* and Soviet prisoners of war.

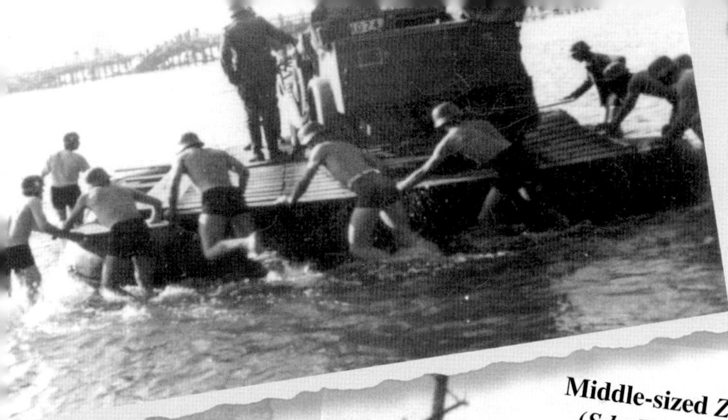

Improvised river crossing in summer 1941.

Middle-sized *Zugkraftwagen* [prime mover] 5 t (*Sdr. Kfz.* 6/2) [*Sonderkraftfahrzeug*: Special purpose vehicle] with 3.7 *Flak* 36.

Captured Soviet *Kampfwagen* BA 10.

SS-Unterscharführer Zumpe.

Ewald Gerhards in the sidecar of his BMW R-12.

Sturmgeschütz III Ausf. B (*Sdr. Kfz.* 142/1) with 7.5 cm *Sturmkanone* 40 (L/24).

Willi Rogmann with *Nahkampfspange* [Close Combat Clasp] in gold on 12/14/44; *Deutsches Kreuz* [German Cross] in gold on 2/8/45.

The Mius position at Ssambek.

On November 17, 1941, in temperatures of -30°C, the *Leibstandarte* moved towards Rostov, occupied the city by November 21, 1941, and formed a bridgehead across the Don. The enemy counterattacks were so violent that the *III. Armee-Korps (mot.)*, against Hilter's orders, again gave up Rostov, and allowed the units to move into a more permanent winter position across the Mius river.

In early December 1941, the *Leibstandarte* moved to positions north of Tanganrog, near Ssambek, and was supposed to be reinforced by the *1. SS-Infanterie-Brigade* because of the heavy losses it had suffered in the previous fighting, and due to countless cases of frostbite. Because of strong attacks against the middle sector, it was impossible to supply the *1. SS-Infanterie-Brigade* from *the 2. Armee* sector.[10]

The *Leibstandarte* remained in its winter quarters until May 24, 1942; it was then transferred to guard the coast in the Mariupol region on the Sea of Azov. Former *SS-Sturmmann* (storm trooper) Willi Rogmann remembers:

> When the sun was shining and it seemed like summer, which was often in this continental climate, we went swimming in the sea and sunbathed a lot. Our skin had become completely pale through the winter, when we never got to take off our clothes. Unfortunately, we were in an area where there were bluffs on the coast, and there were only a few places where you could swim. Despite that we took advantage of this often, and we were soon brown as a Negro. We were very indulgently treated by our Führer and Unterführer at this time; probably they had orders for this from higher up.

Redeployment to the *15. Armee* in France began on July 2, 1942.

10 See section: *18. SS-Freiw-Panzer-Grenadier Division Horst Wessel.*

SS-Division (mot.) Leibstandarte SS Adolf Hitler

Already on February 21, 1942, Adolf Hitler had ordered that the formation be reorganized as a *Division* on the Sennelager troop training grounds. Because of the situation on the front, however, the remainder of the *Leibstandarte* was only able to pull out of the Mius position in May 1942; in July 1941, it was withdrawn from the Mariupol sector. It was not sent to the Sennelager training grounds in any case–only the *VI.* and *VII. Bataillion* were deployed there–but rather to France, because of Hitler's concern about an invasion. The *V.* (former) *Wach-Bataillon* was eventually given the number *VII. Batallion.*

After it was supplied with the *Panzer-Abteilung*, which was formed with three *schwere Panzer-Kompanien* starting on February 1, 1942, on the Wildflecken troop training, as well as the *leichte Panzer-Abteilung*, which followed in October 1942, the formation was organized as follows:

DIVISIONSSTAB
SS-Infanterie-Regiment 1
  I.-III. Bataillon
SS-Infanterie-Regiment 2
  I.-III. Bataillon
SS-Aufklärungs-Abteilung
SS-Artillerie-Regiment
  2 Abteilungen (leichte Feldhaubitzen* 10.5 cm*)
  1 *Abteilung (schwere Feldhaubitzen* 15 cm*)* [11]
SS-Panzerjäger-Abteilung
  3. Kompanien
SS-Panzer-Regiment
  I. Abteilung (1.-4.)
  II. Abteilung (5.-7.)
SS-Sturmgeschütz-Abteilung
SS-Flak-Abteilung
SS-Pionier-Bataillon
***SS-Nachschubdienste* [Supply Service]**
***SS-Verwaltungsdienste* [Administration Service]**
***SS-Sanitäts-Abteilung* [Medical Detachment]**
***SS-Veterinär-Kompanie* [Veterinary Company]**
SS-Nachrichten-Abteilung

11 Deployed with orders on March 22, 1940; originally no *schwere Abteilung* was provided.

After a field parade on July 29, 1942, before *Generalfeldmarschall* von Rundstedt on the Champs-Elysees in Paris, the *Leibstandarte* marched into their cantonment area at Evreux-Melun-Fontainebleau, south of the Seine river. In early November 1942, the troops moved to the Line of Demarcation with as-yet unoccupied southern France. *SS-Division (mot.) Leibstandarte SS Adolf Hitler* marched into the Toulon region, possibly to carry out a surprise attack in order to occupy the city and harbor, where most of the French Mediterranean fleet was located. Even as this operation was being carried out on November 27, 1942, most of the ships succeeded in scuttling themselves. As a result, the French Army of the Armistice was disarmed.

The SS-Panzergrenadier-Division Leibstandarte SS Adolf Hitler

On November 24, 1942, the formation was renamed the *SS-Panzer-Grenadier-Division Leibstandarte SS Adolf Hitler*. It was not reorganized–already formed with a *Pazer-Regiment* instead of a *Panzer-Abteilung*, the *Division* already basically had the strength of a *Panzer-Division*. Unlike the organization of the *Heer*, the two *Infanterie-Regimenter*, renamed *SS-Panzergrenadier-Regimenter 1* and *2*, had three instead of two *Bataillone*, as usual in the *Waffen-SS*.

After the units still had been deployed for barely three weeks to guard the Mediterranean coast, they were transferred back to northern France.

On December 31, 1942, the *Divisionskommando* reported their strength:

Officers	Other Ranks	Total
678	20,166	20,844
3.3%	96.7%	100%

With these reinforcements, the formation reached its *Soll-Stärke* [authorized strength], and was again fully operational after six months of rest and refitting in France. As a result of the tragedy of Stalingrad it was sent back to the Eastern Front, starting on January 11, 1943. Travelling through Amiens-Antwerp-Hamburg-Kaliningrad-Riga-Minsk-Vitebsk-Bobruisk, the units reached the area of Kharkov on January 22, 1943. They were concentrated

The *Leibstandarte* paraded before *Generalfeldmarschall* Runstedt on the Champs-Elysees on July 29, 1942, and then marched into its cantonment area at Evreux-Melun-Fontainebleau.

first at Chuguyev, on the Donets river, and were put at the disposal of the *OKH.*

On February 3, 1943, SS-*Panzergrenadier Division Leibstandarte SS Adolf Hitler* was cleared for action in the sector of the *SS-Panzer-Korps* of *Armee-Abteilung Lanz (Heeresgruppe Don)* [Army Group Don], and was to incorporate the remnants of the *298. Infantrie-Division*, which was retreating from the east, on the Donets.

In opposition to what was its original mission, which was to take the offensive in cooperation with the other *Divisionen* of the *SS-Panzer-Korps*, *SS-Panzergrenadier-Division Leibstandarte SS Adolf Hitler* was immediately pushed back, and was initially engaged in defensive fighting in the area southeast of Kharkov between Chuhuiv and Samostje Sidki. Within days, the units had to retreat to a position along the Donets, from south of Merefa near Samostje Sidki towards Ochotschaje/Okhoche, and from there westwards towards Krasnograd.

After the *SS-Panzer-Korps* commanding *General, SS-Obergruppenführer* Hausser, gave up Kharkov against Hitler's orders on February 14, 1943, the *Leibstandarte* was engaged, under the command of *Armee-Abteilung Kempf*, in fierce defensive battles in the region of Krasnograd until the end of February 1943.

On February 28, 1943, the *Division* was sent to support *SS-Panzergrenadier-Division Totenkopf*, which was launching an attack in the *4. Panzer-Armee* sector for a counter-stroke to the east. As part of German operations in the area around Kharkov, on March 3rd, *SS-Panzergrenadier Division Leibstandarte SS Adolf Hitler* was again attached to the *SS-Panzer-Korps* (*4. Panzer-Armee*) to lead a unified attack.

Starting on March 4, 1943, the *Division* (command post: Krasnograd) pushed forward, now in a northerly direction to Valki. From here, the units first arrived in the area east of Olshany on March 9, 1943, and finally moved northwest of Kharkov. Two days later, the units had already reached the area north of Kharkov, and turned southwards. In the northeast part of the city, which they first reached, *SS-Panzergrenadier Division Leibstandarte SS Adolf Hitler* encountered heavy and difficult street fighting. On March 14, 1943, Kharkov was recaptured. The *Leibstandarte* temporarily took over the function of *Standortkommandantur* [garrison headquarters] in the city.

Already on March 16, 1943, the *Division* moved northwards to Belgorod, and was able to reach the Donets. By the end of March 1943, the formation was in the Kharkov area for refitting. Its losses in the previous fighting–167 Führer and 4,373 other ranks killed in action, wounded, or reported missing–

were compensated for by around 4,000 replacements by the end of June 1943; these included many *Volksdeutsche* from southeastern Europe! *Luftwaffe* troops–mostly members of the *Heimatflak* [Homeland anti-aircraft units]–were also integrated into the *Division* as the so-called *Hermann-Göring Spende* [Herman Göring's contributions]. Former *SS-Rottenführer* [SS Corporal] Willi Rogmann remembers:

> When I returned to the outfit after my leave, it was now at rest in Kharkov. We had hard training service, and the many *Luftwaffenkameraden* [comrades], who had meanwhile been assigned to us, had to be integrated with us.

By the end of June 1943, the formation moved from the refitting area at Kharkov to west of Olschany. In the sector of the *Großverband* [large task force–redesignated as the *II. SS-Panzer-Korps* on July 1, 1943–*SS-Panzer Grenadier Division Leibstandarte SS Adolf Hitler* moved into starting positions east of Tomarovka (about 25 km northwest of Belgorod) for the German summer offensive In the *Kursker Bogen* [the Kursk salient or bulge].

On June 5, 1943, the German summer offensive began with Operation *Zitadelle* [Operation Citadel]; the Red Army had prepared itself well to counter it. The German attacks got stalled suffering heavy losses, not only in the bottomless mud on the ground due to the rain, but also even on the first day due to the in-depth Soviet defenses!

SS-Panzer Grenadier Division Leibstandarte SS Adolf Hitler was deployed on the left flank of the *II. SS-Panzer-Korps*; on the next day the *Leibstandarte*, in fierce fighting with enemy tank units, was able to reach the 20 km distant area of Lutschki. On July 9, 1943, the *Division* moved to the northwest.

The Red Army launched repeated tank counterattacks from the wooded area about 10 km southwest of Prokhorovka against the *Leibstandarte* troops, who were pushing forward from the west to Prokhorovka. On July 12, 1943, some 150 Soviet tanks and self-propelled guns succeeded in overrunning the *Division* position. In well-maneuvered action, *SS-Panzer Regiment LSSAH* was able to destroy some 90 of them, and the *Grenadiere* another 30.

After it became clear that the objectives could not be realized in the conditions on the battlefront, Hitler called off Operation *Zitadelle* on July 13, 1943; for this operation, he ordered Operation *Roland* to be launched in the local area. This operation was to hold the lines that German units had reached, and shatter the enemy forces stationed to the west. Three days

later, the order came that *SS-Panzergrenadier Division Leibstandarte SS Adolf Hitler*, among others, was to be pulled out of the front and be redeployed to the area of Oboyan for Operation *Roland*. The *SS-Panzergrenadier Regiment 2 LSSAH* initially remained in its position, and was briefly placed under the command of *SS-Panzer Grenadier Division Totenkopf*.[12]

On July 17, 1943, the Red Army went on the offensive against the *6. Armee* on the Mius, and against the *1. Panzer-Armee* on the middle Donets, and further preparations for Operation *Roland* were halted. The forces provided–including the again complete *SS-Panzergrenadier Division Leibstandarte SS Adolf Hitler*–redeployed to the region west of Belgorod, and finally marched through Kharhov to the area of Stalino, 400 km distant. During Operation *Zitadelle*, the *Division* had lost 474 killed in action and some 1,700 wounded in 11 days.

12 The *4. Panzer-Armee* was, at this time, about 40 km to the south; the *9. Armee* had only advanced about 20 km in the north. They were now more than 120 km apart from each other! It was no longer possible to meet in Kursk – instead, the *4. Panzer-Armee* would have had to make a thrust towards the *9. Armee* beyond Kursk, since the time and the Soviet forces made success appear very questionable.

On March 14, 1943, the *Leibstandarte* re-occupied Kharkov.

Panzer IV Ausf. F with *Ostkette* [tank treads for the East] (Sdr. Kfz. 161).

Panzer IV Ausf. F; note the Ostkette [tank treads for the East] (Sdr. Kfz. 161).

The *Panzer III*, with 5 cm *KwK 39 L/60* (weight 23 tons and 5 man crew), was part of the standard equipment of the *SS-Panzergrenadier Divisionen* until the summer of 1943.

Walter Malchow, *Deutsches Kreuz* in gold, on 9/2/43

Walter Schüle

Panzer-Division members were awarded *Panzerkampfabzeichen* [Panzer Combat Badges] in silver for 3, 25, 50, 75, and 100 days active duty; members of other units were awarded the badges in bronze.

The *Sicherungsraum* of the *SS-Panzergrenadier Division LSSAH* in Italy

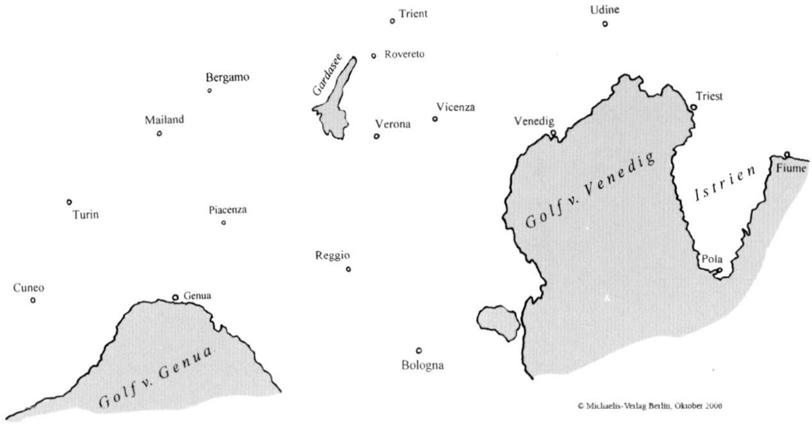

After it was deployed to recapture the so-called Mius Line, the formation was then transferred to Italy, starting on July 29, 1943. Four days earlier, Benito Mussolini had been arrested by the Italian king. On August 3, 1943, the first transports arrived at Innsbruck-Wörgl and Rosenheim, and drove in motorized march over the Brenner Pass to the Trento-Rovereto-Lake Garda region. The caterpillar-tracked vehicles were sent to Bologna. The formation's first cantonment was in the area between Verona-Reggio-Piacenza-Bergamo.

As the so-called *Alarich-Verband* [Alaric's unit], the *Division*, beginning on September 8, 1943, took part in disarming Italian troops–60,000 men in Turin alone. The Italians were sent to the Brenner, where *Landesschützen* [territorial or regional defense] units in particular ran the transport, and brought them to Germany for internment. The *Sicherungsraum* [secured area] was extended westwards to the French border, especially by the SS-*Panzergrenadier Regiment 2 LSSAH*. It was during these operations that the villages of Bove and Castellar, in the Cuneo region (about 70 km south of Turin), were burnt down on September 19, 1943, and parts of the population shot. To the east, the *Sicherungsraum* area extended to Udine. Just four days earlier, in Meina, on Lake Maggiore, members of an *SS-Panzer-Grenadier Regiment 2 Kompanie* arrested about twenty Jews who had escaped from Greece and Italy and shot them on the orders of the *Batallion* leader, *SS-Hauptsturmführer* Röhwer. The trial of the *SS* members at the Osnabrück *Schwurgericht* ended on July 5, 1968, with the conviction of all the defendants.[13]

13 In 1968, the Italian authorities filed charges at the *Staatsanwaltschaft* [District Attorney] in Stuttgart. On December 11, 1968, the *I. Große Strafkammer* [Upper Criminal Court] decided to end the prosecution of the accused, since their guilt could not be proven.

On September 19, 1943, the *OKW* ordered *Heeresgruppe B* to put down the uprising in Istria. Under the *Generalkommando SS-Panzer-Korps*, in addition to a number of *Heer* units, the reinforced *SS-Panzergrenadier Regiment 1* was deployed there on September 26, 1943. By September 29th, the majority of the partisans who had been trapped in the area were able to escape to the north and northwest.

After this operation, which ended on October 12, 1943, another *Säuberungs* Operation [mopping up operation] was launched northeast of Fiume on October 16, 1943. Again under *Generalkommando II. SS-Panzer-Korps, SS-Panzergrenadier Regiment 1* was redeployed for this operation. As the *Division* was concentrated at Vienna for transportation to the heavily embattled Eastern Front, the *Regiment*, which was being used for *Bandenbekämpfung* [fighting banditry], was pulled out of this action on October 29, 1943. Wilhelm Rogmann remembers the time in Italy:

> On July 29, 1943, to our total surprise, we were put on the train and transported from Russia to an unknown destination (as always). Already during the train trip, we were reinforced with convalescents, and all sorts of new replacements. At this time it was again young German volunteers ... On August 3, 1943, we were taken off the train just before reaching Innsbruck, and continued on in a *mot-Marsch* [motorized march]. Now it was clear that we were on the way to Italy. Our *Bataillon's* journey ended in Roveretto, a lovely town south of South Tyrol. Our Kompanie was quartered in a school. We *Unterführer* had a classroom for ourselves. Then we moved to Turin, where there were about 60,000 Italian soldiers. Our weak *Bataillon* occupied the railway station and the Fiat plant. We experienced a lot here–including partisans–but things kept within limits. Beginning in November 1943, our great time in Italy ended: our worst time, with the heaviest losses, began in Russia.

The 1. SS-Panzer-Division Leibstandarte SS-Adolf Hitler

The formation was given the new name of *1. SS-Panzer-Division* on October 22, 1943, and, for this purpose, the *VII. (Wach-) Bataillon* from Berlin, among others, was attached to the *Division*. Otherwise, the formation's existing organization remained unchanged. The two *Panzergrenadier-Regimenter* were numbered 1 and 2 in the serial numbering of *Waffen-SS* military units.

The units of troops were redeployed to the 4. *Panzer-Armee* sector near Kiev by November 3, 1943. Placed under command of the *XXXXVIII. Panzer-Korps*, on November 10, 1943, the *SS-Panzer-Division Leibstandarte SS Adolf Hitler* launched a counterattack northwards, from the region southwest of Fastiv (about 65 km southwest of Kiev). In heavy fighting, the German forces made a successful strike against the enemy tank units, which had pushed forward from the Kiev area, stabilizing the precarious front situation.

Although the Germans were still able to annihilate some of the Soviet formations during the next few weeks, on Christmas 1943, the Red Army succeeded in breaking through the German lines on a broad front in the direction of Zhitomir. The *1. SS-Panzer-Division*, thus pushed back towards Berdichev (about 45 km south of Zhitomir), on December 31, 1943, reported the following strength:

Officers	Unterführer	Enlisted Men	Total
481	3,807	16,299	20,587
2.3%	18.5%	79.2%	100%

Following heavy fighting in the sector of the nearly shattered *4. Panzer-Armee* south of Berdichev, the German forces were encircled in the Cherkassy pocket by the end of January 1944; the formation was then ordered to move to the *III. Panzer-Korps* behind the east flank of the *1. Panzer-Armee* in the area north of Uman. Up until February 15, 1944, the German relief forces tried to fight their way through to the encircled troops to the northeast. Deterred by the mud and Soviet anti-aircraft fire, the operation was unsuccessful, however.[14]

By the end of February 1944, the units had moved into positions at Tikich, and from there formed up on February 16, 1944, at Lysyanka, for the drive to relieve the trapped units. Under intense Soviet artillery and tank fire, as well as continuing air strikes, about 34,000 men reached the German positions on February 17, 1944.

After this mission, the *1. SS-Panzer-Division* was sent back to the *XXXXVIII. Panzer-Korps* (*4. Panzer-Armee*), which was concentrated at Tarnopol, to prevent an envelopment of the *Armee's* western flank. Making heavy attacks, by mid-March 1944, the German forces were able to stabilize the situation on the *4. Panzer-Armee* right flank in the 100 km-wide area between Tarnopol and Proskurov [Khmelnytskyi].

14 See Chapter: 5 *SS-Panzer-Division Wiking*.

After the Red Army again broke through at the boundary between the *4.* and *1. Panzer-Armee* on March 20, 1944, and advanced to the Dniester, three days later, those elements of the *4. Panzer-Armee* still stationed east of the Zbruch river at Husiatyn (about 65 km southeast of Tarnopol)–including what remained of the *1. SS-Panzer-Division*–were placed under command of the *1. Panzer-Armee*, as *Divisionsgruppe Mauss*. They were supposed to stop the enemy advance on both sides of the Zbruch and re-establish contact with the *4. Panzer-Armee* on the Sereth river at Terebovlia – an illusory command.

On March 24, 1944, *Heeresgruppe Süd* ordered the surrounded *1. Panzer-Armee* to fight its way through to the northwest to the *4. Panzer-Armee*. For this mission, the *Divisionsgruppe Mauss* units were placed under command of *Korpsgruppe* [Corps Group] *Chevallerie*.

Five days later they succeeded in establishing a bridgehead to the west, at Skala, on the Zbruch river (about 35 km northwest of Kamyanets-Podilsky). On April 1, 1944, in heavy snowfall, the troops also succeeded in forming a bridgehead over the Sereth river at Lisowce (about 30 km west of Skala). When the *II. SS-Panzer-Korps*[15] was concentrated for the relief mission on April 4, 1944, the *1. SS-Panzer-Division* units in the *Divisionsgruppe Mauss* sector had to cover the northern flank of the breakout groups at Chortkiv, on the Sereth.

When the Germans then briefly succeeded in re-establishing contact between the relief forces and the surrounded units at Buchach on April 6, 1944, they were able to consolidate the front between the *4.* and *1. Panzer-Armee* during the following days.

What remained of the *1. SS-Panzer-Division* was pulled out of the fighting in mid-April 1944 and transferred to the area of Lviv. From here, on

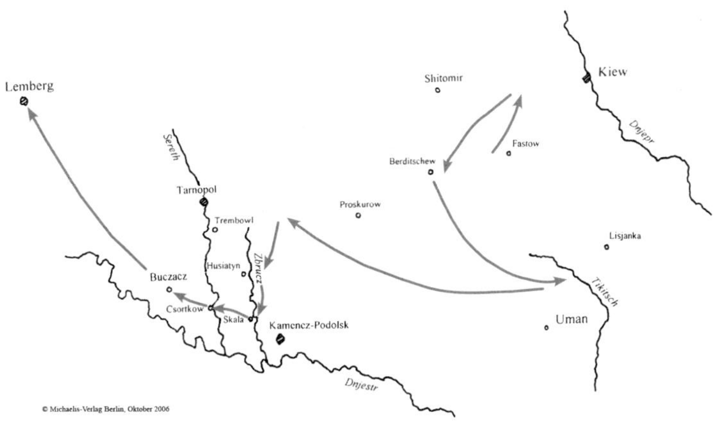

15 Cf. Chapter *9.* and *10. SS-Panzer-Division*.

April 18, 1944, they were transported to Belgium for defense against the expected invasion. About a week later, the formation started refitting and retraining near Turnhout. Herbert Kühl remembers:

> After the end of the battle for the Cherkassy pocket on February 27, 1944, the commander of *SS-Panzer-Aufklärungs-Abteilung 1* ordered me to stay in Uman, to finally repair almost 20 defective *Schwimmwagen* [amphibious vehicles]. Our unit was supposed to repair the vehicles so they could be driven again. Because of all the repeated redeployments we had to tow the vehicles along, and this was a burden on the detachment. When the situation around Uman got rough, I sent five repaired vehicles–against orders–to the *Abteinlung*, which I assumed was around Vinnitsa. I myself left the city with the remaining 13 *Schwimmwagen* before the fall of Uman on March 10, 1944. With no contact to our own unit, we made our way over the Dniester to Kishinev, in Bessarabia. There we refueled at a *Wehrmacht* filling station and reached Chernivtsi without problems. To our relief, we were able to rejoin our Division and the *SS-Panzer-Aufklärungs-Abteilung*. In Chortkiv, we were attacked by the Russians–they had just broken through. As dusk fell, we left the place going southwards and, after a few kilometers, got stuck fast on the road among withdrawing *Heer* and *Luftwaffe* supply columns. There were no combat units. It was clear to us that to get out of there, we had to get over the Dniester. The frozen ground beside the road seemed usable for off-road vehicles. I sent the remaining *Schwimmwagen* across the open ground with the order to cross the Dniester, to put up in the first village, and to put up a visible sign so that we would be able to see the shelter they went to. From behind, T-34s and mounted infantry were approaching. The three of us took cover in the right-side ditch. Our Russian *Hiwi* [*Hilfswilliger*: volunteer] Ivan lost his nerve and crawled out of the ditch; he was shot dead by a barrage of machine-gun fire. Our Opel car went up in flames, and we were trying to reach a forest about 300 m away over the open fields. There were about 30 soldiers gathered there. We held a council of war and looked for an officer to take over the leadership. A *Luftwaffe Stabsartz* [medical captain] refused it, and so I took over the command. I kept to my intention to reach the Dniester. There, we came upon a Hungarian bridgehead *Sicherung* [security detachment] that was just then dismantling things. German *Pioniere* [sappers] urged us to cross the bridge. Once we were across the Dniester, I disbanded our little group of stragglers. Shortly afterwards, the bridge was blown up.
>
> In the next village we found signs pointing to our Division–we

Sturmgeschütz III Ausf. G (Sdr. Kfz. 142/2) with 7.5 cm Sturmkanone L/48 of the SS-Sturmgeschütz-Abt. 1.

SS-Oberscharführer Fritz Henke, awarded the *Ritterkreuz* on 2/26/44.

SS-Unterscharführer of the SS-Sturmgeschütz-Abt. 1.

Panzer IV Ausf. G (Sdr. Kfz. 161/1) with 7.5 cm KwK 40.

L/43 and members of SS-Panzer Regiment 1.

At times, for camouflage, soldiers covered up their sleeve insignia.

Ambulance driver with Ukrainian women helpers.

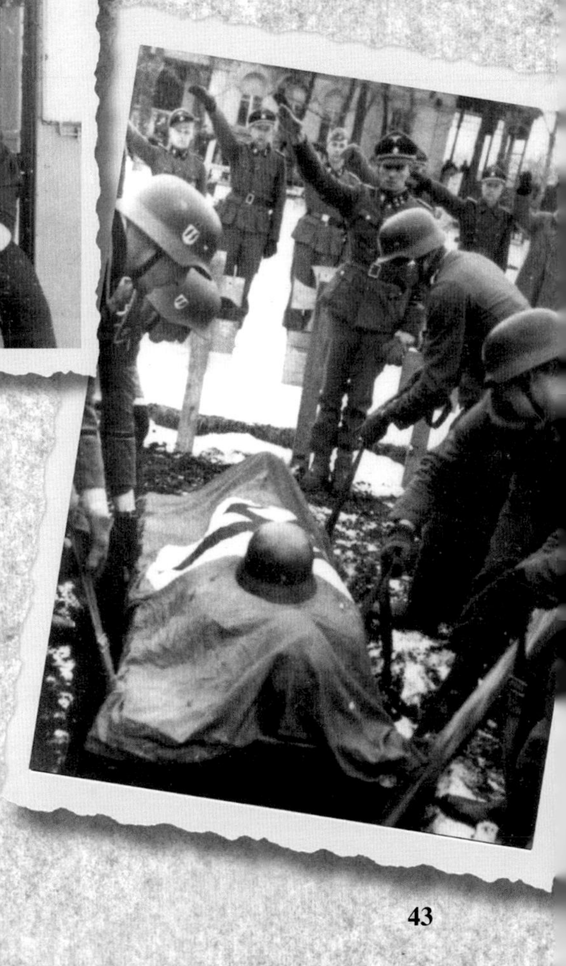

SS-Sturmbannführer [SS Major] Peiper, commander of the III. (gp.) [gepanzert: armored] / *SS-Panzergrenadier Regiment 2* on 2/24/43 at the burial of *SS-Obersturmführer* [First Lieutenant] Westrup (*12./SS Panzergrenadier Regiment 2*).

were together again. We got a short, deep sleep as the night was ending, and in the morning we set out. Without a goal, we moved off to the west–we did not have any map information available. The traffic got denser, and going over a deeply snowed-up pass in the Wooded Carpathians, we reached an ethnic German village on April 1, 1944. In the evening, the residents' happy company took us away from the precarious situation we were now in; they gave us wine, bacon, bread, and onions, as well as singing. The next day, our journey continued. We also had a goal again–Lviv, 400 km away [German: Lemberg]. As we were leaving, we marveled at the peaceful idyll of the village–how long would it continue? Dressed in their traditional clothes, the people hurried to the church on Palm Sunday. Because of the muddy paths they wore short wooden pattens or stilts, which were strapped on the lower legs and were left outside the church.

Our road lay through Munkacs, in Carpatho-Ukraine, northwards to Lviv, which we only reached days later, because we kept running out of fuel. When we got to Lviv, we reported to the *Frontleitstelle* [forward directing center for personnel in transit]. We learned that the LSSAH had been sent to Belgium. We would still be able to find the remaining units 200 km away at the Heidelager SS troop training grounds. Equipped with marching orders, we managed to complete the last leg. We were lucky: the meat-butchery company of our Division took us in. Then the train took us and the remaining vehicles to Belgium. In Turnhout, we rejoined *SS-Panzer-Aufklärungs-Abteilung 1*. Our odyssey was over.

Although the Allied troops landed in Normandy on June 6, 1944, the German leadership assumed that there would be a second invasion at Calais. To counter this, *1. SS-Panzer-Division*, which had been recuperating for about six weeks in the Bruges-Ghent area, was redeployed on June 10, 1944, to the *LXXXIX. Armee-Korps*. However, because of the situation developing at Caen on June 28th, at first *SS-Panzergrenadier-Regiment 1 LSSAH* was sent to join the *I. SS-Panzer-Korps* and was placed under the command of the *12. SS-Panzer-Division Hitlerjugend*. On June 30, 1944, the rest of *1. SS-Panzer-Division* reported this nominal strength:

Officers	Unterführer	Enlisted Men	Total
478	2,860	16,353	19,691
2.4%	14.5%	83.1%	100%

Moved on July 6, 1944–four weeks after the start of the invasion–into a staging area at Bretteville-sur-Laize (about 12 km south of Caen), beginning on July 11, 1944, the *SS-Panzergrenadier-Regiment 1 LSSAH* took over a front sector between Maltot and Caen. On July 15, 1944, it was redeployed to the line at St-Andre-sur-Orne and Frénouville (about 3 km south of Caen). The heavy enemy naval gunfire and the continuous attacks by enemy air forces brought enormous losses during fighting which at times resembled trench or fixed-position warfare. The battles around Caen were certainly among the worst in World War II. A former member remembers:

> The closer it came to mid-year, the more frequently the Allied bombers and low-flying aircraft came to visit us. Things already were starting to crack badly. On June 3, 1944, the village of Testelt got its first two war dead. They were two Belgian railway workers who were killed by fighter-bombers. Mind you not by German, but American airmen.
>
> By this time, enemy warships were cruising off the Dutch coast. This was certainly intended more as a diversion to sidetrack us from the actual invasion landing sites in Normandy. But because our leaders assumed that the invasion has been launched there, we were sent to Holland in June 1944 in forced marches. When we got there, the Allies landed in Normandy. For two days, we lay at a Dutch village called Dreibruck. Suddenly, bombs and shrapnel were flying around our ears. The air was full of iron and gunfire whistled around us. We heard the first screams of comrades who were wounded and saw comrades fall silently as they were hit. My *Schütze 2* [second gunner] on an lMG [*leichtes Maschinengewehr*: light machine gun] was severely wounded. Three days later, the next second gunner lost his foot, cut clean off by a shell splinter.
>
> In a forced march, we went by train to Normandy. With all our youthful readiness for duty, we young men wanted to stop the landed enemy forces. This will developed unbelievably by old and young alike. Our *7. Kompanie* moved into a position on a slope, with a front side which inclined towards the village of Verson. Our company head, *SS-Hauptsturmführer* Brinkmann, put an sMG [*schweres Maschinengewehr*: heavy machine gun] in position near a pasture hut. To secure this an lMG was set up, which tilted backwards in position. That was my MG. On the morning of July 11 or 12, 1944, an enormous firing came down on us. Due to a direct hit, the heavy machine gun was out of action. Suddenly silence, and only English shouts and voices in front of us. My lMG clattered away. Next to me was the youngest of the company–he had done his training in Beverloo with the *SS-Panzer-Division Hitlerjugend*, and had remained there due to sickness when the *HJ-Division* was transported to France. He was

> now my third 2nd gunner in just a matter of days. He was physically the weakest among us, and many times I'd carried his ammunition box on our training marches. But now he was the strongest, at the decisive moment. It was rattling, cracking, and banging, and suddenly, my lMG wasn't shooting anymore. The bolt mechanism was broken. Suddenly we were afraid we couldn't hold off the enemy any more. But suddenly the quiet little 2nd gunner was there–he had the replacement bolt in his hand. While he shouted "Gerhard, hold them off! Throw it! Take hand grenades!" he wrenched the lMG out of my hand. Then he turned the rifle butt, wrenched the cocking slide back, the spring and bolt out, new bolt in, then the spring, the butt went in, the belt put on–barrel and bolt interlocked after shutting the cover, and the machine gun was firing again. During this time he was hit repeatedly by gunfire! I got a part of a hand grenade that exploded at the edge of our fox hole in my back. He shot down an enemy who came up in front of us with his handgun. Helmut had sat up erect to do that. Then he was hit in the neck and his blood splashed in my face. A bullet hit me at the same time in the left armpit and penetrated the shoulder blade.
>
> The enemy overran our position–they thought I was dead. Our *Kompanie* leader threw the enemy back, personally leading the *Kompanietrupp* [HQ personnel] to get us out of there–a dead soldier and myself, wounded!

Because *Panzer* forces are not fixed-position troops, and because, in addition, the enemy had broken through at Avranches, almost all German *Panzer* formations were pulled out to the sector of the *XXXXVII.* and *II. SS-Panzer-Korps* southwest of Caen. Beginning August 7, 1944, they were to launch Operation *Lüttich* [Liège] to retake Avranches.

For this mission, elements of *SS-Panzergrenadier Regiment 2*, *SS-Panzer-Aufklärungs-Abteilung 1*, and *SS-Panzer Regiment 1*, as well as an artillery detachment *(Sfl.* [*Selbstfahrlafette*: self-propelled gun carriage]) of the *II. SS-Panzer-Korps* were placed under the command of the *1. SS-Panzer-Division*, and pushed forward towards Juvigny-Mesnil-Adelee (about 7 km northwest of Mortain). Elements of *SS-Panzergrenadier Regiment 1* were stationed under command of the *84. Infanterie-Division* south of Vire. Under the rolling attacks by the enemy air force, the operation stalled after reaching Mortain. Already by August 8, 1944, the *Oberbefehlshaber West* called off the offensive–the units were thrust into defense.

As elements of the II Canadian Corps succeeded in joining up with those of the U.S. XV Corps, who were fighting their way from the opposite direction, at Trun, on the Dives river on August 17, 1944, the battle-weary remnants of the *1. SS-Panzer-Division*–positioned south of Trun, together with some 80,000 other German soldiers–were surrounded in the Falaise pocket.

Three days later, elements of the *1. SS-Panzer-Division*, together with the *3. Fallschirmjäger-Division*, were supposed to force a breakthrough to the east, between St. Lambert and Chambois. The break-out was an inferno. Crowded together in a small area, the soldiers were victims of enemy artillery, tanks, and fighter planes. Only about 20,000 German soldiers managed to escape across the Seine. The remains of the *Leibstandarte* withdrew after fierce rear guard action at Louviers, across the Seine at Rouen on August 29, 1944, and were there briefly put under the command of *Divisionsgruppe* [a temporary combat group or unit] *Graf von Schwerin.*[16]

Individual *Kampfgruppe*–constantly coming up against U.S. troops and Belgian partisans–pulled back through Charleroy, towards Burg Reuland. At the same time, the first *Division* elements were sent to Siegburg for refitting and retraining in early September 1944. In Stadtkyll, north of Prüm, after a few days rest, a regiment-strong *Kampfgruppe* was reconsolidated from the remains of the two *Panzergrenadier-Regimenter* and combat-support units; on October 10, 1944, the *12. Volks-Grenadier-Division* [People's Grenadiers] (*LXXXI. Armee-Korps*) was sent to the region of Würselen, near Aachen. While one *Batallion* remained in the *12. Volks-*

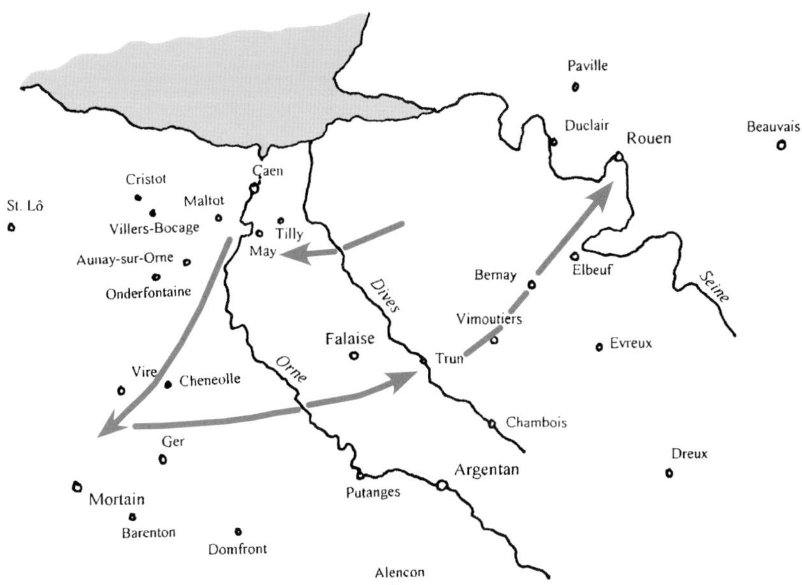

16 The remnants of this *Division* and the *1., 2.,* and *12. SS-Panzer-Division* were reconstituted under the commander of the *116. Panzergrenadier Division*.

Grenadier Division, another one was placed in command of the *246. Volks-Grenadier Division* in Aachen. On October 16, 1944, Aachen was surrounded, and surrendered five days later. What remained of the *SS-Batallion* tried to break through to Würselen. On October 25, 1944, a few reached the positions of the *3. Panzergrenadier Division*.

In mid-October 1944, most of the shattered *1. SS-Panzer-Division* was concentrated in the area of Lübbecke (about 30 km east of Osnabrück) for refitting. In the preceding weeks, the units had lost almost all of their heavy equipment and had to be completely re-equipped. By July 1944, the formation had to report the following personnel losses, assumed captured, killed in action, or wounded:

Officers	Unterführer	Enlisted Men	Total
87	520	3,294	3,601

Including temporary attachments from the *Luftwaffe* and the *Kriegsmarine*, as well as convalescents and newly-trained recruits from the *SS-Panzergrenadier-Ausbildungs-und Ersatz-Bataillon 1* [Training and Replacement Battalion 1], on November 4, 1944, the *Division* again reached the following strength:

Officers	Unterführer	Enlisted Men	Total
553	3,109	17,303	20,965
2.6%	14.8%	82.6%	100%
633	4,128	13,787	18,548
3.4%	22.3%	74.3%	100%

Thus, the *Tagesstärke* [number of troops under command on that day] was higher than the *Sollstärke* [authorized strength]! In mid-November 1994, the formation was redeployed to the Jülich-Mechernich-Düren region. In preparation for the Rundstedt offensive, the units were also supplied with materiel with surprising speed. On December 10, 1944, the *Division* reported the following:

	Authorized	Actual	Incoming
Panzer IV	34	34	-
Panzer V "Panther"	34	38	-
Panzer VI Tiger[17]	45	15	30
Sturmgeschütze	21	22	-
***Schwere Pak* 7.5 cm**	25	25	-
Leichte Feldhabitzen	-	30	-
Schwere Feldhaubitzen	-	18	-
10 cm *Kanonen*	-	4	-

After about seven weeks of rest, the formation marched out on December 13, 1944, for the upcoming Ardennes offensive (the Battle of the Bulge) to the area of Blankenheim. The plan stipulated that the *1. SS-Panzer-Division* should proceed in two spearheads. To accomplish this, the reinforced *SS-Panzergrenadier-Regiment 1* had first to reach the railway bridges at Huy and Amay, and the reinforced *SS-Panzer Regiment 1* had to reach the bridge at Hermalle and build bridgeheads across the Meuse.

On December 16, 1944, Operation *Wacht am Rhein* [Operation Watch on the Rhine] was launched with the attack of the *12. Volks-Grenadier-Division* and *3. Fallschirmjäger-Division* in advance of the *1. SS-Panzer-Division*. After the *3. Fallschirmjäger-Division* failed to win much ground, *1. SS-Panzer-Division* got their order to go into action already in the afternoon. By the evening of the next day, *Panzergruppe Peiper* had reached Stavelot and *Gruppe Hansen* the village of Recht. It was there that the *Panzergruppe* became involved in the Malmedy events.[18]

In the early afternoon of December 19, 1944, the *Panzer* group reached the area of La Gleize-Stoumont (25 km west of Stavelot), where the advance finally stalled. After U.S. troops encircled the units near Stoumont-La Gleize and were able to hit many of their vehicles with bazookas, on December 24, 1944, the remaining troops–after blowing up their last vehicles–fought

17 Assumed.

18 On December 17, 1944, there was a brief gun battle near Malmedy between *Panzergruppe Peiper* and an American field observation detachment, during which some 200 U.S. soldiers were captured. When two POWs tried to reach the nearby forest, the German guards began to use their weapons, and then panic broke out in the entire group. As the mass of Americans now tried to escape, machine gun firing started, killing about 80 enemy soldiers. In 1946, the trial of 74 members of *1. SS-Panzer-Division* began. They had signed confessions under physical and psychological coercion. The sentences – some of death or life imprisonment – were changed to limited detention after the methods used emerged during public review in the U.S., and *SS-Sturmbannführer* Peiper was released from prison December 22, 1956.

their way back to the positions of the reinforced *SS-Panzergrenadier Regiment 1 LSSAH* near Wanne. During the action, there had also been a number of clashes with Belgian civilians and resistance fighters!

On December 29, 1944, the deployable parts of the *Division* were put under the command of *Armeegruppe Lüttwitz (5. Panzer-Armee)*. Initially, the *SS-Panzergrenadier-Regiment 2 LSSAH* moved to the area southeast of Bastagone and attacked in the sector of the *XXXXIX. Panzer-Korps* to the northwest, from the area northwest of Harlange. In cooperation with elements of the *3. Panzergrenadier-Division*, they were to encircle the U.S. troops in Bastogne. In the unsuccessful fighting, the *Division* suffered heavy losses; after the offensive was halted from January 10, 1945, it was withdrawn from the *HKL* [*Hauptkampflinie*: main combat line] and ordered to the area east of St. Vith. Here again, it was put under the command of the *I. SS Panzer-Korps* and transported to the Cologne area.

Redeployment to Hungary began a few days later. For the upcoming *Plattenseeoffensive* [Lake Balaton offensive], the Division was camouflaged as *Ersatz-Staffel Totenkopf* [replacement echelon]. On February 12, 1945, it had the following:

	Officers	Unterführer	Enlisted Men	Total
Actual	513	3,165	15,377	19,055
	2.7%	16.6%	80.7%	100%
Authorized	615	4,037	13,723	18,375
	3.3%	22.0%	74.7%	100%

By mid-February 1945, the formation was concentrated in the area south of Raab. To destroy the Soviet Gran bridgehead–Operation *Südwind* [Operation Southerly Wind]–the formation moved 70 km northeast, to the assembly area Farnad (26 km east of Neuhäusel). From here, the units attacked on February 17, 1945, initially towards Gywa; after heavy fighting, they reached Murzsla and the Gran. Having taken Parkany, the *1. SS-Panzer-Division Kampfgruppen* turned northwards and occupied Köhidgyarmat, Kemend, and Beny. On February 24, 1945, they destroyed the Soviet bridgehead. Already by the next day, *Ersatz-Staffel Totenkopf*, with a strength of 18,871 men, was redeployed through Komárom to the area west of Veszprem-Várpalota, and by March 6, 1945, moved into initial positions for Operation *Frühlingserwachen* [Operation Spring Awakening] in the area about 6 km west of Kalóz (some 30 km south of Székesfehérvár

[German name: Stuhlweißenburg]). During the subsequent offensive in the thaw, they were able to initially capture Kalóz and Deg, and on March 12, 1945, after hard and bloody fighting, cross the Sio Canal at Simontornya.

Once the Red Army itself launched a large-scale offensive three days later, the troops were withdrawn behind the Székesfehérvár–Lake Balaton line. The total *Division* losses in the nine days of fighting were as follows:

	Officers	Other Ranks
Killed in Action:	6	205
Wounded	16	1,059
Missing:	1	148

On March 17, 1945, the formation, operating again from that day as *1. SS-Panzer-Division Leibstandarte SS Adolf Hitler*, reported a mobility of 68% and an armory of the following:

Panzer IV	**14**
Panzer V Panther	**14**
Panzer VI Tiger	**9 (assumed)**
Sturmgeschütze	**4**

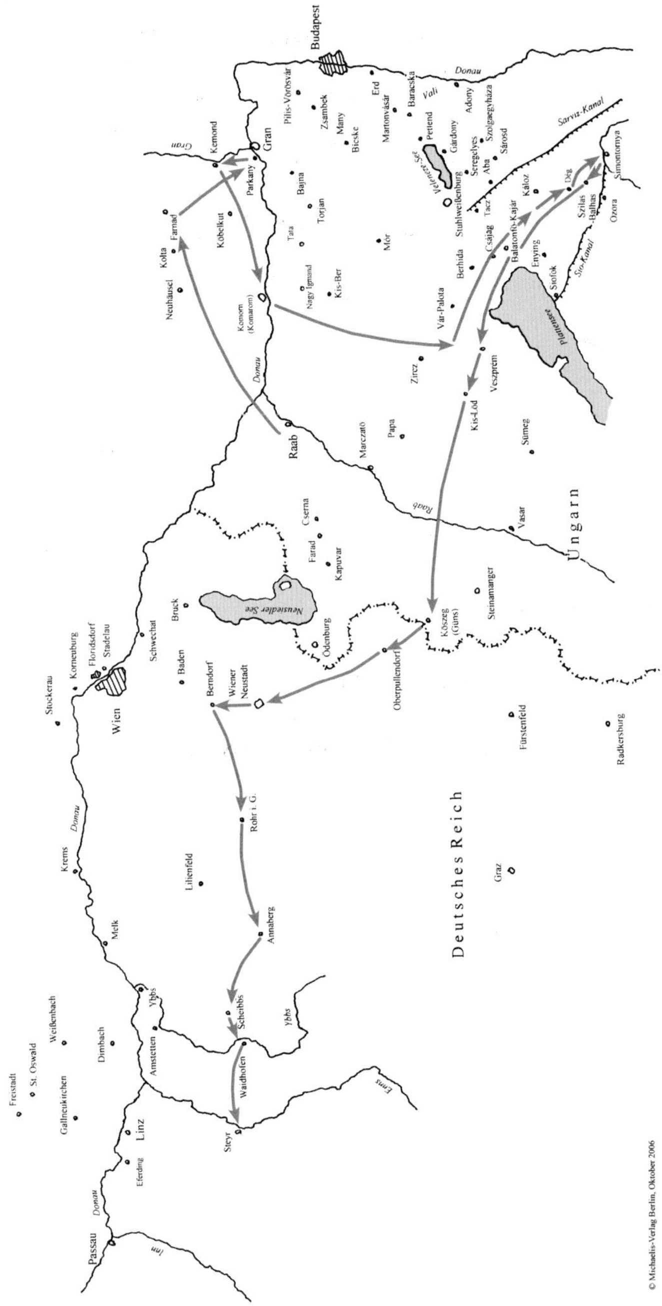
Budapest
Donau
Gran
Kemond
Parkany
Farnad
Kolta
Neuhäusel
Köbelkut
Komorn (Komarom)
Tata
Bajna
Torjan
Zsambek
Pilis-Vörösvár
Many
Bicske
Erd
Martonvásár
Baracska
Vali
Adony
Pettend
Gárdony
Velencze-See
Szolgaegyhaza
Seregelyes
Aba
Sárosd
Sarviz-Kanal
Stuhlweißenburg
Tacz
Csajag
Balatonfö-Kajár
Káloz
Dég
Szilas-Balhas
Simontornya
Ozora
Enying
Siofok
Sio-Kanal
Plattensee
Berhida
Vár-Palota
Mór
Kis-Ber
Nagy Igmand
Zircz
Veszprem
Kis-Löd
Sümeg
Papa
Marczato
Raab
Vasar
Ungarn
Cserna
Farad
Kapuvar
Neusiedler See
Bruck
Ödenburg
Köszeg (Güns)
Steinamanger
Oberpullendorf
Wiener Neustadt
Berndorf
Baden
Schwechat
Stadelau
Floridsdorf
Korneuburg
Stockerau
Wien
Fürstenfeld
Radkersburg
Rohr i. G.
Deutsches Reich
Graz
Lilienfeld
Annaberg
Krems
Melk
Ybbs
Scheibbs
Waidhofen
Steyr
Enns
Amstetten
Dimbach
Weißenbach
St. Oswald
Freistadt
Gallneukirchen
Linz
Eferding
Passau
Inn
© Michaelis-Verlag Berlin, Oktober 2006

Artillerie-Batterien	*3 leichte*
	3 *schwere*
	1 *Kanonen-Batterie* (10 cm)
	2 *Nebelwerfer* [rocket artillery] *Batterien*

Thus, *SS-Panzer-Regiment 1* had the strength of about three companies, which were reconstituted into the *I. Abteilung*. Unable to establish a continuous front, the *1. SS-Panzer-Division* pulled back with heavy losses, initially to Veszprem. When the Red Army overran the region on March 24, 1945, the units retreated to the area of Kislöd. After crossing the Raab, the remnants of the units reached the region near Wiener Neustadt by way of Köszeg-Oberpullendorf on April 1, 1945.[19]

Under heavy pressure from the Red Army, they next retreated towards Berndorf (about 12 km south of Baden). Reinforced by the *II./SS-Panzer-Regiment 1*, which was following them, and which had been deployed as infantry, they engaged in heavy fighting. From this area, the troops retreated to the region of Rohr im Gebirge. On May 2, 1945, they marched through Annaberg to the area of Scheibbs (about 35 km west of Lilienfeld). During the surrender, the remnants of the *Division* attempted, by going through Waidhofen an der Ybbs, to reach Steyr an der Enns, and thus the line of demarcation. Herbert Kühl remembers:

> In the last days of March 1945, *SS-Panzer-Aufklärungs-Abteilung 1* crossed the Reich frontier and moved into the area of Deutschkreutz/Burgenland, the so-called *Reichsschutz-Stellung* [Reich protective position], which had a great name, but was no more than a continuous trench. With the last drop of gasoline, on prime movers and armored personnel carriers with their treads knocked off and without rubber blocks, we reached our destination. The drivers' curses could be heard a long way when the treads came off on the sharp turns.
>
> Our *Kommandeur–SS Hauptsturmführer* [SS captain] Wawrzinek–asked me, "What do we do about the treads? We don't want to have to walk at the very end." I replied that I saw no way to get our hands on treads through official channels. Earlier deliveries had labels, "*Gleiskettenlager* [caterpillar tread depot] *XVII*." This Roman numeral indicated *Generalkommando XVII* in Vienna. After a short deliberation, the commander ordered: "You're leaving tomorrow for Vienna; look for the tread depot and bring back some treads. Figure out how many trucks you need and make some empty space."
>
> The next morning, six trucks equipped with driving and marching orders and a requisition for 40 sets of treads drove to Vienna.

19 When about 60 km of area between had been yielded between March 24-26, 1945, on March 27, 1945, Hitler ordered that the Waffen-SS Divisonen should discard their sleeve insignia.

> Arriving at the tread depot, I asked a *Feldwebel* [sergeant], who told me that he was only allowed to dispense anything with the allocation of the OKH. We got into an argument. Finally, he asked for orders from his superiors in the acting *Generalkommando*. I drove there–the windows and doors were open, and documents stamped "Secret" were swirling around in the corridors. The sight was depressing. Several *Abteilungen* and the Major we were looking for were on the way to Linz, I found out. Back in Prater, I explained to the *Feldwebel* about his Major. His response, "Take what you need–we're getting out of here."
>
> We didn't just stare, our jaws dropped. Six or seven of these huge depots were filled with treads, from a *Kettenkrad* [half track motorbike] to a *Königstiger* ["king tiger," the Tiger II tank]–one depot had sets of rubber blocks in boxes. Using trolleys, we quickly loaded our trucks. These impressions let us figure out why we were now operating on German soil.
>
> *Just get out of here*. By midday, we were on the way back to Deutschkreutz. When we got there, we unloaded a set for every prime mover and every armored personnel carrier. We changed the treads quickly. The *Kommandeur* was pleased with us and said, "Now we can go on to the end." A little later, on April 1, 1945, we lost our last revered *Kommandeur* along with several comrades due to a direct hit on the command post.

By this time, almost 50% of the remainder of the unit consisted of former members of the *Wehrmacht*. The history of the *Division* indicates that it–for propaganda purposes–was given preference. While other German formations which had been decimated on the Eastern Front were disbanded, every six months, the *Leibstandarte* –altogether thus for about a year's time–was pulled out of active service and refitted!

In 1945, due to temporary attachments from the *Luftwaffe* and the *Kriegsmarine*, the formation realized a strength of nearly 20,000 men. However, this could only partially increase its operational capability, due to the replacements' lack of infantry training, inadequate equipment, and insufficient fuel.

It achieved no greater successes in active service than did other proven *Waffen-SS* formations, such as the *20. Waffen-Grenadier-Division der SS (estnische Nr. 1)* [20th Waffen-SS Grenadier Division (Estonian No. 1)] on the Narva front, or the *Wehrmacht*. Thus, the units differed–at least initially–primarily in the members' appearance: the *Leibstandarte* was to be known as being formed of notably "racially" selected men.

Panzer VI Tiger I with 8.8 cm *KwK* (*L/56*) (*Sdr.Kfz. 181*).

SS-Obersturmführer Wittmann was the most successful German *Panzer* commander, with 138 destroyed enemy tanks.

Panzer VI Tiger I
(Sdr. Kfz. 181)
with 8.8 cm KwK 36 L/56.
Length: 8.45 m;
Width: 3.56 m;
Height: 3 m;
Weight: 54 t;
5 man crew.

Members of the *SS-Panzer-Division Leibstandarte SS Adolf Hitler* in tropical uniform. The photograph was possibly taken in Italy in summer 1943.

Panzer VI in 1945.

2

SS-PANZER-DIVISION DAS REICH

The SS-Verfügungstruppe

SS-Standarte 1 Deutschland was formed from the *Politische Bereitschaften* of the *Allgemeine SS* in the summer of 1934 in Munich; it was ultimately organized in four *Sturmbanne*. In 1935, Hilter gave *SS-Standarte 1* the name *Deutschland* at the *Reichsparteitag* [Nazi Party rally]. After participating in the Austrian operation, in March 1938 the *II. Sturmbann*, which consisted of emigrant Austrian National Socialists, was assigned to the initial formation of the *SS-Standarte 3 Der Führer*. In October 1938 it took part in the Sudetenland operation, and then was reclassified as a motorized *Standarte*. Ordered to return to Munich after the occupation of the rest of Czechoslovakia in March 1939, the *Standarte* was redeployed in mid-July 1939 to *Ostpreußen* [East Prussia] to officially participate in the Tannenberg Memorial celebration. Placed under the command of the *I. Armee-Korps*, the formation was given intense *Sturmausbildung* [assault training] at the Stablack troop training ground. In mid-August 1939, it was incorporated into the *Ostpreußen Panzer* formation (*Panzer-Division Kempf*).

SS-Standarte 2 Germania was formed in Hamburg in the summer of 1934 from *Politische Bereitschaften*, and was organized into three *Sturmanne*. In 1936, Hitler gave *SS-Standarte 2* the name *Germania* at the Nuremberg Rally. In March 1938, the *Sturmbanne* took part in the Austrian operation;

about half a year later, they were redeployed for the upcoming Sudetenland operation, to the Königsbrück troop training grounds in Dresden. Afterwards, the formation was reclassified as a motorized *Standarte* and was again sent to the Königsbrück troop training grounds. From here on, the *Standarte* took part in the occupation of the rest of Czechoslovakia in March 1939. The *Sturmbanne* were then deployed as guard formations for the *Reichsprotektor* [representative of the Nazi German government] in the protectorate of *Böhmen und Mähren* in Prague. Reassembled in Königsbrück, the *Standarte* was transferred to Silesia, and took part in the Polish campaign under command of the *14. Armee*. At the end of September 1939, the formation was integrated into the *SS-Verfügungs-Division* at the Czech troop training grounds at Brdy-Wald [Brdy forest] (east Pilsen).

SS-Standarte 3 Der Führer was formed in spring 1938 in Vienna from the *II./SS-Standarte 1 Deutschland* and more Austrian volunteers, and was organized in three *Sturmbanne*. In 1938, *SS-Standarte 3* was awarded the name *Der Führer* at the Nuremberg Rally by Hitler. By October 1938, the *Standarte* had already participated in the Sudetenland operation. It was then regrouped into a motorized *Standarte* and participated in the occupation of Czechoslovakia in March 1939. In July 1939, the *Sturmbanne* took over duty as guard formations of the *Reich Protektor Böhmen und Mähren* in Prague from *SS-Standarte 2 Germania*. In mid-September 1939, it was then redeployed to the Waldkirch area in the Black Forest, on the Western Front. From there, the *Standarte* was ordered in October 1939 to the Brdy-Wald Czech military training area east of Pilsen for the formation of the *SS-Verfügungs-Division*.

SS-Verfügungstruppen Artillerie-Standarte was established in June 1939 at the *Heer* Artillery School at Jüterbog. Some 2,000 infantrymen, who had previously served with *schweren Maschinengewehr-* and *Infanteriegeschütz-Kompanien*, were assigned for this purpose. Organized in three *leichte Abteilungen*, the formation was transferred to East Prussia in mid-August 1939, and there placed under the command of *Panzer-Division Kempf*. The later *SS-Hauptscharführer* [*SS* Master Sergeant] Fred Zura remembers:

> Personnel from all sectors were assigned to Jüterbog, near Berlin, to the *Heer Artillerie-Schule* for the formation of the *SS-Artillerie-Regiment* of the *Verfügungstruppe* in June 1939. I was ordered with a number of men to the *I. Abteilung*. First used as a dispatch rider for the regimental staff, after three days I became a *Fernsprechtruppführer* [telephone section squad leader]. After about two months of training we were driven to Kiel, and from there went by ship to

> Königsberg [now Kaliningrad]. Our staff was ready for us on the Kilgris manor. At first, life and just hanging around on the manor went on as usual. We had plenty of time after work to roam through that bleak area. There was a small shop, with the usual daily extra food in stock. The beer tasted best to us, until the storekeeper's old father came by with his homemade *Bärenfang* ["bear trap," a honey liqueur]. This was wonderful, but don't underestimate it! In a nutshell, in just a short time we bought out the old man's entire stock.

SS-Verfügungstruppen Fla-Maschinengewehr-Abteilung [anti-aircraft machine gun] was formed in June 1939 at the Bergen military training grounds, initially only at company strength.

In August 1939, the unit was transferred to East Prussia and moved into quarters in Bladiau (about 40 km southwest of Kaliningrad). While the *Kompanie* was ultimately placed under the command of *Panzer-Division-Kempf*, organization of the other two *Kompanien* began in Radolfzell. These were added to the *SS-Verfügungs-Division* in November 1939.

SS-Verfügungstruppen Aufklärungs-Abteilung was formed in late May 1939 by reconstituting other units in Ellwangen (Jagst), with two *Kradschützen-Kompanien* [motorized rifleman], as well as a *Panzerspäh-Zug* and a *Panzerabwehr-Zug*. It was redeployed to East Prussia as early as July 1939 for the autumn maneuvers there. In August 1939, it was integrated into *Panzer-Division-Kempf*.

SS-Verfügungstruppen Panzerabwehr-Abteilung was formed in June 1939, in the short term by reconstitution of other units in Ellwangen. After the personnel were then used to form the *SS-Artillerie-Standarte*, in August 1939, it was preliminarily disbanded. In September 1939, re-formation began in Ellwangen, and by the end of October 1939, the formation was transferred to the *SS-Verfügungs-Division* in the Pilsen area. On April 1, 1940, it was renamed the *SS-Panzer**jäger**-Abteilung*.

SS-Verfügungstruppen Pionier-Sturmbann was formed in early 1935 in Dresden, and was organized into three *Stürme* [*SS* companies]. In March 1938, the *Sturmbann* took part in the Austrian operation, in the Sudetenland in October 1938, and in March 1939 in the occupation of the rest of Czechoslovakia. Ordered to return to Dresden, the SS-*Pioneer Sturmbann* was redeployed in mid-August 1939 to Oberglogau, and attached to the *XV. Armee-Korps* for the upcoming Polish campaign as *Korps-Pioneer-Batallion*. At the end of October 1939, it was integrated into the *SS-Verfügungs- Division*.

Members of the *SS-Verfügungstrupe*.

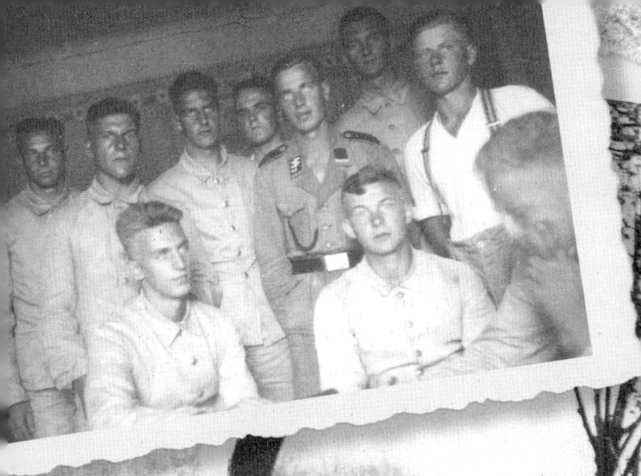

Training also included estimating distances.

SS-Verfügungstruppen Nachrichten-Sturmbann was formed in early 1935 in Berlin-Adlershof, and in March 1938 took part in the Austrian operation. In May 1938, the *Sturmbann* was sent to Unna, in Westphalia. In the summer of 1938 the *Stürme*, ordered to the Alten-Grabow troop training grounds, took part in October 1938 in the Sudetenland operation, and were motorized afterwards. In March 1939, it participated in the occupation of Czechoslovakia. Ordered to return to Unna, the *SS-Nachrichten-Sturmbann* was ordered in the summer of 1939 to take part in the 25th anniversary celebration of the Battle of Tannenberg in East Prussia. On August 10, 1939, it was incorporated into *Panzer-Division-Kempf.*

Panzer-Verband Ostpreußen (Panzer Division Kempf)

The *Aufstellungsbefehl* [initial organization order] to form *Panzer-Verband Ostpreußen*, also called *Panzer-Division Kempf* after its commander, was issued in July 1939. The formation was set up by combining *Heer* troops and elements of the *SS-Verfügungstruppe*. The reasons for this action included both that the *Wehrmacht* leadership wanted to bring the *SS* units closely into the *Heer* chain of command for active duty, and also wanted to rapidly form a *Panzer* force in East Prussia for the upcoming Polish campaign without attracting the attention of enemy intelligence by the transfer of a full *Panzer-Division* from the Reich.

Panzer-Verband Ostpreußen was organized as follows:

Panzer-Regiment 7 (Heer)
SS-Standarte 1 Deutschland
Panzer-Abwehr-Abteilung 511 (Heer)
SS-Aufklärungs-Abteilung Pionier-Bataillon 505 (Heer)
SS-Artillerie-Standarte Verwaltungs-Dienst 171 (Heer)
Sanitäts- und Nachschub-Dienste (Heer)

Since the *Division* had only one motorized *Infanterie-Regiment*, its infantry strength was what it should be, but was not sufficient to prepare the *Panzer-Regiment* to break through enemy positions on a broad front.

While *SS-Standarte 3 Der Führer* was deployed on the *Westwall* [West Wall, also known by the Allies as the Siegfried Line], *SS-Standarte 2 Germania* was placed under the command of *AOK 14* [*Armeeoberkom-*

mando, Field Army Command], and the *SS-Pioneer-Sturmbann* under the *10. Armee*. Their operational deployments are discussed at the end of this chapter.

In mid-August 1939, *Panzer-Verband Ostpreußen* was assembled in the *1. Armee-Korps* sector in greater Osterode, and then transferred to the area of Neidenburg, about 50 km distant. On August 25, 1939, the formation moved into the assembly areas across from the Polish Mlawa position. The order to attack for the next day was revoked, and at first the units moved back into their barracks. On August 31, 1939, they again moved into the assembly areas; the next day, the German forces attacked in the direction of Mlawa. The offensive stalled under the fierce defensive fire and due to a deep anti-tank ditch. As a result, in the evening of September 2, 1939, the units were pulled out and marched to the area of Willenberg.

Placed under command of the *Korps z. b. V.* [*Korps zur besonderen Verwendung*: for special deployment], *Panzer-Verband Ostpreußen* was supposed to assume active duty at Ciechanów and hit the enemy at Mlawa from the rear, from the southeast. After several fierce battles in the outpost area, they were able to take Ciechanow the next day without a fight. After the Polish troops had withdrawn from Mlawa, the formation was assigned to attack the Polish fortress Rozan, on the Narew (about 50 km east of Ciechanów), on September 5, 1939. Just as in front of Mlawa, the units got bogged down in heavy defensive fire and had to be withdrawn to the line of departure. After heavy fighting and facing the danger of being encircled, the Poles retreated from Rozan on September 7, 1939. *Panzer-Division-Kempf* then received orders to move north to support the *XXI. Armee-Korps* from the south, enabling it to advance to Lomza. Here too, Polish resistance had blocked success.

On September 10, 1939, the *Division* halted the advance to Lomza, and moved in forced march to Brok, on the Bug river (about 40 km southeast of Rozan). Here, it was to capture the Polish units taking evasive action to the northeast from Warsaw. This led to heavy fighting on September 12, 1930, while other elements had already pushed forward to the area of Siedlce (about 65 km southeast of Brok). From there, the units marched in a southwesterly direction to Maciejowice, on the Vistula river, and there fended off all Polish counterattacks. As the ring was closed around Warsaw on September 16, 1939, the formation was next ordered to attack the Modlin Fortress. Attached to the *II. Armee-Korps* in the region northeast of Modlin at Nasielsk (about 110 km away), *Panzer-Division-Kempf* relieved the *228. Infanterie-Division* in the siege ring. In the face of the threatened assault on the fortress, the Poles surrendered on September 29, 1939.

On October 7, 1939, *Panzer-Verband Ostpreußen* held a passing out parade in Neidenburg. Afterwards, the *SS-Verfügungstruppe* units marched into the region of Pila [German: Schneidemühl]-Deutsch-Krone [now Walcz, Poland], and from there travelled by train to Dresden. In motorized march, they reached the Brdy-Wald training grounds near Pilsen, where they were integrated into the *SS-Verfügungs-Division*.

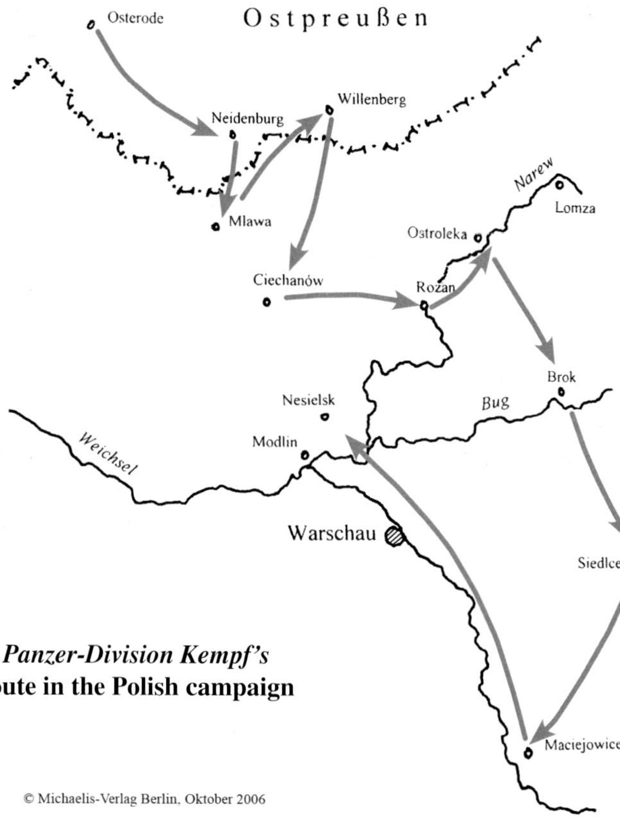

***Panzer-Division Kempf's* route in the Polish campaign**

SS-Standarte 2 Germania was concentrated on September 1, 1939, in the area north of Ratibor-Althammer, at the disposal of the *VIII. Armee-Korps*. Two days later, it was placed under command of the *Grenzabschnitt-skommando 3* [Border Sector Guard Command]. The *Standarte* initally marched toward Sosnowiec; then, from September 7, 1939, towards Krakow. There, the troops were allocated to other formations. The *I.* and *III./SS-Standarte 2 Germania* were assigned to the *XXII. Armee-Korps* and deployed to protect its flanks. This led to fierce battles in Jaworow.

The *II. Batallion* remained with the *VIII. Armee-Korps*, and was stationed on the San river September 12, 1939. In heavy fighting, here it attempted to build a bridgehead near Krzeszow (about 50 km southeast of Sandomierz). Three days later, it was placed under command of *XXII. Armee-Korps* and transferred through Przemysl to Chyrow (about 25 km south of Przemysl). On September 18, 1939, the *Regiment* was reassembled, and shortly thereafter ordered to the Brdy-Wald training area.

Deployment of *SS-Standarte 2 Germania*

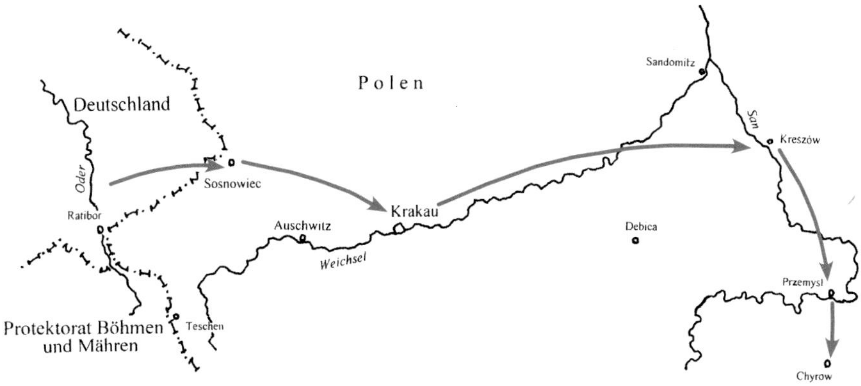

The *SS-Pioneer-Sturmbann* was attached to the *XV. Armee-Korps* in late August 1939, in the region of Świbie [Schwieben]-Zwieborn-Krupski Młyn [German: Kruppmühle]. On September 4, 1939, it first engaged in fighting with straggling Polish troops near Lelow (about 40 km southeast of Czestochowa). Two days later, the *Sturmbann* reached Kielce (about 110 km east of Czestochowa). On September 8, 1939, the formation was deployed directly on the front for the first time, north of Ostrowiec, to prevent Polish troops from escaping.

On September 12, 1939, fighting ended in the Lysa mountains. The next day, the *Sturmbann* was deployed to build a bridge over the Vistula at Annopol. On September 20, 1939, it was again transferred to the front between Borki-Nowe Budy on the *HKL*. After the *XV. Armee-Korps* had cordoned off Modlin from the south and west, the *SS-Pioneer-Sturmbann* carried out mopping-up operations in the Puszcza forest.

On September 24, 1939, it was placed under the command of the *XIII. Armee-Korps* for the attack on Warsaw. After heavy fighting southwest of the Polish capital on September 26, 1939, Warsaw surrendered the next day. On September 28, 1939, the *Sturmbann* marched back to the *XV. Armee-*

Korps and was sent to rest positions at Czechowicze. On October 1, 1939, the unit was commanded to go to the Brdy-Wald training ground east of Pilsen, in the *Protektorate Böhmen und Mähren*.

Deployment of the *SS-Pionier-Sturmbann* in the Polish campaign

The SS-Verfügungs-Division

There, the *SS-Verfügungs-Division* was organized in tripartite formation, i.e., consisting of three *Infanterie-Regimenter* as follows:

DIVISIONSSTAB
SS-Standarte 1 Deutschland
SS-Standarte 2 Germania
SS-Standarte 3 Der Führer
SS-Aufklärungs-Abteilung
SS-Artillerie-Standarte
SS-Panzerjäger-Abteilung
***SS-Fla-MG-Sturmbann* [*Fliegerabwehr*: anti-aircraft]**
SS-Pionier-Sturmbann
SS-Nachschubdienste
SS-Verwaltungsdienste
SS-Sanitäts-Abteilung
SS-Veterinär-Kompanie
SS-Nachrichten-Abteilung

Already by December 1939, *SS-Standarte 3 Der Führer* was taken out of the Division formation and transferred by motorized march to the *X. Armee-Korps* in the area of Datteln, near Recklingshausen. For the remaining units, their period at the training ground was focused primarily on training for finely tuned operations in Division formation. Fred Zura remembers:

> In the period from October 14 to December 1, 1939, we were stationed at the Jince-Cenkow training grounds in Prague. Himmler came for an inspection and was received by our *Regimentskommandeur*. At the same time, the *Reichsführer* inspected the *Stabsbatterie* [headquarters battery], and he presented some decorations. As *Fernsprechtruppführer*, I received the Iron Cross 2nd Class from his hand.

At the end of November 1939, the *Division* began its move to Würzburg, to *Generalkommando XIV*. On January 24, 1940, it was ordered to the Münster area, to *AOK 18*. On February 6, 1940, the formation–without *SS-Standarte 3 Der Führer*–was sent to the *XXVI. Armee-Korps*.[20]

The *SS-Aufklärungs-Abteilung* was placed under the command of the *254. Infanterie-Division* at Kleve for a short period on February 9, 1940. Remaining in the Kranenburg area (about 8 km west of Kleve) after Febru-

20 Deployment of *SS-Standarte 3 Der Führer* will be discussed separately.

ary 12, 1940, on May 9, 1940, the *Abteilung* was alerted. Together with *Heer* elements, it was to take at least one bridge over the Maas-Waal Canal and then occupy the bridge at Grave. The next day, the troops crossed the Dutch border. Since they only achieved a partial success, the order came on May 11, 1940, to march back to the *SS-Verfügungs-Division.*

On May 1, 1940, they reported an overall strength of:[21]

Officers	Unterführer	Enlisted Men	Total
593	3,058	17,354	21,005
2.8%	14.6%	82.6%	100%

This formation had also been alerted on May 9, 1940. Two days later, the troops marched across the Rhine at Rees (about 18 km southwest of Bocholt), and on May 12, 1940, the first elements crossed the Dutch border east of Gennep. Here the *SS-Aufklärungs-Abteilung* again reached the *Division* formation.

Together, the troops advanced to Hilvarenbeek (about 25 km south of s'Hertogenbosch). After an initial order on May 13, 1940, to push forward to Belgium and Antwerp as rapidly as possible, the next day came the order that part of the *SS-Verfügungs-Division* was to stop the shipping on the Westerschelde.

On May 15, 1940, the *SS-Verfügungs-Division*–still without *SS-Standarte 3 Der Führer*–was assigned by the *XXVI. Armee-Korps* to move against the islands of South Beveland and Walcheren. For this mission, the *Division* elements still stationed at the siege front in front of Antwerp were redeployed to join them, except for *SS-Regiment 2 Germania*. The first heavy fighting, primarily against French troops, began near Ossendrecht; the Dutch forces only rarely put up any cohesive resistance. When Fortress Holland capitulated, the only further battle was in Zeeland against the French and British forces stationed there. On May 17, 1940, there was fierce and costly fighting during the conquest of the island of Walcheren, across the narrow causeway from South Beveland.

Already the next day, the units were relieved here by elements of the *225. Infanterie-Division* and marched to the assembly area at Hasselt (about 70 km southeast of Antwerp). *SS-Standarte 2 Germania* also arrived here from the siege of Antwerp, and *SS-Standarte 3 Der Führer* from the command of the *207. Infanterie-Division.*

21 With *SS-Standarte 3 Der Führer* and the *SS-Aufklärungs-Abteilung.*

Amsterdam
Haarlem
Isselmeer
„D.F."
Niederlande
Veenendaal
Doesburg
Arnheim
Issel
Westervoort
Nimwegen
Kranenburg
Beveland
Walcheren
Maas
Grave
Kleve
Bocholt
Rees
sHertogenbosch
Ossendrecht
Gennep
Rhein
Hilvarenbeek
Dünkirchen
Antwerpen
Calais
Belgien
Hasselt
Lille
la Bassé
Arras
Cambrai
Somme
Arve
St. Quentin
Hirson
Deutsches Reich
Roye
Montdidier
Soissons
Paris
Seine
Romilly
Troyes
Maas
Frankreich
Chatillon
Dijon
Chateurenault
Le Creusot

SS-Standarte 3 Der Führer was placed under command of the *207. Infanterie-Division* on May 10, 1940, and took part in the battle for the so-called *Ijsselstellung* [Ijssel position] at Doesburg, as well as, beginning the next day, for the *Grebbestellung* near Westervoort (about 8 km southeast of Arnhem). After taking these positions, the *Standarte* was redeployed to Amerongen (about 8 km southwest of Veenendaal). From here, the units marched through Amsterdam to Haarlem and were temporarily deployed to secure the coast. On May 16, 1940, the *SS* members were released from the *207. Infanterie-Division*, and they marched to the *SS-Verfügungs-Division* assembly area.

Restored to full strength, the *SS* formation marched on May 20, 1940, from Hasselt to Hirson, about 150 km distant, and was then placed under command of the *XXXXI. Armee-Korps*. With the line of attack towards Calais, fighting started north of Arras on May 23, 1940. There, fiercely contested bridgeheads were thrust across the La Bassee Canal at Guerbecque and St. Venent. The battle for the Forêt de Nieppe [Nieppe Forest] (about 25 km west of Lille), launched on May 27, 1940, brought the hardest fighting during the Western campaign.

On June 1, 1940, around 2,000 men arrived from Germany as replacements for the *SS-Verfügungs-Division*, which had just been taken out of active service, and were sent to the area between Arras and Cambrai for refitting and retraining. After a few days rest and integration of the enlisted men, the Division was placed under the command of the *XVII. Armee-Korps* on June 6, 1940. After crossing the Somme river, there was fighting on the Arve river on both sides of Roye; then the formation advanced to Montdidier. On June 9, 1940, it was taken out of active service and concentrated north of St. Quentin. The next day, the *IV. (schwere) Abteilung* arrived for the *SS-Artillerie-Regiment*.

On June 13, 1940, the *Division* was placed under command of the *XIV. Armee-Korps*, and marched into the Soissons region. The units were to follow the *Panzer-Divisionen* to cover their flanks and clear the areas they were crossing of enemy stragglers. Two days later, the men secured the Seine crossing between Troyes and Romilly. They then marched in two columns through Chattilon to Le Creusot, on the demarcation line. On June 21, 1940, the formation assembled north of the Loire at Châteaurenault (some 30 km northeast of Tours).

After the Armistice Agreement of June 25, 1940, the *SS-Verfügungs-Division* was redeployed on the Spanish border at Biarritz. Fred Zura remembers:

> Our staff moved into quarters in the town of Dax, near Biarritz. In the center there were hot spring fountains. Bathing in the Bay of Biscay, we didn't notice that the undertow had pulled us into the open sea. From land, they had seen that we were adrift and sent a boat to bring us back. None of us had known anything about how dangerous the undertow could be. That could have been very risky.
>
> We *Unterführer* got at lot of experiences and impressions during a short trip to Spain. At the border crossing in Irum, the Customs officials caught our eyes with their hats with feather plumes. In St. Sebastian, we briefly gathered local knowledge and, of course, exchanged all kinds of information.

In early July 1940, the *Division* was ordered to the Netherlands, near The Hague. There, the units moved into the following quarters:

DIVISIONSSTAB	**AMERSFOORT**
SS-Standarte 1 Deutschland	**Hilversum, Amsterdam**
SS-Standarte 2 Germania	**Apeldoorn**
SS- Standarte 3 Der Führer	**Meppel, Almelo**
SS-Aufklärungs-Abteilung	**Culenborg, Leerdam**
SS-Artillerie-Standarte	**Amersfoort, Arnheim**
SS-Panzerjäger-Abteilung	**Ede**
SS-Fla-MG-Sturmbann	**Moerdijk**
SS-Pionier-Sturmbann	**Ermelo**
SS-Nachrichten-Sturmbann	**Amersfoort**
SS-Nachschubdienst	**Hengelo, Enschede**

Then came refitting and retraining, including personnel replacements and replenished materiel, as well as training the units for the planned landing operation against England. In addition, the units were given *Heer* designations as regiments, battalions, etc.

On December 1, 1940, *SS-Regiment 2 Germania* was redeployed to the newly raised *SS-Division Wiking*. As a replacement, the *SS-Verfügungs-Division* got *SS-Infanterie-Regiment (mot.) 11*, which at the time was still deployed to guard the coast.

SS-Obergruppenführer **Hausser, commander of** ***SS-Division Das Reich*** **from October 1939 to October 1941.**

SS-Brigadeführer **[Brigade commander] Bittrich led the** ***Division*** **from October to December 1941.**

"Died in the service of France."

French colonial soldiers taken as prisoners of war.

Destroyed and captured French tanks: Renault 35 model.

Members of *SS-Standarte Germania*.

After the Western campaign, the *SS-Verfügungs-Division* was quartered in modern barracks at Steenwijk.

The SS-Division Das Reich (mot.)

After the *SS-Verfügungs-Division* was renamed the ***SS-Division Deutschland (mot.)*** on December 3, 1940, and transferred on December 15, 1940 to the *XXXXI. Armee-Korps (1. Armee)*, stationed in the area around Vesoul (about 60 km west of Belfort), it was then re-named the ***SS-Division Reich (mot.)***[22] on January 28, 1941.

At the same time the name was changed, a *SS-Sturmgeschütz-Batterie Reich* was formed to support the *Infanterie*, and an order issued for an *SS-Kradschützen-Batallion Reich*. The *Kradschützen-Batallion* was intended to relieve the *Aufklärungs-Abteilung*, allowing it to take responsibility for its own task of reconnaissance.

After nine months in France, the *Division* was put on alert, and redeployed to the *XXXXI. Armee-Korps* sector for the Balkans campaign, travelling through Belfort-Alsace and the Black Forest to the area of Donaueschingen. On April 2, 1941, the *Division* reached Braunau am Inn, and on April 6, 1941, the units of troops marched through Hungary towards Romania. When they arrived at Timisoara, they had covered some 1,500 km in about eight days.

For the imminent deployment, the *SS-Infanterie-Regiment 11 (mot.)* which still had no combat experience, was first deployed as a *Korps-Reserve*. The remaining part of the *Division* was to push forward on April 11, 1941 from the Denta region (about 45 km south of Timisoara) towards Belgrade, and occupy the Danube bridges there. Because the routes were barely passable, due to the weather conditions, the units initially reached Alibunar under great physical stress, and partly on foot. Belgrade was captured the next day, through a stratagem of one *SS-Kradschützen-Bataillon Reich Kompanieführer*. He drove with a few soldiers directly through the city to the German Embassy, and from there informed the Mayor of the Yugoslav capital about the–alleged–impending bombardment. As a result, the Mayor handed the city over to *SS-Hauptsturmführer Klingenberg*.

22 Thus, the *Division* troops, except for the three motorized *Infanterie-Regimenter*, all received the name *Reich* – i.e., *SS-Artillerie-Regiment Reich*.

The *SS-Standarte Der Führer* parade on Hitler's birthday, 4/20/1941, in the Serbian Banat region.

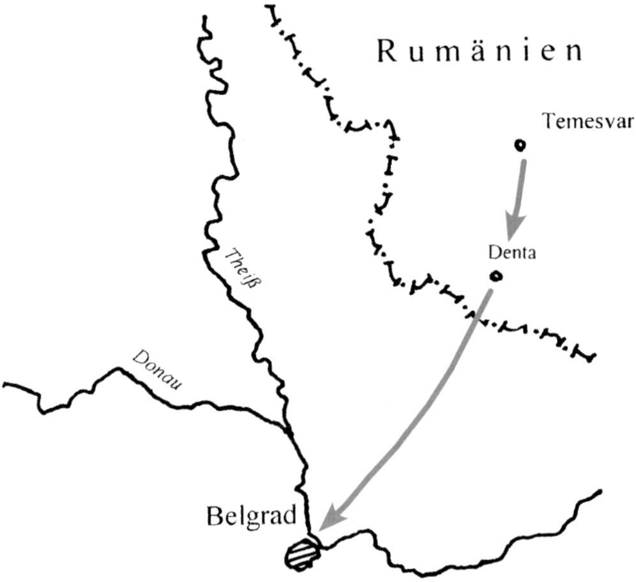

The same day, *SS-Infanterie-Regiment 11* was sent to join the *Division*. When Yugoslavia capitulated on April 18, 1941, *SS-Division Reich* undertook securing the region between the Tisza and Danube rivers and the Romanian and Hungarian borders. When the formation marched off to its rest area at Linz-Eferding-Traunsee, some 600 Romanian *Volksdeutsche* war volunteers joined the units.

On June 5, 1941, the formation was redeployed for the upcoming Russian campaign to the *XXXXVI. Panzer-Korps (Panzergruppe 2)* in the *Generalgouvernement* [Government General, the administrative region set up in occupied Poland]. Initially concentrated east of Lublin and deployed as a *Korps-Reserve*, on June 26, 1941, *SS-Division Reich* was assigned to carry out mop-up operations against the left-behind and scattered enemy units in the area between the Soviet roadways (highways) 1 and 2. On the completely overcrowded roadways, the motorized German columns at times could make no progress for several hours.

On June 28, 1941, the units were to push forward towards Minsk from the area of Slutsk and Kopyl, which they had reached in the meantime. On the next day, the 19,021 *Führer*, *Unterführer*, and *Enlisted Men* of *SS-Division Reich* experienced their first military combat near Losza. On July 1, 1941, the units reached Cherven. While *SS-Infanterie-Regiment 11* was assigned to comb through the forests, the other units of troops advanced across the Berezina river to the Dnieper.

Intense and bloody fighting occurred there, along the Stalin Line. The *Division* succeeded in getting across the river on July 11, 1941, between Shklov and Mogilev, and reached the Desna river at Elnya (about 70 km southeast of Smolensk). They engaged in their heaviest fighting yet in the area around Elnya; there, the Red Army, using its air superiority and vast expenditure of human and materiel resources, was able to totally decimate the German forces. The artillery barrages recalled the World War I mechanized warfare at Verdun! The *XXXXVI. Panzer-Korps'* commanding *General* vicariously documented the *SS-Division Reich's* struggle:

After one of the intense defensive battles on the Elnya northeast front, *Gruppe Förster* of the *1./SS-Kradschützen-Bataillon*, which was assigned to secure the *Kompanie* left flank, was found as follows:

> The *Gruppenührer*, *SS-Unterscharführer* Förster, with his hand on the pin of his last hand grenade, shot in the head.
>
> *Schütze 1*, *SS-Rottenführer* Klaiber, his machine gun still at his shoulder and just firing it, shot in the head.
>
> *Schütze 2*, *SS-Sturmmann* Buschner; *Schütze 3*; and *SS-Schütze* Schyma all dead in the foxholes.
>
> The solo messenger, *SS-Sturmmann* Oldeboerhuis, dead at his machine, kneeling with his hand on the control lever, fallen in the moment when he was to deliver the last message.
>
> The driver, *SS-Sturmmann* Schwenk, dead in his foxhole.
>
> Of the enemy, only dead bodies to be seen, lying in hand-grenade range in a semicircle around the *Gruppe* position.
>
> A model for the term "defense!" We stand in awe before such heroism!
>
> I have requested that these names be published in the Honor Roll of the German *Heer*.
>
> Between June 24 to July 27, 1941, there were as follows:

	Officers	**Other Ranks**
Killed in Action:	23	577
Wounded:	76	1,672
Missing:	1	62

Without ammunition for their own artillery because of the supply problems, and lacking air support, the units in the Elnya bridgehead were literally mown down by the enemy. By August 8, 1941, *SS-Division Reich* had been

The *SS-Division Reich* advance in summer 1941.

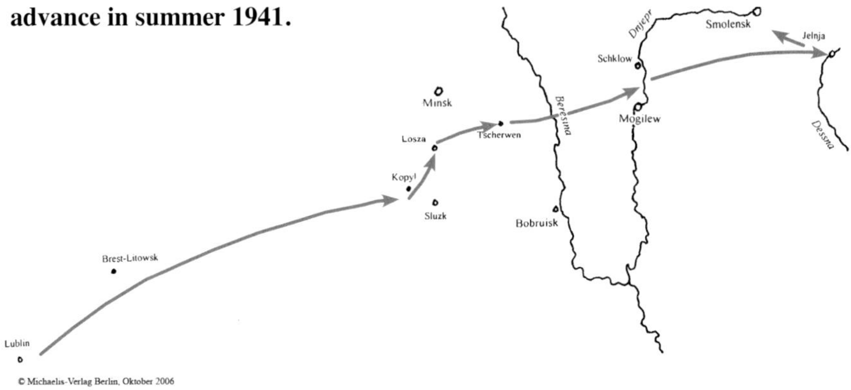

relieved by the *15. Infanterie-Division* and, after a short rest, took over positions between Smolensk and Elnya.[23]

At the end of August 1941, the *SS* formation was sent about 1,700 men as replacements, and was set in march to the *XXIV Panzer-Korps*, which was about 380 km distant in the area of Awdejewka (about 50 km northwest of Konotop). On September 6, 1941, they encountered heavy fighting and Red Army counterattacks at the Makoschin bridgehead over the Desna. In the course of annihilating the Kiev pocket, *SS-Division Reich* pushed forward to Priluki on September 16, 1941. After fierce battles, the units then had to redeploy to Romny, about 80 km away, to reinforce the *Heer* forces stationed there in defense against intense relief attacks by the Red Army. On September 23, 1941, the battle for the Kiev pocket ended.

The *Division* was withdrawn from the area and transferred to the *XXXX. Panzer Korps (Panzergruppe 4)*. The units moved into rest quarters west of Roslavl and were again reinforced by replacements. On October 6, 1941, during the encirclement of Bryansk and Vyazma, the units moved by way of Juchnov to Gshatsk. A few days later, the breakthrough through the Moscow defensive line was launched at Elnya. The men were back in the sector where they had experienced such heavy fighting and large losses in the summer. In the advance to Moscow, *SS-Division (mot.) Reich* overran Mozhaisk on October 18, 1941.

While battling for the breakthrough, elements of the *Division* also secured the rear area. There they not only took large numbers of prisoners of war, but also secured large amounts of war materiel. On October 22, 1941, *SS-Infanterie-Regiment 11* was divided between the other two motorized regiments, to compensate for their high losses. It was never re-formed,

23 Elnya was abandoned by German troops on September 2, 1941.

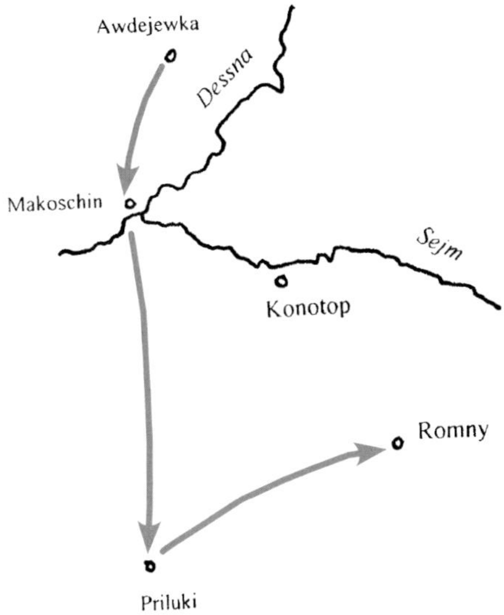

although initially that had been planned. From June 24 to October 23, 1941, SS-*Division (mot.) Reich* had recorded a total of over 8,000 men killed in action, wounded, and missing.

Following the *10. Panzer-Division*, the formation advanced beginning on October 26, 1941, through Rusa towards Istra, which was taken on November 26, 1941, after fierce fighting.

The attack on Moscow was immediately launched again, at temperatures of -45°C, and without adequate winter clothing. As a result, the Germans occupied Lenino (about 17 km west of Moscow) on December 3, 1941.

Two days later, the Red Army began a major offensive; the German units had little they could deploy to defend themselves. Suffering maximal losses, *SS-Division (mot.) Reich* succeeded in holding the positions at Lenino. Then, on December 9, 1941, it was ordered to pull back across the Istra river at Istra anyway, and move into winter positions.

Three days later, the *XXXXVI. Panzer-Korps* took over command there of the front sector before Moscow. Although the positions along the Istra offered good defensive potential, they had to be abandoned, because the Red Army succeeded in outflanking the *XXXXVI. Panzer-Korps* on its flanks. To prevent encirclement, *SS-Division (mot.) Reich* had to keep retreating westwards. They were only able to establish a sustainable *HKL* at the Rusa position, northwest of Rusa.

As the situation worsened–lack of re-supply, heavy losses of materiel and men due to the terrible freezing temperatures, and heavy attacks by Siberian forces–these positions were also abandoned on January 16, 1942.

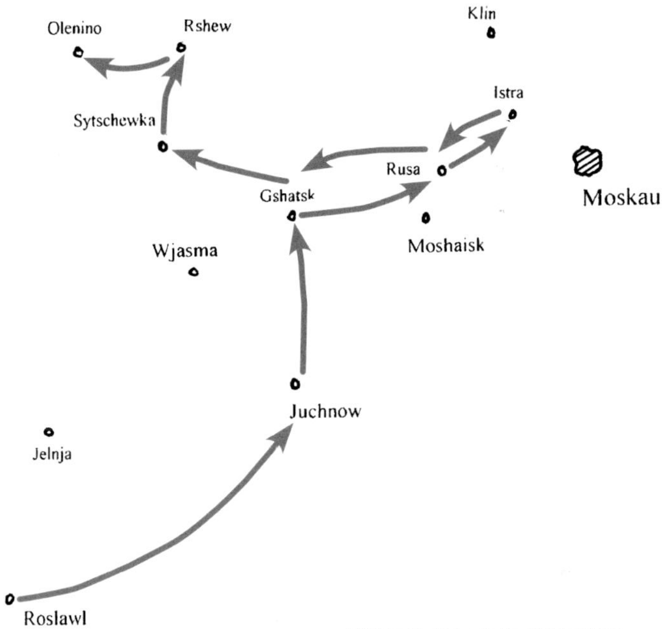

The *SS-Division* marched to Gshatsk, to redeploy from there to the fiercely combatted sector at Sychevka (about 120 km west of Rusa). On January 4, 1942, the Red Army pushed through the German *HKL* at Rzhev, about 40 km to the south. Fred Zura remembers:

> In Istra–near the church–the Russians landed a direct hit on our combat support train. Our *Nachrichtenzugführer* [signal platoon leader] Ernst Wittwer fell. We had to bury him by the church. I had a splinter injury, and Klaus Schaal was slightly injured. To the right of our firing position, a *Heer* unit had prematurely abandoned its position.
>
> In the freezing cold of about -50 degrees, I went on a countermarch with Günther Haar, both of us with our boots wrapped in straw–thankfully without frostbite! We got horse blankets from the first *Wehrmacht* unit we ran into, so that we–lice-infested–could get some rest. Also, the comrades in the horse-drawn unit had plenty of meatballs to eat made of their dead horses. The next day we were able to move further back, until we found our own units. It was here at these rear units we got to see the winter clothes that we had so urgently needed at the front....

The units, again placed under command of the *XXXXVI. Panzer-Korps*–except for *SS-Regiment 3 Der Führer*–formed up at Sychevka for a counterattack on January 21, 1942. *SS-Regiment 3 Der Führer* was assigned further north, directly at Rzhev, to the *256. Infanterie Division* in the *VI. Army Corps*, in order to re-close the gap in the front in coordination with other forces. This was realized on January 28, 1942. The Soviets immediately launched attempts to re-establish contact with the now-encircled Red Army formations; as a result, on February 10, 1942, most of the *SS-Division Reich* was transferred to the front lines at Rzhev.

As a result of heavy winter fighting against a numerically and materially far superior enemy, the units in the *HKL* along the Volga melded together in such a way that ever-more *Kompanien*–in some cases even *Batallionen*–were disbanded and their men distributed among those which remained.

This made it possible to still hold the positions and crush those enemy forces which had broken through. On February 17, 1942, the fighting ended in the pocket southwest of Rzhev. Already the next day, *SS-Division Reich* was detached from the positions and concentrated in the rear areas west of Rzhev.

While elements of the *Division*–including *SS-Regiment 3 Der Führer*–were transferred to Germany for reorganization, the *1. Generalstabsoffizier*, *SS-Standartenführer* Ostendorff built up a regiment-strength *Kampfgruppe* from remnants of the remaining units.

Under command of the *XXXXVI. Panzer-Korps*, *SS-Kampfgruppe Reich* moved to the region of Olenino (about 35 km northwest of Sychevka) on March 2, 1942. Until it was taken out of active service and transferred to Germany to form the successor *SS-Panzergrenadier-Division Das Reich* on June 1, 1942, the *Kampfgruppe* remained engaged in repeated heavy and extremely costly fighting in the area of Olenino.

_SS_ members examine a captured Soviet T-26 tank with interest.

A damaged German _Panzer IV. Ausf. E._

Repairing a _DKW 350 [Dampf-Kraft-Wagen_: steam power vehicle].

A distinctive signpost…

Schwere Zugkraftwagen 12 t (Sdr. Kfz. 8) with a 21 cm *Mörser* [howitzer].

... and forward-deployed *Artillerie* observer.

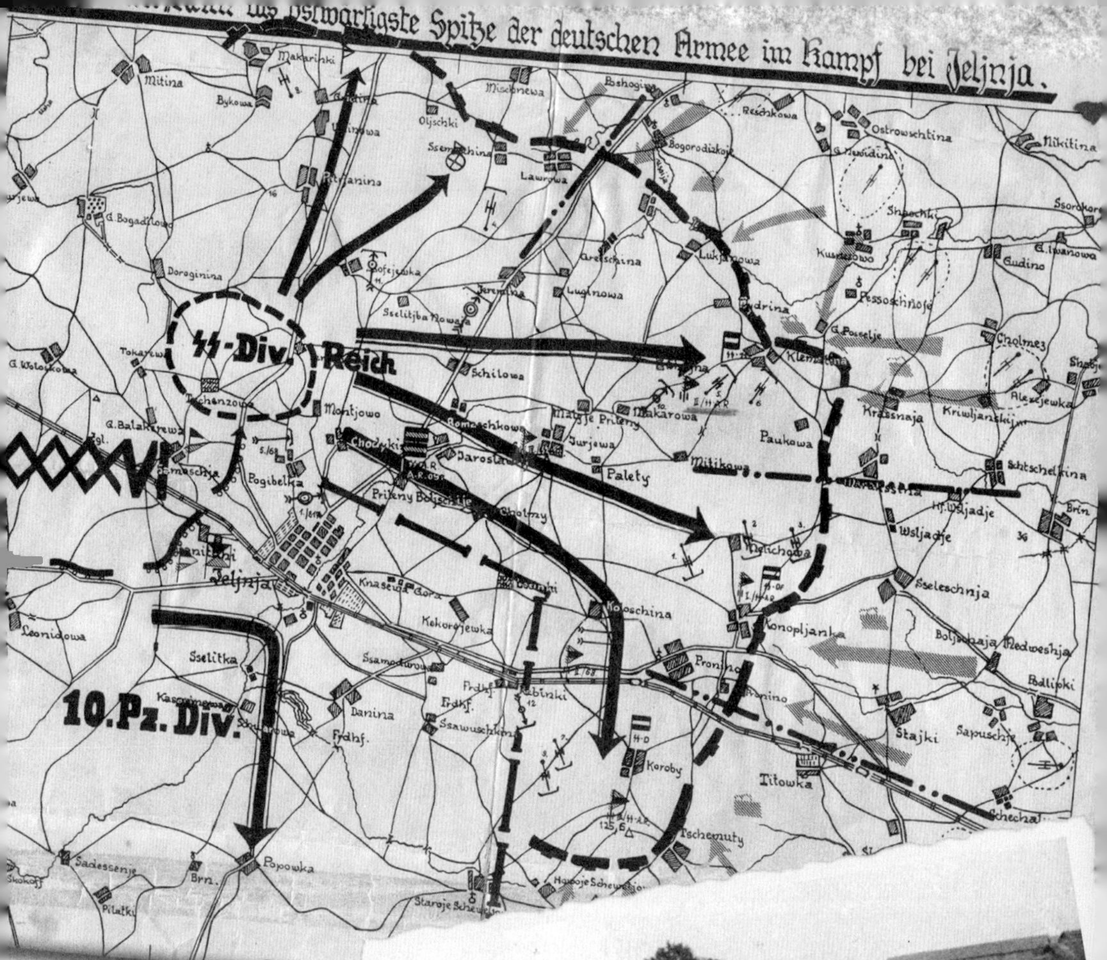

Enlisted Men of *SS-Regiment Der Führer* with captured Soviet flags.

Heinz Twesmann was awarded the Iron Cross at Elnya.

5 cm *Pak 38 Riegel* [anti-tank oblique defense line].

Members of *SS-Artillerie-Regiment 2* and a 10.5 cm *leichte Feldhabitze 18*.

SS-Gruppenführer **Kepper**, *Kommandeur* **of** *SS-Panzergrenadier-Division Das Reich* **between April 1942 and March 1943.**

SS-Gruppenführer **Krüger (center) led the** ***Division*** **from March to November 1943.**

SS-Panzergrenadier-Division Das Reich

Initial measures to re-establish the *SS-Regiment 3 Der Führer* began at the Fallingbostel troop training area in March 1942. In April 1942, *Stämme* [groups of cadre] arrived from other *Division* units, except for *SS-Kampfgruppe Reich*, which remained on the front.

In May 1942, and renamed the *SS-Division* **Das** *Reich*, it was newly activated in the organization of a *Panzergrenadier-Division*:

DIVISIONSSTAB
SS-Panzergrenadier-Regiment 1 Deutschland
I.-III. Bataillon
SS-Panzergrenadier-Regiment 2 Der Führer
ditto-the *III. Bataillon (gp.* [*gepanzert*: armored]*)*
schnelle SS-Schützen-Regiment* [fast rifle regiment] *Langemarck
***I. Bataillon* (former *SS-Kradschützen-Btl. Reich*)**
***II. Bataillon* (former *SS-Infanterie-Regiment 4*)**
SS-Aufklärungs-Abteilung Das Reich
SS-Artillerie-Regiment Das Reich
SS-Panzerjäger-Abteilung Das Reich (mot.)
SS-Panzer-Abteilung Das Reich
SS-Flak-Abteilung Das Reich (mot.)
SS-Pionier-Bataillon Das Reich (mot.)
SS-Nachrichten-Abteilung Das Reich (mot.)
SS-Nachschubdienste Das Reich (mot.)

In July 1942 the formation, still designated the *SS-Division Das Reich*, and with a strength of nearly 20,000 troops, was transferred to France, to the *7. Armee* in the area of Le Mans. Placed under the command of the regrouped *SS-Panzer-Korps* on August 12, 1942, the units were then sent on to the St. Lô area on October 1, 1942.

At the same time, the *schnelle SS-Schützen-Regiment Langemarck* was again disbanded. The *II. Bataillon* ultimately formed the *II. Abteilung* of the now-to-be-reconstituted *SS-Panzer-Regiment*. The *I. Bataillon* again became an *SS-Kradschützen-Bataillon*. In addition, an *SS-Sturmgeschütz-Abteilung* was established to replace the still-lacking *Panzer-Abteilung*.

The *Division*, which was, in part, in an almost peace-time reorganization for some six months, attained an outstanding operational strength with the supply of young *SS* volunteers from Germany and being fully provided with weapons and equipment. In addition, with the formation of a *Panzer-Regiment* instead of an *Abteilung*, it already had the organization of a *Panzer-Division*.

Effective as of November 9, 1942, the formation was initially designated:

SS-Panzergrenadier-Division Das Reich

During the occupation of France that same month, *SS-Kradschützen-Bataillon Das Reich* took part in the occupation of Toulon on November 27, 1942. In the *SS-Panzer-Korps* sector, the *Division* also secured the coast against potential Allied landing attempts.

In early December 1942, it was moved to the region south of Rennes, from where, with a strength of:

Officers	Other Ranks	Total
599	16,513	17,112
3.5%	96.5%	100%

Transfer then began to the heavily embattled Eastern Front.

By the end of January 1943, *SS-Panzergrenadier-Division Das Reich* reached the assembly area of the *SS-Panzer-Korps* west of Kharkov and was put under command of *Heeresgruppe B* as an operational reserve.

Although the German leadership indicated that *SS-Panzer-Korps* units should not be deployed split up, the three *Divisionen* of the *Korps (Leibstandarte SS Adolf Hitler, Das Reich*, and *Totenkopf*) had to be sent into action immediately, to support the front. *SS-Panzergrenadier-Division Das Reich* units were ordered to the area northeast of Kharkov up to Valuiki, on the Oskol river, for this mission.

Already within a few days, the troops had to retreat towards Volchansk, and on February 9, 1943, moved into positions across the Donets. At the same time, the Red Army outflanked the *SS-Panzer-Korps* lines both to the north and south, and thrust forward in a pincer movement to encircle Kharkov and the *SS-Panzer-Korps* units.

Pushed back towards Kharkov, and in danger of being encircled, the commanding *General* of the *SS-Panzer-Korps* decided on the night of February 15, 1943, to abandon the city, against Hitler's explicit orders. *SS-Panzergrenadier-Division Das Reich* was commanded to concentrate behind the front near Krasnograd (about 90 km southwest of Kharkov), in order to again take the offensive from there.

On February 19, 1943, the attack was launched on both sides of the Orel and the Samara, initially southwards to the *4. Panzer-Armee*, and then to pivot eastwards to the region of Pavlograd. From here, the *Division* moved on February 25, 1943, in a northeasterly direction to Losowaja. After fierce fighting, the units pushed forward until March 6, 1943–on roads which were

Sturmgeschütz III Ausf. G (Sdr. Kfz. 142/2) **with 7.5 cm** *Sturmkanone 40 L/48*.

The later *SS-Obersturmbannführer* and *Kommandeur* of *SS-Panzer-Regiment 2*, Christian Tychsen. Awarded the *Ritterkreuz* on 4/6/43, *Eichenlaub* [oak leaf cluster] on 12/10/43 (Killed in action on 7/28/44).

Formation of the *II. (Panther)/SS-Panzer-Regiment* in summer 1943.

When the Soviet tanks surpassed the *Panzer II* with 5 cm *KwK 39*, the *Panzer IV* and *Sturmgeschütz III*, with their 7.5 cm guns, primarily became the long-term backbone of German Panzer weaponry.

Capturing a Russian village.

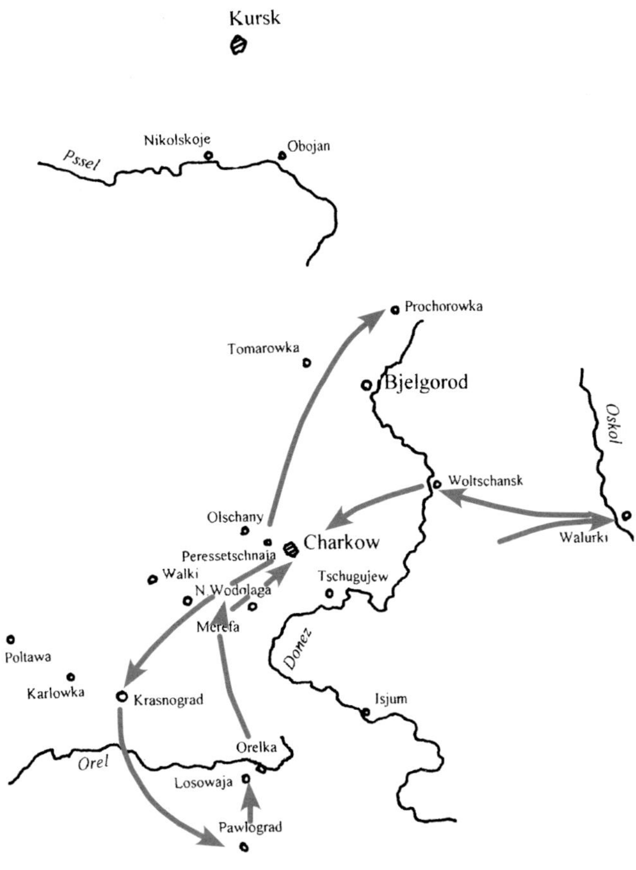

barely passable, even for tracked vehicles–to Novaya Vodolaga (about 36 km southwest of Kharkov) and Merefa (about 21 km south of Kharkov).

As the *SS-Panzer-Korps* kept advancing, the enemy began to again evacuate Kharkov on March 11, 1943, leaving behind stronger rear guards. On the evening of March 14, 1943, the city was once more in German hands. The German forces immediately kept pushing forward, and reached Belgorod on March 18, 1943. They then proceeded to mop up enemy forces in the area west of the Donets.

Between January 30 and March 20, 1943, the *Division* lost altogether (killed in action, wounded, and missing):

Officers	Other Ranks	Total
102	4,396	4,498

Because the formation was to be refitted after this costly fighting ended, it was transferred in April 1943 to the *SS-Panzer-Korps* sector near Peresichna (about 13 km west of Kharkov). Here, in addition to the supply of both materiel and personnel replacements–for the first time primarily *Volksdeutsche* from Romania–the *SS-Kradschützen-Bataillon*, among others, was disbanded. The *SS-Aufklärungs-Abteilung* took over their personnel.

At the end of June 1943, the *Division* moved its starting positions west of Belgorod for the upcoming German summer offensive, Operation *Zitadelle*. On July 5, 1943, the units concentrated in the *SS-Panzer-Korps* sector at Beresoff; by the next day, they were already in the area of Lutschki. The rain, and the total clogging of the roads being used for the advance, hampered both combat missions and supply.

Despite the fierce counterattacks launched by the Soviets, *SS-Panzergrenadier-Division Das Reich* was able to get to the area 3.5 km in front of Prokhorovka by July 11, 1943. On that day, the *SS* force had:

***Panzer III* (5 cm long)**	**34**
Panzer IV	**18**
Panzer VI Tiger	**1**
T 34 (captured tanks)	**8**
***Befehlspanzer III* [command *Panzer*]**	**7**
Sturmgeschütze	**27**
***Pak* 5 cm**	**30**
***Pak* 7.5 cm (*mot. Z.*) [*Zug*: platoon]**	**16**
Pak* 7.5 cm (*Sfl.	**3**
***Pak* 7.62 cm (*r.* [*russisch*: captured Russian]) (*Sfl.*)**	**9**

"The greatest tank battle in history" was fought the next day at Prokhorovka. Overall, some 1,200 Soviet and German tanks faced each other in battle within a very confined area. After heavy enemy counterattacks, the offensive was stopped on July 17, 1943: the *9. Armee* formations in the northern sector, in particular, were not able to win the required ground to the south, and were themselves forced into serious crisis situations by the Red Army.

SS-Panzergrenadier-Division Das Reich lost the following in some 12 days of major battles:

	Officers	Other Ranks
Killed in action	17	456
Wounded	46	1,842
Missing	-	23

A former member recalls an incident during Operation *Zitadelle*:

> We lay overnight in a ravine, and drove the next morning at first through a not-too-thickly planted grain field. Here, several of our *Panzer* ran over mines. We were funneled through the minefield to reach a village in front of us. In the center of the village was a sand trap, where one of our *Pak* was set up. We proceeded to the outskirts of the village, where there was another *Pak* moved into position. When we drove around with our *Beobachtungs-Schützenpanzerwagen* [observation armored personnel carrier] (Sdr Kfz 250), we got a radio message to come back to the *Abteilung*. But this was prevented when suddenly three T-34s with mounted Red Army soldiers rolled into the village. We positioned our *SPW* [*Schützenpanzerwagen*] behind a pile of straw and jumped off. Since one T-34 had meanwhile seen us, it raced towards the *SPW* at full throttle and rammed it, as often happened in the tank battle at Prokhorovka. Our proven *Beobachtungs-SPW*, which had given us such good service, and protected us despite its thin armor, was a pile of junk. The T-34's joy was short. Immediately after, it was shot by one of the *Paks* in the village.

After the Western Allies landed in Sicily, the *SS-Panzer-Korps* was withdrawn from the front already on July 18, 1943, and concentrated west of Belgorod for transfer to Italy. However, because of the situation developing for the *6. Armee* on the Mius, the *Korps* was immediately marched off again to the Stalino area, about 300 km away.

On July 30, 1943, the *Division* joined the *Großverband* [large formation], now designated the *II. SS-Panzer-Korps*, to attack the Soviet bridgehead over the Mius south of Kuybyshev (about 80 km east of Stalino). The heavy defensive fire from the Red Army caused the German forces to consider ending the operation, until *SS-Panzergrenadier-Regiment 2 Der Führer* managed to take a strategically important hill in a surprise attack, thus creating the conditions to push into the enemy bridgehead. In four days of fierce fighting, the *SS-Panzergrenadier-Division*, along with other units, had again successfully stabilized the situation and thrown the enemy back over the Mius.

By August 4, 1943, the *Division* was ordered back to *Armee-Abteilung Kempf* in the already fiercely-combated region of Kharkov, which cancelled the potential transfer to Italy. Redeployed to the Bogoduchow area (about 25 km northwest of Kharkov), the units engaged in fierce offensive and defensive battles, initially in the *XI. Armee-Korps* sector, and then in that of the *III. Panzer-Korps*. Pressed towards Korotish (about 10 km southwest of Kharkov), *SS-Panzergrenadier-Division Das Reich* took part in the Battle of Kharkov. After abandoning the city on August 23, 1943, the Germans began their withdrawal through Poltava to the Dnieper on September 2, 1943

The first elements of the *Division* crossed the river at Kremenchug on September 25, 1943, and immediately moved about 150 km to the northwest, near Kanev. The Red Army had already established a bridgehead across the Dnieper there. The *Division* was deployed until early November 1943 around the Soviet bridgehead; after the Red Army broke through at Kiev, it was transferred on November 6, 1943, to the *XXXXVIII. Panzer-Korps* near Fastiv.

Starting on November 21, 1943, the units were pulled out of their positions and moved to the area east of Zhitomir; there, in the sector of the *XXXXVIII. Panzer-Korps*, they were to force the enemy back to Kiev. Due to the intense and almost uninterrupted fighting during the past months, the *Division* fighting strength was only about 20% of its authorized strength. The *I./SS-Panzergrenadier-Regiment 2 Der Führer*, among others, was disbanded and reconstituted with reinforcements from the 10. *SS-Panzergrenadier-Division* from France. During the period August 1-December 1, 1943, the formation, meanwhile designated the *2. SS-Panzergrenadier-Division Das Reich*, had lost a total of 7,436 men! These included the following:

	Officers	**sonstige Dientsgrade**
Killed in Action	46	1,438
Wounded	157	5,638
Missing	1	156

Because of such losses, the first elements of the *Division* were pulled out of action on December 17, 1943, and were sent to the Stablack troop training grounds in East Prussia for reorganization. A *Kampfgruppe* that remained at the front southeast of Radomyshl in brigade strength was organized as follows:

SS-Panzergrenadier-Regiment Das Reich[24]
2 Panzer-Kompanien
1 Aufklärungs-Schwadron
2 Artillerie-Batterien
***2 Werfer-Batterien* [rocket launchers]**
1 Pionier-Kompanie
1 schwere Infanterie-Geschütz-Kompanie
2 Sturmgeschütz-Batterien
1 Flak-Batterie
1 Nachrichten-Kompanie
Versorgungs-Einheiten

In the *XXXXVIII. Panzer-Korps* sector, the so-called *SS-Panzer-Kampfgruppe Das Reich*, reported this strength:

Officers	Unterführer	Enlisted Men	Total
163	994	5,241	6,398
2.5%	15.5%	82.0%	100%

It took part in the heavy defensive fighting in the region west of Berdichev. On February 14, 1944, the *Kampfgruppe* was put under the command of the *LIX. Armee-Korps*, which redeployed it to the area of Starokonstantinov (about 100 km west of Berdichev).

Starting on March 4, 1944, in defense against the Soviet Union spring offensive launched the day before there was heavy fighting around Starokonstantinov until March 9th. During this period, more *Stämme* were pulled out of action for the reconstitution of the *2. SS-Panzer-Division Das Reich* and sent to Germany.

The *SS-Panzer-Kampfgruppe Das Reich*, reduced by this process, and by the losses in killed and wounded, to barely 1,000 men, was placed under the command of the *XXIV. Panzer-Korps* in the sector of the almost encircled *1. Panzer-Armee* on March 18, 1944.

The *Kampfgruppe* lost almost all its remaining vehicles on March 25, 1944, and marched southwards to Kamenets-Podolsky during the next few days. From here, it moved westwards in the so-called *Wandernden Kessel* ["wandering," or moving pocket] of the *1. Panzer-Armee*. After reestablishing contact with the German front and renewed deployment in battle on April 13, 1944, two days later the *Kampfgruppe* was given a movement order to France, with embarkation in Halicz, for reconstitution of the *2. SS- Panzer-Division*.

24 Formed from the operational remnants of the *Panzergrenadier-Regimenter*.

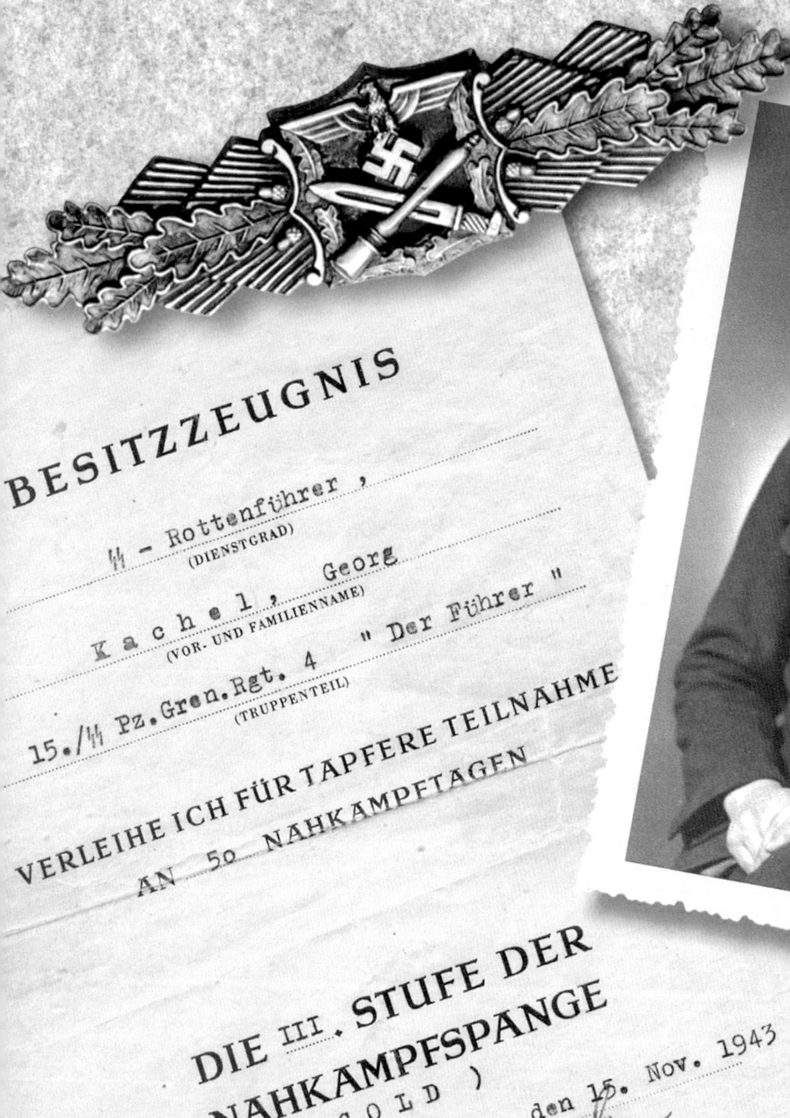

BESITZZEUGNIS

ᛋᛋ - Rottenführer ,
(DIENSTGRAD)

Kachel, Georg
(VOR- UND FAMILIENNAME)

15./ᛋᛋ Pz.Gren.Rgt. 4 " Der Führer "
(TRUPPENTEIL)

VERLEIHE ICH FÜR TAPFERE TEILNAHME
AN 50 NAHKAMPFTAGEN

DIE III. STUFE DER
NAHKAMPFSPANGE
(i. G O L D)

Rgt.Gef.Std., den 15. Nov. 1943
(ORT UND DATUM)

(UNTERSCHRIFT)

ᛋᛋ-Obersturmbannführer u.Rgt.Kdr.
(DIENSTGRAD UND DIENSTSTELLUNG)

(STEMPEL)

The *Nahkampfspange* could be awarded for 15, 30, or 50 days of close combat, in bronze, silver, or gold.

The 2. SS-Panzer-Division Das Reich

On January 24, 1944, the *SS-FHA* ordered refitting and retraining of the *2. SS-Panzergrenadier-Division*, and reclassified it as the ***2. SS-Panzer-Division Das Reich***.

To accomplish this, already in December 1943 the first *Stämme* were pulled out of active service in Russia and redeployed to the Stablack military training grounds in East Prussia. On February 2, 1944, the reorganized formation was sent to the *Oberbefehlshaber West* in France as its operational reserve in the Bordeaux region.

In fact, the *Division* retained its existing structure; it was only renamed. As of October 1943, the *Panzergrenadier-Regimenter* had been given the following numbers:

SS-Panzergrenadier-Regiment* 3 *Deutschland
SS-Panzergrenadier-Regiment* 4 *Der Führer.

On April 9, 1944, the *Division*, with a strength of some 12,000 men, was transferred to the Montauban-Toulouse region, about 200 km to the south-east. Placed under command of the *LVIII. Panzer-Korps*, refitting was carried forward and the *Division* cantonment area secured against French partisans.

Materiel and personnel replacements only arrived by the end of May 1944, with the result that most of the around 9,000 replacements still had not received any training. The majority were *Volksdeutsche* from Romania and Alsace-Lorraine.

After the Allied landing in Normandy on June 6, 1944, *2. SS-Panzer-Division Das Reich* was alerted and ordered to join the *LXVI. Armee-Korps* in the Limoges-Tulle sector, about 200 km to the north. This mission was also to clear the area of *Maquisards* at the same time. On an almost daily

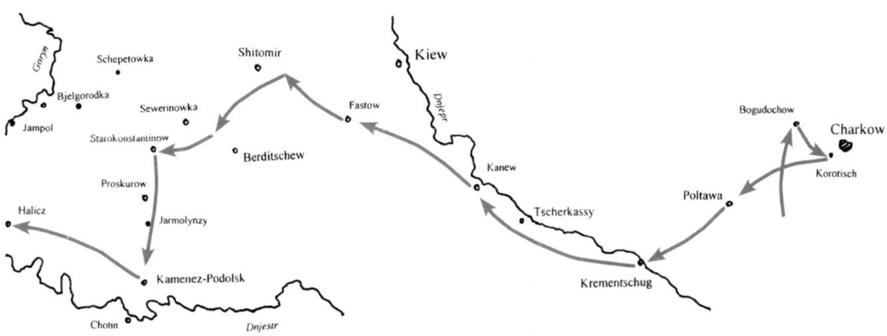

basis, the *Maquisards* were attacking both individual German vehicles and entire villages or towns throughout the region. In Tulle—as just one town—64 members of the *III./ Sicherungs-Regiment 95* had been found dead; some of them had been mutilated by the partisans. In response, the Germans hanged 98 French hostages.

These operations escalated when *SS* forces searching for *SS-Sturmbannführer* Kämpfe, *Führer* of the *III. (gp.)/SS-Panzergrenadier-Regiment 4 Der Führer*, who had fallen into the hands of the partisans, raided the village of Oradour-sur-Glane on July 10, 1944. After weapons and ammunition were found in many houses, *SS-Sturmbannführer* Dieckmann, *Führer* of the *I./SS-Panzergrenadier-Regiment 4 Der Führer*, had some 180 civilians shot. The German side investigated these events, but the investigation was abandoned after Dieckmann fell in Normandy.[25]

On June 9, 1944, members of the *Pionier-Zug* of *SS-Panzer-Aufklärungs-Abteilung 2* hanged 99 suspected *Maquisards* in Tulle after over 100 German soldiers, murdered and sometimes badly mutilated by the Resistance, had been found in and around the town.

Two days later, the *2. SS-Panzer-Division* moved through Poitiers and Tours to the area south of Le Mans. From here, the formation was ordered into the region southeast of St. Lô. When the first units arrived at the *LXXXIV. Armee-Korps* on June 16, 1944, they had marched along an approach route of over 300 km.

Not yet fully concentrated, the order came on June 26, 1944, for a regiment-strength *Kampfgruppe* of the *2. SS-Panzer-Division Das Reich* to go into action in the area southwest of Caen, about 50 km to the southwest.

British troops launched heavy attacks there two days later. On June 29, 1944, the so-called *SS-Kampfgruppe Weidinger* was briefly placed under the command of the *9. SS-Panzer-Division Hohenstaufen*.

The *Divisionkommando* reported their overall strength on June 30, 1944:

Officers	Unterführer	Enlisted Men	Total
528	3,387	16,269	20,184
2.6%	16.8%	80.6%	100%

25 In 1953, the higher military court in Bordeaux initially sentenced two members of the *Kompanie* to death; eventually, along with other defendants, they were given long prison terms. The former *Regimentskommandeu, SS-Obersturmbannführer* Weidinger, wrote about the events in his book *Kameraden* in 1962: "The tragedy of Oradour was terrible for the French population, and, humanly speaking, the behavior of *Sturmbannführer* Diekmann was inexcusable and incomprehensible to all of us .... Oradour was exclusively the consequence of the failure of a single officer, who had never received a command for such an inhuman act. He acted contrary to the express order of his *Regimentskommandeur*, to whom he simply presented a *fait accompli* after his return."

Caption: Josef Winkler, a *Volksdeutscher* from Slovakia, was first inducted into the *Waffen-SS* in summer 1944, and ultimately served in the *SS-Panzergrenadier-Regiment 3 Deutschland*.

Erfolgreiche deutsche Gegenangriffe in der Normandie

Abwehrschlacht größten Ausmaßes – Hohe Feindverluste

Aus dem Führerhauptquartier, 26. Juli. Das Oberkommando der Wehrmacht gibt bekannt:

Im Verlauf der schweren Kämpfe südlich Caen gelang es dem Feind, westlich der Straße Caen—Falaise in unsere Stellungen einzubrechen und weitere Infanterie- und Panzerkräfte nachzuführen. Unsere fanatisch kämpfenden Truppen verhinderten jedoch das Ausweiten der feindlichen Einbrüche und traten dann in den Nachmittagsstunden zum Gegenangriff an. Nach erbitterten Kämpfen waren am Abend die alten Stellungen wieder voll in unserer Hand. Die Verluste des Feindes sind hoch. 18 Panzer wurden abgeschossen.

Auch nordwestlich St. Lo tobt eine Abwehrschlacht großen Ausmaßes. Nachdem die ersten feindlichen Angriffe, die unter stärkster Artillerie- und Luftwaffenunterstützung vorgetragen wurden, abgewiesen waren, gelang es dem Feind an einigen Stellen in unsere Front einzudringen und die Straße St. Lo—Periers nach Südwesten zu überschreiten. Gegenangriffe sind im Gange.

Seit den heutigen Morgenstunden haben die Kämpfe mit großer Wucht auch auf den Raum nördlich Periers übergegriffen.

Schlachtflieger griffen feindliche Bereitstellungen im Landekopf mit gutem Erfolg an und beschädigten vor der Küste ein großes Transportschiff schwer. In Luftkämpfen wurden elf feindliche Flugzeuge abgeschossen.

Im südfranzösischen Raum wurden wiederum 110 Terroristen im Kampf niedergemacht.

Schweres V 1-Vergeltungsfeuer liegt weiterhin auf dem Großraum von London.

In Italien hat der Großangriff gegen den Raum südlich Florenz begonnen. Der erwartete Durchbruch ist dem Gegner nicht gelungen. Erst nach schwersten Kämpfen und unter besonders hohen Verlusten konnte er geringen Geländegewinn erzielen. Weitere Angriffe gegen unsere neuen Stellungen wurden zerschlagen.

Nördlich Arezzo und beiderseits des Tiber scheiterten feindliche Angriffe unter Abriegelung örtlicher Einbrüche. An der adriatischen Küste trat der Feind erneut zum Angriff an. Heftige Kämpfe sind dort noch im Gange.

Kampffähren der Kriegsmarine beschädigten vor der westitalienischen Küste zwei britische Schnellboote.

Bei Angriffen auf Nachschubgeleite in der Aegäis brachten Sicherungsfahrzeuge der Kriegsmarine, Bordflak und Jagdflieger von 15 angreifenden Bombern sieben zum Absturz.

In Galizien brachen zwischen dem oberen Dnjestr und Lemberg zahlreiche von Panzern unterstützte Angriffe der Sowjets blutig zusammen. Im Stadtgebiet von Lemberg warfen unsere Truppen den Feind im Gegenangriff zurück.

Im Abschnitt einer Armee wurden in der Zeit vom 14. bis 23. Juli 553 feindliche Panzer abgeschossen. Hierbei hat sich die hamburgische 20. Panzergrenadier-Division unter Führung von Generalleutnant Jauer besonders ausgezeichnet.

Im Kampfraum zwischen oberem Bug und Weichsel gewann der Feind gegen den San und den Raum von Lublin weiter Boden. Südöstlich Lublin wurden dagegen alle feindlichen Angriffe zerschlagen.

Zwischen Brest-Litowsk und Grodno, sowie östlich und nordöstlich Kauen scheiterten alle feindlichen Durchbruchsversuche an der zähen Abwehr unserer Divisionen.

Auch an der Front zwischen Dünaburg und dem Finnischen Meerbusen errangen unsere Truppen gegen alle Durchbruchsangriffe der Bolschewisten einen vollen Abwehrerfolg. 47 feindliche Panzer wurden dort abgeschossen.

Hauptmann Weißenberger, Gruppenkommandeur in einem Jagdgeschwader, errang an der Ostfront seinen 200. Luftsieg.

Feindliche Bomberverbände griffen Orte in West- und Südostdeutschland an. Besonders in Stuttgart entstanden durch einen erneuten Terrorangriff Schäden und Personenverluste.

Einzelne feindliche Flugzeuge warfen außerdem Bomben auf das Gebiet der Reichshauptstadt und auf Orte in Ostpreußen.

Luftverteidigungskräfte brachten 51 feindliche Flugzeuge zum Absturz.

2 cm *Flak* 38.

Since a number of units were still stationed in southern France to complete their training, only some elements were deployed in Normandy. The formation's fighting power also could not be compared with that of earlier times, because the often forcibly conscripted *Volksdeutsche* at times made up 50% of the *Division*.

On July 2, 1944, the *Kampfgruppe*, after suffering losses of a total of 846 killed in action and wounded, was withdrawn from active service and ordered back into the *Division* assembly area at St. Lô. In the critical situation which had developed since July 4, 1944, the commanding *LXXXIV. Armee-Korps* assigned the incoming elements of the *2. SS-Panzer-Division*, divided into a number of battle groups, to be placed under the command of other formations. As a result, units were assigned to the sector of the *353. Infanterie-Division* northeast of St. Germain, and to the *17. SS Panzergrenadier-Division* northwest of St. Lô.

Beyond this, the *2. SS-Panzer-Division* command also took over its own front sector northeast of Periers (about 25 km northwest of St. Lô) on July 6, 1944; after fierce fighting, it pulled back on July 27, 1944, to a line south of Periers.

When U.S. forces to the east succeeded in breaking through the German front in the direction of Granville, it became apparent that the Germans were being forced into a pocket at Coutances (about 25 km southwest of St. Lô). To escape encirclement the order was issued to move south, and to attempt to break through at Granville on July 29, 1944, towards Avranches. Then-*Stabsscharführer* [Staff Sergeant] Fred Zura remembers the retreat:

> In the fighting during the retreat my supply train was scattered by the combat unit, so we moved alone through enemy territory. Suddenly, we were under heavy enemy fire from artillery and strafing by the Seine, and could not find a bridge far and wide. Then two men of the *Munitionsstaffel* [ammunition supply echelon] reported to me; they had been boatmen on inland waterways. We found a large barge, and by night they brought us and all our vehicles to the other bank with it. Despite all the "Christmas trees" [German popular term for marker flares] and bombs, we lucked out in getting all our motor vehicles safely across the river. The men in the outfit were dead tired. After a few days, we found our battery and detachment again. For saving all the vehicles, I was given the *Kriegsverdienstkreuz I. Klasse* [War Service Cross 1st class]."

Moving once more into defensive positions at Percy, by August 5, 1944, the units had pulled back into the region east of Mortain. From here, already the next day the units took part in Operation *Lüttich*, with the aim of recapturing Avranches, about 35 km distant. A questionable mission for troops who had only just escaped from the pocket, and had lost the bulk of their heavy weapons and equipment.

Reinforced by a *Kampfgruppe* from the *17. SS-Panzergrenadier-Division Götz von Berlichingen*, the *2. SS-Panzer-Division Das Reich* was supposed to occupy Mortain on August 7, 1944. The enemy's materiel superiority, especially its absolute air superiority, caused the Germans to quickly abandon the offensive. After heavy American counterattacks, they began to withdraw to their original positions on August 11, 1944. The operation had resulted in large numbers of casualties and even more materiel losses, but brought no success.

In chaotic circumstances and under continuous air strikes, on August 15, 1944, the units were ordered through Flers (about 35 km northeast of Mortain) to the area of Argentan, in order to halt the American drive to the north there.

While elements of the *Division* were engaged in heavy fighting against U.S. troops the next day at Trun (about 20 km north of Argentan), the remaining elements were to concentrate south of Vimoutiers (about 15 km northeast of Trun) as a *Heeresgruppenreserve*. When the Allies succeeded in closing off the Falaise pocket on August 19, 1944, the *2. SS-Panzer-Division Das Reich*–now again assembled–as part of the *II. SS-Panzer-Korps*, remained outside the pocket.

On August 20, 1944, the units formed up to break through the pocket from south of Trun. In the chaos of constant artillery and tank shelling and waves of fighter-bomber attacks, only some of the troops were able to escape from the pocket.

The *2. SS-Panzer-Division* secured the escape of these troops and, on August 23, 1944, redeployed to the Elbeuf area. Already the next day, they were engaged in fighting with Allied forces striving to prevent the German troops from crossing the Seine. In the intense bombing attacks, a large number of the remaining vehicles were lost. On August 28, 1944, the *Division* abandoned the bridgehead between Rouen and Elbeuf and was ordered to the region east of Rouen.

The troop units, moving by way of Montidier (about 30 km southeast of St. Amiens), reached the Belgian border near Hierson on August 31, 1944. In early September 1944, the remnants of the *Division* at Givet (about 15 km southwest of Dinant) moved into positions on the Meuse.

By September 7, 1944, the positions across the Ourthe river south of Liège were retaken. Often with no contact with other units, the *Division*–now under command of the *I.* SS *Panzer-Korps*–under constant pressure from the enemy (including many partisan attacks), pulled back by way of Stavelot to the *Westwall* west of Prüm (about 60 km northwest of Trier).

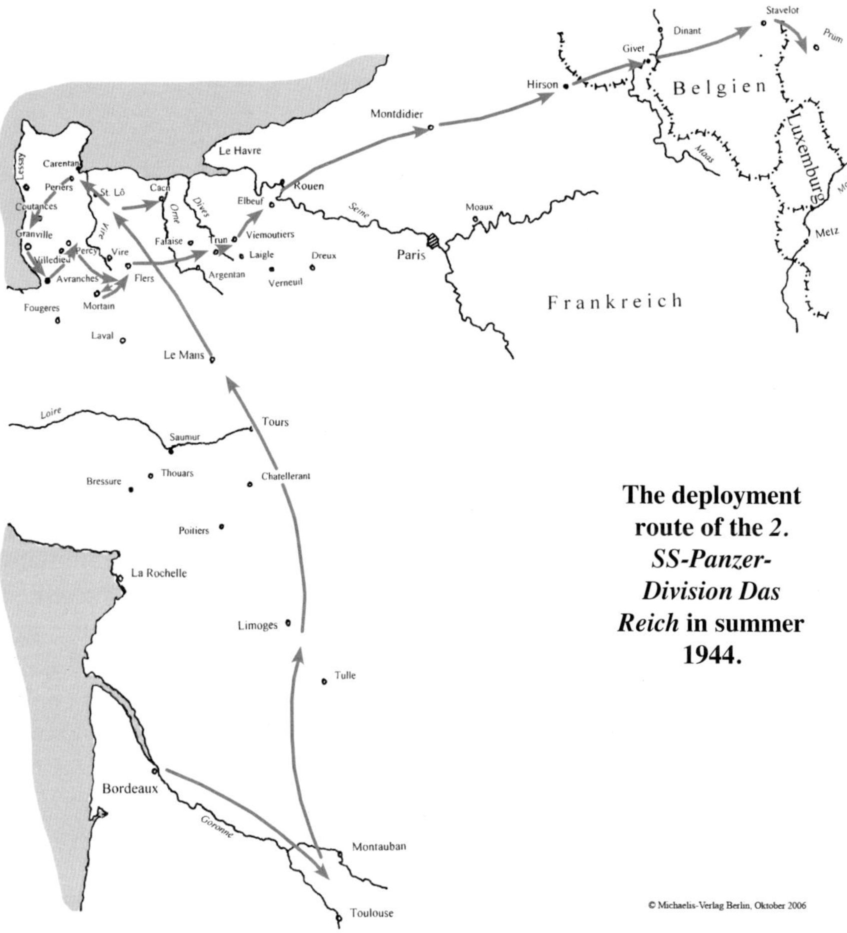

The deployment route of the *2. SS-Panzer-Division Das Reich* in summer 1944.

In a sector about 30 km long, they moved into bunker positions, and the units were reinforced by *Wehrmacht* elements. The defense of the *Westwall* was improvised, because no preparations had been made there. Since the bunkers could not provide required security under massive enemy fire, field positions were set up between the bunkers which were easier to hold.

On September 20, 1944, the formation reported its strength:

	Officers	Unterführer	Enlisted Men	Total
Actual	312	2,228	9,817	12,357
	2.5%	18.0%	79.5%	100 %
Authorized	614	3,923	13,260	17,797
	3.5%	22.0%	74.5%	100%

SS-Panzer-Regiment 2, then being reconstituted, was not included in the *Tagesstärke*. The *Regiment* had some 2,000 men, so the actual total strength was about 14,300 men.

Facing repeated fiercely-contested offensive and defensive battles, *2. SS-Panzer-Division* was again briefly placed under the command of the *LXVI. Armee-Korps* in mid-October 1944. At the end of the month, it was finally pulled out of the *HKL* and redeployed to the area south of Paderborn for refitting and retraining.

Until November 12, 1944, there were attempts to reinforce the units with personnel and equipment for the upcoming Rundstedt offensive. Initially ordered the next day to the region of Krefeld-Rheydt-Grevenbroich, *2. SS-Panzer-Division Das Reich* moved on December 13, 1944, to the area west of Cologne. At this time it reported its strength:

	Authorized	Actual
Panzer IV	30	28
Panzer V Panther	60	58
Sturmgeschütze	28	48
***schwere Pak* 7.5 cm**	28	18
leichte Feldhaubitzen	-	36
schwere Feldhaubitzen	-	22
10 cm *Kanonen*	-	5

With more than 14,000 men, the formation had, at least nominally, attained a sufficient personnel and exceptionally strong materiel authorized strength. However, there were limiting circumstances: there was very little fuel for the vehicles and only limited ammunition for the guns available, and the replacements were inadequately trained. These were made up of, in addition to 17- and 18-year-old Germans from the Reich, primarily commandeered members of the *Luftwaffe* and *Kriegsmarine*, as well as older *Volksdeutsche*–some from Slovakia–and foreign volunteers.

On December 15, 1944, *2. SS-Panzer-Division Das Reich* moved into its assembly area for the Ardennes Offensive at Euskirchen, and formed, together with the *9. SS-Panzer-Division Hohenstaufen* in the *II.* SS *Panzer-Korps*, the reserve for the *5. Panzer-Armee*. On December 21, 1944, moving by way of Jünkerath, the units crossed the border to Luxembourg at Dasburg, five days after the beginning of the great Western offensive. Lack of fuel and congested streets and roads caused many difficulties. At least the weather still did not allow a large-scale deployment of Allied air forces.

On December 23, 1944, the first intense fighting occurred in Baraque Fraiture (about 6 km southwest of Lierneux). Next came heavy fighting in the area of Grandmeril, during the attempt to push toward Liège. The reinforced *SS-Panzer-Aufklärungs-Abteilung 2*–under command of the *12. Volksgrenadier-Division*–was to support the encirclement of U.S. troops in the area of St. Vith on December 24, 1944. This resulted in extremely intense fighting.

Clearing weather brought Allied air superiority to bear. Waves of bombardment hit the units, and they were strafed by low-flying aircraft. As the U.S. Army launched a counteroffensive with this support on January 4, 1945, after more fierce and very bloody battles, on January 17, 1945, the *2. SS-Panzer-Division* was ordered to withdraw behind the *Westwall* to east of Prüm.

This concentration was delayed by lack of fuel and spare parts for the damaged weapons and vehicles. Without any comprehensive opportunity to rectify the shortages, in early February 1945, transport began for the forthcoming German *Plattensee-Offensive* in Hungary.

For camouflage, the *2. SS-Panzer-Division Das Reich*, concentrated near Farad-Csorna (about 50 km east of Sopron [German: Ödenburg]), was first designated the so-called *Ausbildungsgruppe Nord* [training group North]. After more personnel replacements arrived–who consisted, however, as was generally the case since the summer of 1944, of barely-trained recruits or members of the *Luftwaffe* and *Marine* not previously deployed as *Infanterie*– on March 1, 1945, the *Divisionskommando* reported a strength of:

19,542 *Führer* and *sonstige Dienstgrade*.

On March 3, 1945, *Ausbildungsgruppe Nord* moved through Raab towards Székesfehérvár. Because of the muddy and congested roads, not all of the units were able to reach the ordered assembly southeast of Székesfehérvár by March 6, 1945.

On March 7, 1945, the *Division* finally formed up without artillery support between Seregelyes and Aba for the costly attack to the southeast. Accompanying *Panzer* got stuck in the mud; the attack foundered. Only on March 11, 1945, did they succeed in gaining ground against the Red Army's fierce defense and counterattacks. Casualties due to massive enemy artillery fire, tank attacks, and shelling by entire *Pak-Riegel* [anti-tank gun defense lines] rose enormously.

During the Soviet's *Wiener Operation* [Vienna Offensive], launched on March 16, 1945, *2. SS-Panzer-Division Das Reich* was pulled out of its positions in the *II. SS Panzer-Korps* sector on March 18, 1945, and concentrated in the area southwest of Székesfehérvár.

The formation–its camouflage designation as *Ausbildungsgruppe Nord* was ended that day–was only about 60% mobile at that time. Its fighting strength had also fallen by approximately 50%, to 5,000 men.

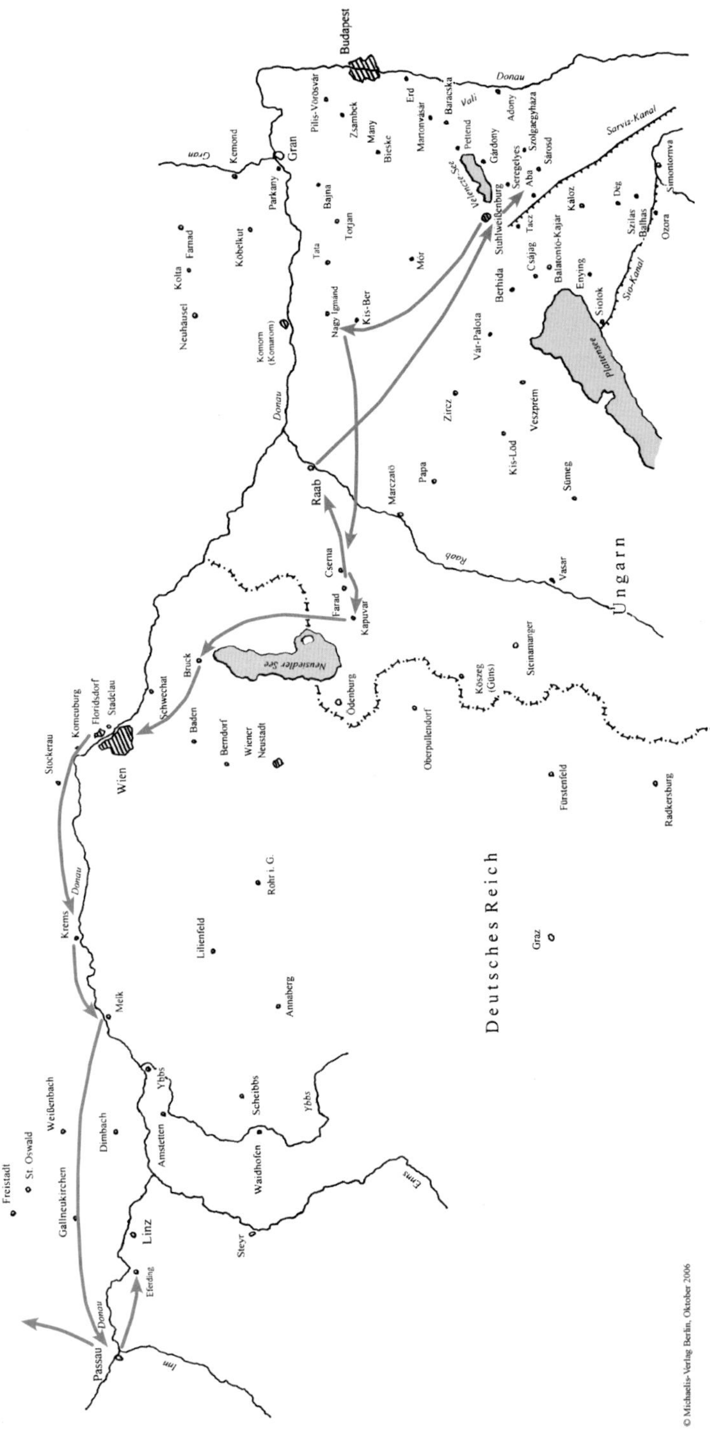
Budapest
Gran
Raab
Kapuvar
Bruck
Wien
Krems
Melk
Ybbs
Linz
Passau
Stuhlweißenburg
Nagy Igmand
Kis-Ber
Plattensee
Neusiedler See
Donau
Raab
Ungarn
Deutsches Reich
Graz
© Michaelis-Verlag Berlin, Oktober 2006

On March 20, 1945, the troop units moved to the area of Nagyigmánd-Kisbér (about 15 km south of Komárom), to re-close the gaps which had emerged here. Four days later, the *Division* was again reinforced with about 2,800 *Marine* members. Their lack of infantry training, however, meant this was nothing but a reinforcement in numbers.

Soviet superiority forced them to withdraw through Csorna to Kapuvar, where they took up positions on March 28, 1945, when the *Division* still had:

Panzer IV	**5**
Panzer V	**2**
Jagdpanzer IV	**2**
Jagdpanzer V	**5**
Sturmgeschütze	**3**
***Feldhaubitzen* 10.5 cm**	**19**
***Feldhaubitzen* 15 cm**	**21**
***Feldkanonen* 10 cm**	**3**

Because there was no coherent German front, the Red Army was able–especially with its strong tank units–to push through the spread-out German formations in many places. This led to chaotic conditions and extremely high casualties. The remnants of the *2. SS-Panzer-D*ivision withdrew by April 2, 1945, east of Lake Neusiedl to Bruck an der Leitha.

From there, the units streamed into the *Verteidigungsbezirk* [defensive area] at Vienna and moved, fighting in delaying tactics, over the Danube Canal. Under extremely heavy Soviet fire, they were able to hold a small bridgehead on the Floridsdorfer bridge until April 13, 1945.

After brief defensive operations in the area northeast of Stockerau, the battered force marched through Krems to Melk. On April 20, 1945, *SS-Panzergrenadier-Regiment 3 Deutschland* was placed under command of the *LXXXIV. Panzer-Korps*, to secure the crossings over the Inn and Danube rivers near Passau. During transport of the remaining troop units to Passau, on April 26, 1945, *SS-Panzergrenadier-Regiment 4 Der Führer* was ordered to the *Protektorat Böhmen und Mähren.* As the majority of the *Division* followed the *Regiment* through Prague to the area northeast of Dresden, *SS-Panzergrenadier-Regiment 3* redeployed from Passau to the area of Eferding (about 20 km west of Linz). On May 5, 1945, the *Regiment* was placed under the command of the *9. SS-Panzer-Division Hohenstaufen.*

The next day, *SS-Panzergrenadier-Regiment 4 Der Führer* received the order to take part in the battle against the uprising which had erupted in Prague. On May 7, 1945, the reinforced *Regiment*, after a 120-km march, came to the relief of the encircled German troops and civilians. After fierce battles with Czech partisans, they were able to make contact with the *Wehrmachtbefehlshaber* [military commander in occupied territory] of Prague. When the surrender was announced, the units attempted to go into American captivity at Pilsen.

This ended the war deployment of the *2. SS-Panzer-Division Das Reich*. As hardly any other *Waffen-SS Division*, this force demonstrated a high level of motivation, training, and combat effectiveness until 1944. Due to enormous casualties, its operational capacity was increasingly reduced during the last year of the war. The poorly trained replacements–by 1945, about 50% of the *Division* were former members of the *Luftwaffe*, *Kriegsmarine*, *Polizei*, or *Hitlerjungend*–and the lack of vehicles, weaponry, and ammunition were the root causes of this loss.

3.

SS-PANZER-DIVISION TOTENKOPF

The SS-Totenkopf-Division

On May 18, 1939, Adolf Hitler declared further, that the *SS-Verfügungstruppen* be limited to a maximum of 20,000 men, and when training was completed, these forces should be consolidated into an *SS-Division*. By doing this, Hitler was taking the *Wehrmachtführung*'s requests into account; already in 1934, they had seen their position threatened by the *SA* [*Sturm Abteilung*: Assault Division] paramilitary party formations.

Just four months later, he revised his declaration and ordered, after discussions with the Chief of the *Ordnungspolizei* [Order Police] and the *Führer* of the *SS-Totenkopf-Verbände (SS-TV)* [*Totenkopf* formations]:

> that those members of younger age groups who are subject to conscription, who are to be found in the *SS-Totenkopfverbände* and in the *Ordnungspolizei* formations, be consolidated into *Regimenter* for the duration of their mobilization, inclusive of their *Führer* and *Unterführer*, to the extent that they are suitable for deployment as front line combat troops; and, after formation as well as outfitting with the *Division* troops which are still lacking, these should, as much as possible, be formed and trained as combat *Divisionen*.

SS-Obergruppenführer **Eicke commanded what became the *SS-Panzergrenadier-Division Totenkopf* until his death on 2/26/1943.**

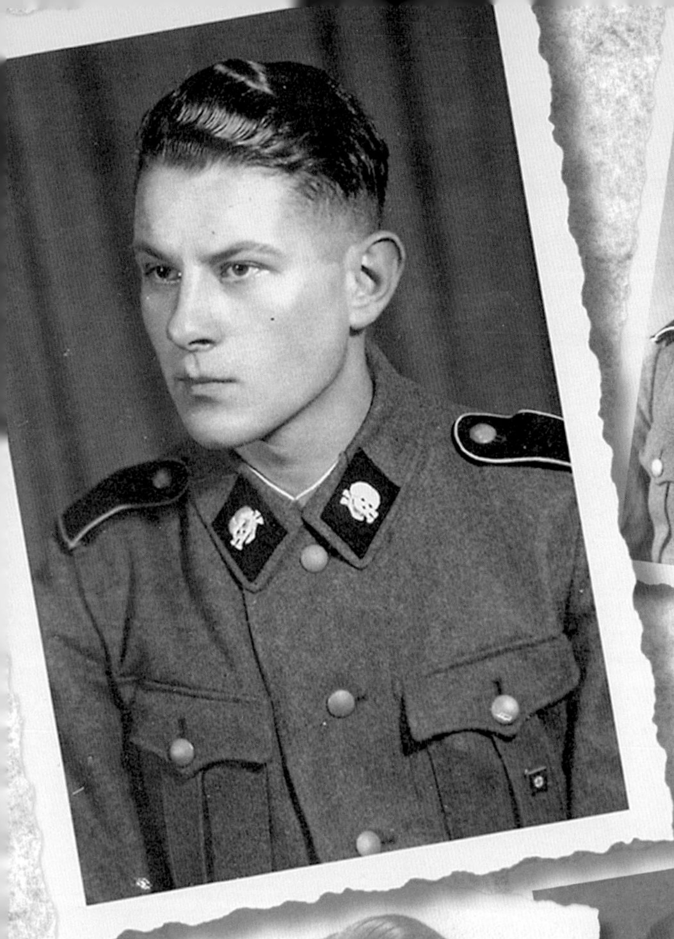

Members of the *SS-Totenkopf-Division*.

Based on their fundamental conceptions, the *Oberbefehlshaber des Heeres*, *Generaloberst* [Full General] von Brauchitsch, and the leader of the *Ersatzheer* [Replacement or Reserve Army], *General* [Lieutenant General] von Fromm, were extremely outraged by this command; Hitler then relented and allowed, at least temporarily, the *Polizei-Division* which was to be newly raised, to be set up within the framework of the *Heer*.

The former *Inspekteur* [Inspector] of the *SS-Totenkopf-Verbände, SS-Gruppenführer* Eicke, was given responsibility for establishing the second *SS-Division*. To do this, about 6,500 *SS-TV* men and 6,000 members–mostly between the ages of 30 and 40–of the reinforced *SS-Totenkopf-Standarten,* were ordered to the *SS* training camp at Dachau. When the local accommodations proved insufficient, the Dachau *KL* [*Konzentrationslager*: concentration camp] was cleared out, and the approximately 2,500 prisoners there were sent to the Buchenwald concentration camp.[26]

The new SS-Division was to be organized as follows:

DIVISIONSSTAB
SS-Totenkopf-Infanterie-Regiment 1[27]
Bataillon
1.-3. Schützen-Kompanie
4. (schwere) Kompanie
Bataillon
5.-7. Schützen-Kompanie
8. (schwere) Kompanie
Bataillon
9.-11. Schützen-Kompanie
12. (schwere) Kompanie
SS-Totenkopf-Infanterie-Regiment 2[28] **(ditto)**
SS-Totenkopf-Infanterie-Regiment 3[29] **(ditto)**
SS-Totenkopf-Aufklärungs-Abteilung[30]
2 *Kradschützen-Schwadronen*
1 *Panzer-Schwadron* [mechanized cavalry reconnaissance squadron]
1. *Zug* with 3 *Skoda-Panzer 10 t.*
2. *Zug* with 3 *Skoda-Panzer 10 t.*
3. *Zug* with 3 *Panzerabwehrkanonen*

26 For the history of the *SS-Totenkopf-Verbände* cf. chapter: The *SS-Totenkopf-Verbände*.
27 Formerly *1. SS-Totenkopf-Standarte Oberbayern*.
28 Elements of *2. SS-Totenkopf-Standarte Brandenburg* and *3. SS-Totenkopf-Standarte Thüringen*.
29 Formerly *SS-Heimwehr Danzig (I. Bataillon),* elements of *3. SS-Totenkopf-Standarte Thüringen (II. Bataillon)*, and *Reservisten (III. Bataillon)*.
30 Elements of *III. /SS-Totenkopf-Standarte 6* in Prague-Ruzyne.

***SS-Totenkopf-Panzerjäger-Abteilung*[31]**
- **3 *Kompanien***

***SS-Totenkopf-Pionier-Bataillon*[32]**
- **3 *Kompanien***

SS-Totenkopf-Nachschubdienste
- **3 *Werkstatt-Kompanien***
- **1 *Nachschub-Kompanie***
- **9 small *Nachschub-Kolonnen* [supply column]**
- **3 large *Betriebsstoff-Kolonnen* [fuel column]**

SS-Totenkopf-Verwaltungsdienste
- ***Verpflegungsamt* [ration supply office]**
- ***Bäckerei-Kompanie* [bakery company]**
- ***Schlächterei-Kompanie* [Butcher]**

***SS-Totenkopf-Sanitäts-Abteilung*[33]**
- **2 *Sanitäts-Kompanien***
- **3 *Krankenkraftwagen-Züge***

SS-Totenkopf-Veterinär-Kompanie

***SS-Totenkopf-Artillerie-Regiment*[34]**
- **3 *Abteilungen (leichte Feldhaubitzen 10.5 cm)***
- **1 *schwere Abteilung*[35] *(schwere Feldhaubitzen)***

***SS-Totenkopf-Nachrichten-Abteilung*[36]**
- **1. *Kompanie (Fernsprecher)***
- **2. *Kompanie (Funker)***

The *Heer* undertook outfitting the formations with weapons and equipment, of which a large amount came from captured Czech materiel. Although it was originally planned to be a *bespannt* [horse-drawn or propelled] *Infanterie-Division*, *SS-Gruppenführer* Eicke was able to motorize the formation.

On December 1, 1939, the *SS-Totenkopf-Division* was redeployed to the Ludwigsburg-Heilbronn area as a *Heeresreserve*. From there, starting on January 30, 1940, the formation was transferred to the Münsingen troop training grounds, where, under command of the *XIV. Armee-Korps*, it was to receive formation training. This was complicated by the weather conditions, including heavy snowfall, however, and the *Divisionskommandeur's* attempts to have the formation moved from the training grounds failed. Two years later, in Russia, they would be faced with even more severe conditions in combat.

31 Formed from *Panzerabwehr-Kompanie Leiner* of the *SS-Heimwehr Danzig* and *Reservisten.*
32 Elements of *SS-VT SS-Pionier-Sturmbanne* and *Reservisten.*
33 Formed from the Sanitätsabteilung of SS-TV Oranienburg.
34 Formed from the II. /SS-Artillerie-Standarte of the SS-VT and the SS-Totenkopf-Artillerie-Ersatz-Abteilung Oranienburg.
35 Raised on the order of March 22, 1940; originally no schwere Abteilung was envisaged.
36 Elements of SS-Nachrichten-Sturmbann of the SS-VT and the Nachrichtenzug of SS-Heimwehr Danzig.

On March 7, 1940, the formation was redeployed to the Brilon-Frankenberg-Korbach-Arolsen region, to be at the disposition of *AOK 2*. On May 1, 1940, the *Division* reported a strength of:

Officers	Unterführer	Enlisted Men	Total
668	2,825	17,818	21,311
3.1%	13.3%	83.6%	100%

When the Western campaign began on May 10, 1940, the *SS-Totenkopf-Division* was redeployed on May 12, 1940, to the area northeast of Cologne as an *OKH-Reserve*. From there, starting on May 17, 1940, the units marched through Jülich to Geilenkirchen, where they were placed under the command of the *4. Armee*. Two days later came the order to go into action, and march in the sector of the *XXXIX. Armee-Korps*, southwest to Cambrai. While the first German troops had already reached the English Channel by May 20, 1940, thus splitting the Allied forces, the *SS-Totenkopf Division*–under command of the *XVI. Armee-Korps*–was deployed to the northwest, against Arras. After some fierce fighting, the German troops succeeded in beginning the destruction of the enemy troops north of the Somme. For the *SS-Totenkopf-Division*–since it still had no *Flak-Abteilung* of its own; it had the *Luftwaffe leichte Flak-Abteilung 73* under its command–this meant an advance to Bethune.

At the La Bassee Canal, the *XVI. Armee-Korps* initially ordered the forces to go on the defensive on May 24, 1940. Two days later, the *Division* crossed the Canal to the northeast, towards Estaires-Fromelles. There can be no discussion of any "severely weakened British troops" whom the *Division* was to face! There was extremely heavy fighting with high casualties. Among the fallen was *SS-Standartenführer* Goetze, former *Kommandeur* of the *SS-Heimwehr Danzig* and current *Kommandeur* of *SS-Totenkopf-Infanterie-Regiment 3*, who was killed in action on May 27, 1940, in the village of Le Paradis. The day before, the Germans had committed a war crime at Le Paradis. There, *SS-Obersturmführer* Knöchlein-Kompanieführer of *SS-Totenkopf-Infanterie-Regiment 2* had 99 British soldiers, who had been taken as prisoners of war, shot. Two of them survived and were able to hide. They were re-taken three days later by a *Wehrmacht* unit and remained in German captivity until the end of the war. After the war, Knöchlein was sentenced to death for this incident and hanged in Hamburg on January 28, 1949. A former member remembers:

> After a social evening with the *Hitlerjugend*, I reported to the *SS-Totenkopf-Verbände* and was inducted into the *2. SS-Totenkopf-Standarte Brandenburg* in October. As a member of a *schwere Kompanie*, I served on an sMG. Accordingly, I was assigned to a watchtower at the Sachsenhausen concentration camp. Fortunately, I never had to shoot. When the German *Wehrmacht* marched into Austria, we were annoyed that we could not go with them, and as the Polish campaign started, we were just as disappointed not to be deployed. But then, with the *SS-Totenkopf-Division* at Arras, as the first enemy shells were flying over our heads, at first we didn't even know what was going on. We got stomach aches already from seeing the first casualties. The British shot so-called dum-dum bullets at us, which caused incredible wounds and violated the Hague Land War orders [Conventions and Regulations concerning the Laws and Customs of War on Land]. When the British came at us on a captured German *Panzerspähwagen* and suddenly opened fire, several *Kameraden* [comrades] were killed or wounded. *SS-Hauptsturmführer* Knöchlein then had about 100 British prisoners of war shot. For us at that time, that was only right–today, of course, you see it in a different way. It is always the wrong people who have to pay.

On May 31, 1940, the *Division* was pulled out of the fighting and, under command of the *XIV. Armee-Korps*, assigned to guarding the coast in the sector between Boulogne and Calais. This was not because they had failed in the fighting, but because they had become redundant, due to the steady narrowing of the pocket of enemy forces; in addition, the German leadership wanted to be able to oppose any renewed British landing attempts. Since the German formations had already broken through the Weygard line, which lay across the Somme-Oisne-Aisne Canal sector, the *SS-Totenkopf-Division* was sent 500 men as replacements, to compensate for the casualties suffered so far. On June 6th, *SS-Gruppenführer* and *Generalleutnant* Eicke reported that his *Division* was again "fully operational." Three days later, the formation was placed under command of the *6. Armee* and ordered to the Peronne area.

On June 14, 1940, it was again placed under command of the *XIV. Armee-Korps*, in the area south of Amiens. Its mission at hand involved, in the heat of high summer, little more fighting than the almost non-combat pursuit of the fleeing enemy. The French troops were totally dejected, and at times simply surrendered voluntarily in large groups. On June 17, 1940, the *SS-Totenkopf-Division* moved further south and occupied the bridges over the Loire at Marcigny, Iguerande, and Pouilly-sous-Charlieu. Three days later, the formation was already west of Lyon! By June 20, 1940, the *XIV. Armee-*

Korps was withdrawn from active service, in order to occupy the Atlantic coast down to the Spanish border, in the sector of *Heeresgruppe B* south and southeast of Bordeaux. Five days later, the ceasefire with France came into effect. The Western Campaign was over.

In the 20 days of fighting, the *SS-Totenkopf-Division* had lost:

	Officers	Other Ranks
Killed in action:	18	321
Wounded:	34	747

On July 13, 1940, the formation was marched to the newly trained *2. Armee* at Avallon, primarily to secure the Line of Demarcation and make it possible to resume training. One special assignment was to guard the Auxerre prisoner of war camp, which held about 15,000 French soldiers.

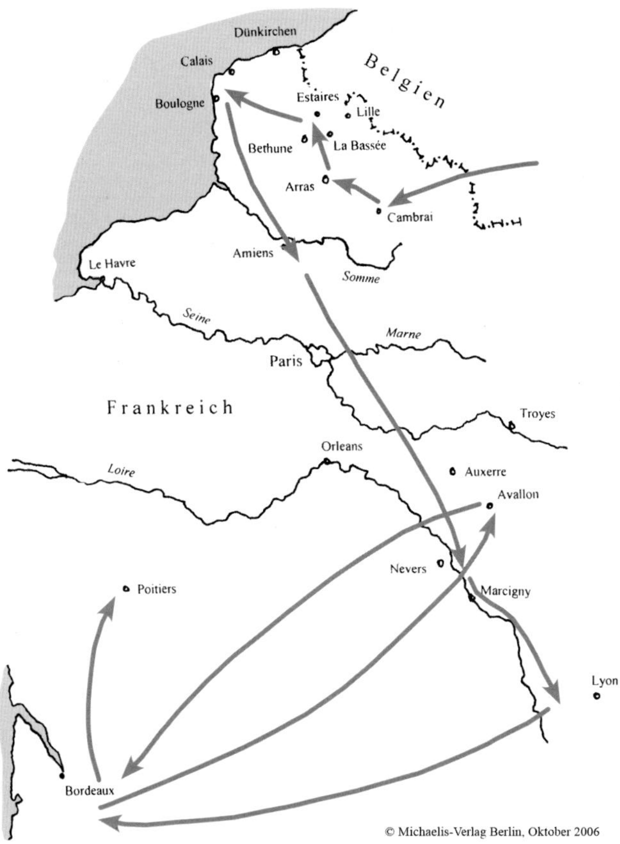

Deployment route of the *SS-Totenkopf* Division in the Western campaign

Members of the *SS-Totenkopf* Division in 1940.

Leo Wilm as driver of a BMW R-12 for *Stab/SS-T.I.R. 3* [*Totenkopf-Infanterie-Regiment*].

The *Kradmeldestaffel* [motorcycle messenger detachment] of *SS-T.I.R*. At center is the *Regimentskommandeur*, *SS-Standartenführer* Goetze.

The several burial places of *SS-Standartenführer* Goetze, *Kommandeur* of *SS-Totenkopf Regiment 3*, who was killed in action in France on 5/25/40.

A captured French Panhard reconnaissance car was immediately used in the fray.

The *SS-Totenkopf* Division in the French campaign.

Schwere Kompanie 8.14 cm *Granatwerfer* [mortar gunners].

French prisoners of war.

SS-Brigadeführer **Keppler (at left front) commanded the** ***SS-Totenkopf-Division*** **from July to September 1941.**

Kübelwagen **[command car]** ***Adler*** **[eagle]** ***3*** **of the** ***SS-Pionier-Bataillon Totenkopf*.**

In early August 1940, the *Division* was sent around 900 men from the replacement units, to compensate for its casualties and to replace older reservists. The retiring older age groups were dismissed from service completely, and took over functions in the replacement troop units or in concentration camps. By the end of the month there was another redeployment already, this time back to the *7. Armee* south of Bordeaux. There, *Division* elements were stationed along the Demarcation Line.

While the *Division* got intensified training in various areas in the sector of the *XXXIX. Armee-Korps*, in April 1941, formation was started for its own lacking *SS-Totenkopf-Flak-Abteilung* at Dachau. This consisted of one *Batterie* with 12 *Geschützen* 2 cm, one *Batterie* with 12 *Geschützen* 3.7 cm, and one *Batterie* with 4 *Geschützen* 8.8 cm.

On April 26, 1941, the formation was placed for a short time under command of the *XXXI. Armee-Korps*; three weeks later, it was commanded to join the *LIX. Armee-Korps* in the Saintes-Poitiers-Niort region. From there, at the end of May 1941, the *SS-Totenkopf-Division* was transported by rail through Marburg-Frankfurt/Oder-Posen to Marienwerder, which it reached on June 10, 1941.

There, in preparation for the imminent *Unternehmen Barbarossa*, it was placed under command of *Panzergruppe 4*. On June 19, 1941, the march began to the assembly areas at Taplacken-Knablacken-Pregelswalde-Sandy Itten.

Three days later, the campaign against the Soviet Union was launched. *SS-Totenkopf-Division* received its order for action for this campaign on June 24, 1941. Following the already far-advanced *Panzer* forces, the formation was to secure the *LVI. Armee-Korps (mot.)* rear areas. On the night of June 25, 1941, the units crossed the Lithuanian border and marched through Ariogola-Kaunas-Vilkomir-Zarasai, towards the Latvian border. On this march, they primarily were to scour through the extensive forest areas for scattered enemy forces. On June 29, 1941, the *Division*, marching in pouring rain in a strength of 18,754 men, reached the bridgehead at the badly damaged Duafgavpils [German: Dünaburg].

There, the formation took over securing the right flank of the *LVI. Armee-Korps (mot.)* and pushed through to the northeast, through Dagda-Bukmuiza-Rosenov, just in front of the Russian border. It had already suffered many casualties just in the maneuvering area before the Stalin Line, which ran from Lake Peipus to Sebesh. The units also scoured the vast forest and swamp areas, where overrun enemy troops had been left behind.

On July 6, 1941, the *Division* emerged from the Rosenov area to break through the Stalin Line to the Opochka-Sebesh road and the village of

Sebesh. In the fields, forests, and swamps, the enemy bunkers for in-depth defense and its strong artillery positions formed such obstacles that *Panzergruppe 4* was considering temporarily calling off the attack. After heavy fighting and extremely high casualties, the *SS-Totenkopf-Infanterie-Regimenter 2* and *3* were able to take Sebesh on the afternoon of July 8, 1941. In this battle, the retreating enemy forces attacked *SS-Totenkopf-Infanterie-Regiment 1*, positioned north of Sebesh to Opochka, from behind. The next day, the *Division* elements stationed near Sebesh reinforced their fellow *Regiment*–which meanwhile had been encircled by enemy units–for the fierce fighting around Opochka. This was finally taken on July 10, 1941. *SS-Oberscharführer* Wieninger (*III. /SS-Totenkopf-Artillerie-Regiment*) wrote during this time to his wife:

> Once again, I am able to dedicate a few spare minutes to you and tell you quickly that I'm healthy and things are going well for me. This war here is by all means totally, totally different from the one against France, and I've never longed so much for quiet and cleanliness as I do right now. You simply can't describe the situation here: you have to have seen it all with your own eyes to be able to understand it! Yes, I can only keep saying that I will be overjoyed when this comes to an end. Not that we are afraid of dying, because we have long been used to that, and if that happens to you, you just can never change it; but the constant rush, all the dirt and dust, always being separate and the loneliness, all the confusion and everything else, is making me over time both physically sick and emotionally disturbed. Now, thank God, we have a good consolation: we aren't fighting for nothing, because this is about our home country, and we are therefore giving our loved ones a secure life. Although many of us will never be able to see our homes again, still it was not for nothing; everything we have to suffer and endure here, will mean our future! We must think this way, and this is how we think–otherwise everything would be much worse! It has just begun again to get unpleasant here with us, some *Kameraden* have caught it again, and soon we will have to get out of this spot. But don't you worry, somehow this war will pass, and we hope that we still be able to come home healthy!

The severity of previous battles was also evident in the casualty figures. In the first four days of fighting in Russia, the *SS-Totenkopf-Division* had more men killed in action and wounded than in the entire 1940 Western campaign:

	Officers	Other Ranks
Killed in action:	30	460
Wounded:	58	1,315

Because of a total loss of nearly 1,800 men, *SS-Totenkopf-Regiment 2* was disbanded, and the remaining troops were divided between the other two *Regimenter*.

Still deployed to cover the *Korps* right flank, the *Division* now marched into the Porchov bridgehead without encountering major combat. From there the units reached Szoltzy, to the northeast. By their constant attacks, Soviet troops inflicted heavy casualties on the German formations in the extremely difficult terrain of woods and swamps. On July 31, 1941, the *SS-Totenkopf-Division* was placed under command of the *XXVIII. Armee-Korps (16. Armee)*. On August 10, 1941, while going on the offensive on the right flank, the formation reported a strength:

Officers	Unterführer	Enlisted Men	Total
399	1,953	12,254	14,606
1.2%	6.0%	92.8%	100%

SS-Oberscharführer Wieninger described the situation very vividly on Aug. 9, 1941:

> By yesterday, we fortunately had survived one of our most difficult and terrible days. It is like a miracle, you could say, that we go through it all right. Everything just all happened at once: we had a thunderstorm, like nothing I had experienced for years, and calculating on this, the Russians tried with all their might and means to take us by surprise. Many hours later, we were in the hole, and this meant also in the water, because due to the incredible thunderstorm, our dugout was of course soon under water. We didn't have a dry speck anywhere on us; the dirty brown muddy water ran down our necks, into our boots, and everywhere else. And then came the enemy's shells; the Russians sent an incredible amount over to us, and there was strike after strike. The crashing of the shells and the storm mingled into a single constant thunder. You could make out nothing any more, the constantly exploding shells around us, the whooshes, whistling and

> crashes all together made us totally whacky. Today our ears were ringing, as if it had only just stopped. If we had not built such good holes, I think fewer of us would have come through, and thank God, we can say that only two men were wounded. So I'm still healthy, as you know now, and my other little troubles are not that bad. The first is our shortage of cigarettes; secondly, there is rarely any water to wash in here in Russia; basically, we only brush our teeth with tea or coffee, and we only shave when we get the chance. I have to let you know one thing, so that you for sure will recognize me when I get back. We are losing our hair – just to mention it (it's happening to all of us), and if the war goes on much longer, I'll have to come home with a damned bald head. So, if I one day stand in front of you without any hair (hoping that I come home well), then don't send me away; it will really be me! These are all just small evils of war, but you take those in stride when everything else is going okay.

Five days later, they broke through the enemy positions in the Mshaga sector at Sakibje and Ugorody (north of Szoltzy) and formed bridgeheads. When the Red Army tried to attack the flanks of the *16. Armee* - which was advancing towards Leningrad - south of Lake Ilmen, the *SS* formation was commanded to the threatened area southwest of Staraya Russa. Starting August 21, 1941, the units were deployed through the Polisst sector for a counterattack towards Lovat. The *SS-Totenkopf-Division*, which had lost 4,854 men through death, injury, and disease (dysentery especially) by the end of August 1941, got some 3,450 replacements during August and September, as well as a *Sturmgeschütz-Batterie* (12 *Geschütze*), which was put under command of the *SS-Totenkopf-Artillerie-Regiment*.

Already on September 5, 1941, the *Division*, together with the *30. Infanterie-Division*, on the orders of the *LVI. Armee-Korps (mot.)*, had to attack on both sides of the Pola to Demyansk. After they reached their goal, on September 12, 1941, the *SS-Totenkopf-Division* formed a *Kradschützen-Bataillon* with five *Kompanien* as a mobile reserve, instead of the disbanded *SS-Totenkopf-Infanterie-Regiment 2*. Now under command of the *II. Armee-Korps*, the formation moved into the Lushno-Kirillowschtschina-Plemewizy positions to meet the expected Soviet attacks. These began on September 24, 1941, in the wake of heavy air attacks with effective tank support. In severe and bloody battles, the formation was able to hold the almost 18-km wide area. In these battles, which lasted for five days, some 200 men were killed in action, and more than 600 were wounded.

The *Division* formed up on October 17, 1941, for the attack on Ljubniza, in the bottomless mud due to the snow and rain. Meeting strong defenses, after initial successes the attack stalled. The units moved into positions on the lines they had reached. To make up for the loss of about 5,100 men since the end of August 1941, in October and November 1941, 2,600 replacements arrived. In the sector of the *X. Armee-Korps (16. Armee)*, the *SS-Totenkopf-Division* proposed in early December 1941 that these positions be enlarged for defense during the winter. Without the necessary winter equipment, nothing the troops had was anything more than merely provisional. Crumpled newspapers stuffed into their uniforms were supposed to protect body heat at temperatures of more than -40° C; they burned fires under the vehicles and weapons to keep their oil fluid and thus ready for use.

The winter positions were hardly rest quarters. The Red Army had already begun to intensify operations by mid-December 1941. The first Soviet winter offensive was launched January 8, 1942. In the *16. Armee* area, the enemy attempted to encircle many German formations between Lake Ilmen and Lake Seliger in a pincer movement. This led to fierce fighting in the maneuvering area before Staraya Russa; in these battles, about 10 *Kompanien* (including *SS-Totenkopf-Division Artillerie* and *Sturmgeschützen*) were divided into different *Kampfgruppe* and deployed into the threatened area. There, they were placed under command of the *18. Infanterie-Division (mot.)*. When the adjacent *290. Infanterie-Division* was also hard pressed, it was also sent attachments from the *SS-Totenkopf-Division*, now under command of the *II. Armee-Korps*. When it became apparent by the end of January 1942 that the *II. Armee-Korps* was being encircled after intense battles, Hitler ordered the area at Demyansk to be held to the last man. On February 8, 1942, the Soviet 11th and 1st Shock Army troops joined at Kobylkino, thus surrounding some 96,000 German soldiers.

SS-Gruppenführer Eicke was given the mission to defend the western front of the pocket, which was to be newly established. By combing through all the *Divisionen*, Eicke was able to pull together about 6,000 men. Constantly under heavy defensive fire, elements continued to be separately encircled by the enemy. These included a 1,500-strong *Kampfgruppe* under the *Kommandeur* of the *SS-Totenkopf-Pionier-Bataillon*, *SS-Sturmbannführer* Ullrich. As of February 12-23, 1942 they were separated from their own lines, and only one-third of the men were able to fight their way out. By the middle of the month, *Generalleutnant* Zorn, who had been flown in, formed *Korpsgruppe z. b. V.* at Demyansk, which took over command in the western pocket of the *290. Infanterie-Division*, *Gruppe Eicke*, and *Arko 105* [*Artilleriekommandeur*: Artillery Commander].

By air transport, *SS-Totenkopf-Division Group Eicke* was delivered 540 replacements in March 1942. After the Red Army initially took Kobylkino and Bjakovo after hard fighting, the attack on Wassiljewschtschina was launched. *SS-Oberscharführer* Wieninger wrote on March 2, 1942:

> As I already told you, it will probably remain the case that there will be another six to eight weeks until our next reunion. You only need to keep the whole situation in mind; we can't be spared from here! It is unfortunately a somewhat different war than our previous campaigns, and then you can't forget, that here in the East, any single civilian is more dangerous than, say, 100 Frenchmen. Here you have to be prepared for anything, and thousands of cases have shown what hordes we have to deal with this time. Of course, we have adapted to the conditions and learned to treat animals like animals!

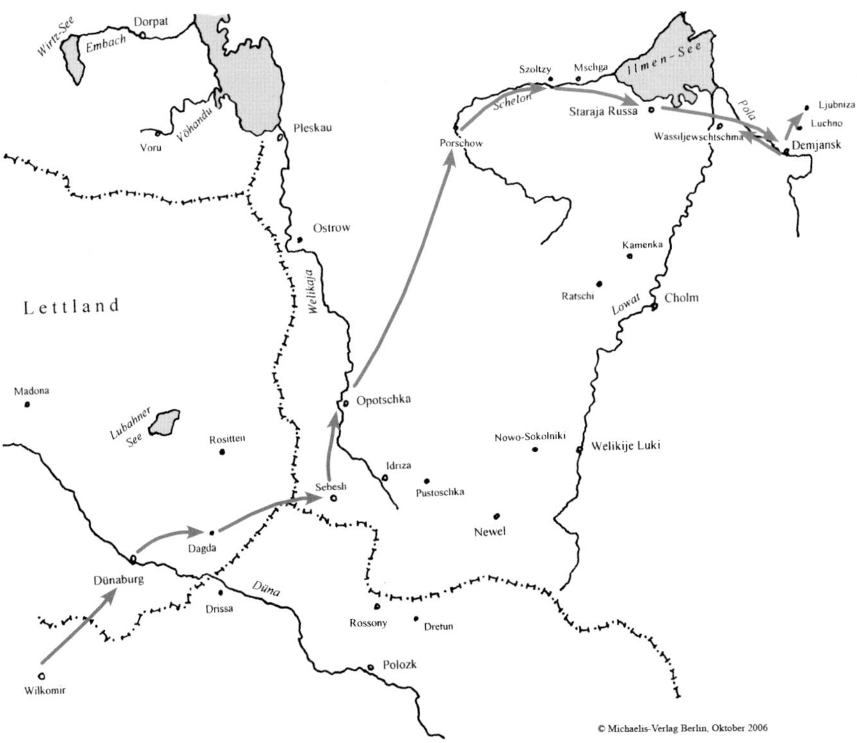

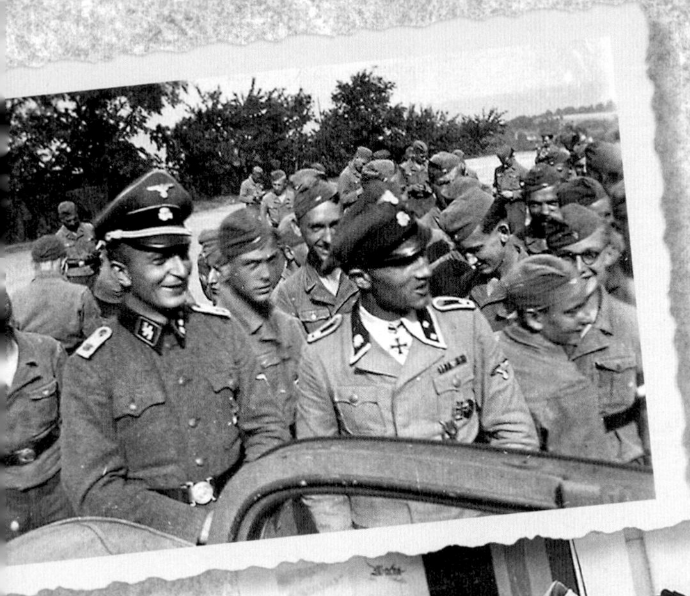

Fritz Christen was awarded the *Ritterkreuz* as a member of the *2./ SS-Panzerjäger-Abteilung Totenkopf* for destroying five Soviet tanks on 10/25/41.

Christien during a promotional campaign for the Waffen-SS with the *Hitlerjugend*.

***3.7 cm Pak* during the advance in the summer of 1941.**

Positions in Demyansk.

Destroyed Soviet weapons and equipment in the Demyank pocket, April 1942.

Sturmgeschütz III Ausf. G.

SS-Hauptsturmführer **Richter, as** ***Batterieführer***
in the ***SS-Sturmgeschütz-Abteilung Totenkopf*****,**
was awarded the ***Ritterkreuz*** **on 4/22/1942.**

Although some 60% of the *Division* was deployed on the west front of the Demyansk pocket, the *Kommandeur* of *SS-Totenkopf-Infanterie-Regiment 1*, *SS-Ober*führer Simon, sent his *Regiment* and *Kampfgruppe* rear units into the original "winter positions" around Lushno.

On April 14, 1942, *Unternehmen Fallreep* [Operation Gangway] was launched for the planned attempt for the German formations to fight out of the pocket. After four days, they had recaptured the strategically important Kobylkino and reached the Lovat river. One week later, the first elements of *Gruppe Seydlitz*, pushing from the outside in the opposite direction, also reached the Lovat – contact had been restored between the German units. By May 1, 1942, the Red Army, after heavy artillery bombardment, launched an attack on the few-kilometer-wide land corridor to Demyansk. In the fierce defensive battles, however, the Germans were able to prevent another encirclement.

On May 8, 1942, *SS-Obergruppenführer* Eicke took over command of the *Korpskommando z.b.V.* and handed over the leadership of his *Gruppe* to the *Kommandeur* of *SS-Totenkopf-Infanterie-Regiments 3*, *SS-Standartenführer* Becker. *Gruppe Eicke* was reinforced on May 20, 1942, by the about 800-strong *Freikorps* [volunteer corps] *Danmark*, which was flown in. On May 30, 1942, the *Division* had an overall strength of:

	Officers	**Unterführer**	**Enlisted Men**	**Total**
Actual	225	722	5,779	6,726
	3.4%	10.7%	85.9%	100%
Authorized	638	2,836	14,058	17,532
	3.6%	16.2%	80.2%	100%

Thus, the *SS-Totenkopf-Division* had just barely 40% of its authorized strength.

Unternehmen Danebrog [Operation Danebrog] was launched on June 3, 1942, to expand the land corridor between the *X.* and *II. Armee-Korps.* In this operation, the Germans succeeded in taking Bol. Dubowize on June 6, 1942. Fierce fighting flared up in this place four days later. While there were continuous smaller and larger operations along the entire front, *SS-Totenkopf-Division*, which had been divided up, was again completely reassembled. For the first time, the formation also received *Volksdeutsche* replacements: Hungarian *Volksdeutsch*e who had been conscripted in to the *Waffen-SS* in the spring of 1942.

After very heavy artillery preparations, on July 17, 1942, the Red Army formed up for the umpteenth time to push into the Bol. Dubowizy-Wassiljewschtschina-Bjakowo land corridor. By July 20, 1942, the *SS-Totenkopf-Division*, after losing 168 killed in action and 457 wounded, had only *Batallion* strength. The casualties had risen by the end of the month to nearly 2,000 men. On a 41km-long front along the Robya (east of the Lovat), it had a combat strength of only 51 *Führer* and 2,685 *sonstige Dienstgrade* – 66 men per kilometer. Leo Wilm remembers:

> One day, we heard that we were surrounded in a pocket. Airplanes supplied us by air. Along with strong attacks at the front, there were more and more partisans active – sometimes reinforced by Red Army members who were parachuted in. Once we got the order to destroy a guerrilla camp. Deep snow hampered our march and I was incredibly hot. When we found the camp and, of course, found no more partisans, I broke into shivers and thought, just don't collapse. We took a couple of baked breads and blew up the camp. When we got back, I reported to the Sani [*Saniäter*: medical orderly], who kept me right there in the medical barracks. I slept all the time and didn't register anything. After 14 days I was released – I had the so-called swamp fever.
>
> The sun was getting warmer by the day, and it started to thaw: it dripped into the bunkers, and the snow walls that used to protect us against fragments and bullets melted. At the beginning of April 1942, the mercury rose in the thermometer, the snow melted away, and the marshes spread. The streams and rivers in the pocket ran free and flooded the countryside.
>
> Despite almost daily attacks by the Red Army, we were able to hold the pocket, and in October 1942 we were loaded up and finally got out of the cursed area south of Lake Ilmen. How many *Kameraden* did we have to leave behind, who are now resting in Russian soil?

In mid-September 1942, due to the sharp fall in combat strength, the formation was redesignated *Kampfgruppe/SS-Totenkopf-Division*.

To face the new heavy attacks expected when the frost set in, *Unternehmen Michael* [Operation Michael] was carried out on September 27, 1942, which successfully held the land corridor Demyansk, and brought the front forward again to the Lovat.

These battles were the last for the *Kampfgruppe/SS-Totenkopf-Division* in the *Festung* Demyansk. On October 12, 1942, came the command to transfer the remaining troop units to France for reorganization. In rail transport, the units reached the area of Poitiers by the end of October 1942, travelling by way of Pskov-Riga-Tilsit-Dirschau-Kassel-Strasbourg-Mulhouse-Belfort-Dijon. A former member remembers:

> The situation in Demyansk was bad. We were always famished – but the ammunition was more important. So our *Kompanieführer* gave us the order to first shoot with our *sMG* when the Red Army had approached to about 30m. These are among the worst memories I have – the waves of Russians charging at us, who were shot by our two flanking *sMG*. The riflemen positioned between them probably only fired a shot when sometimes one got through ... even then, that was already hard for me! For my service as *sMG-Schütze* in Demyansk, I received the EK I [*Eisernes Kreuz*] – after I received the EK II before Staraya Rusa in the summer of 1941.

The SS-Panzergrenadier-Division Totenkopf

On June 24, 1942, the *SS-Führungshauptamt* ordered the reorganization and reformation of the *SS-Totenkopf-Division* on the Sennelager troop training grounds near Paderborn. Since only individual *Stämme* – as well as convalescent wounded and men on leave – could be taken out of active service, this reorganization was initially just a theoretical matter.

On July 10, 1942, the *SS-FHA* announced the training of a *schnelle Regiment* [fast regiment] as part of the reorganization of SS-*Panzergrenadier-Division Totenkopf*. It was to be formed from the remnants of *SS-Infanterie-Regiment 9*, which was previously deployed on the Northern Front, as well as the *Division Kradschützen-Bataillon*.

The reorganization first took form on August 20, 1942, with Hitler's order that 6,000 volunteers for the *Waffen-SS*, who were still employed in the *RAD* [*Reichsarbeitsdienst*, national labor service], should be immediately released and called up for the *Division*. The organization was to be carried out in France, after the developments in the West, *i.e.*, the Allied commando raid on Dieppe.

In early September 1942, the organizational staff and the cadre units left the Sennelagertroop training grounds and were transferred to the French Mailly le Camp training grounds at Troyes. The *Divisionsstab* moved into quarters in Bordeaux, where the units were also gradually sent to join them. When Hitler ordered the same month that the *Divisionen Leibstandarte*, *Das Reich*, *Totenkopf*, and *Wiking* were to get a second *Panzer-Abteilung*,

zugleich Personalausweis
Nr. 33/II/44-3
für
(Dienstgrad)
den
ab 1.10.1939
(Datum)
ab 1.2.1940
ab 1.5.1940
(neuer Dienstgrad)
ab 1.9.1944
Beschriftung und Nummer der Erkennungsmarke
Blutgruppe A
Gasmaskengröße 2
Wehrnummer
1
geb. am 29.9.1913 in
(Ort, Kreis, Verw.-Bezirk)
Stand, Beruf Student
Religion
Personalbeschreibung:
Gestalt stark
Größe 181 cm
Haar blond
Gesicht oval
Augen blau
Bart keinen
Besondere Kennzeichen (z. B. Brillenträger): keine
Schuhzeuglänge 29
Schuhzeugweite
(Vor- u. Zuname, eigenhändige Unterschrift des Inhabers)
Die Richtigkeit der nicht umrandeten Angaben auf Seite 1 und 2 und der eigenhändigen Unterschrift des Inhabers bescheinigt
28. XI. 1940
den
II/SS-T.J.R.3
(Ausfertigender Truppenteil, Dienststelle)
(Dienststempel)
SS-Untersturmführer und Adjutant
(Eigenh. Unterschrift, Dienstgrad u. Dienststellg. d. Vorges.)
2
Bescheinigungen über die Richtigkeit der Zusätze und Berichtigungen auf Seiten 1 und 2
Lfd. Nr.
Art der Änderung
auf Seite
Datum
Truppenteil
Unterschrift
Dienstgrad und Dienststellung
SS-Untersturmführer und Adjutant

SS-Hauptsturmluhrer Uebelacker was awarded the following decorations: *Ehrennadel* [Badge of Honor] of the *SS-Heimwehr Danzig*; *EK II* and *I*; *Infanterie-Sturmabzeichen* [Infantry Assault Badge] in bronze; *Verwundetenabz* [Wounded Badge] in black and silver; *Ostmedaille* [Eastern Front Medal]; *Demjanskschild* [Demyansk shield]; and the *Nahkampfspange* in bronze.

as well as a *Sturmgeschütze-Abteilung*, the organization of the formation – designated as the ***SS-Panzergrenadier-Division Totenkopf*** since November 9, 1942 – appeared as follows:

DIVISIONSSTAB
SS-Panzergrenadier-Regiment 1 Totenkopf
I. (SPW.)-III. Bataillon
SS-Panzergrenadier-Regiment 3 Theodor Eicke[37]
I.-III. Bataillon
SS-Schützen-Regiment Thule
I.-II. Bataillon
SS-Panzer-Regiment[38] ***Totenkopf***
I. Abteilung **with three** ***Kompanien***
II. Abteilung **with four** ***Kompanien***
SS-Artillerie-Regiment Totenkopf
SS-Aufklärungs-Abteilung Totenkopf
SS-Panzerjäger-Abteilung[39] ***Totenkopf***
SS-Sturmgeschütz-Abteilung Totenkopf[40]
SS-Pionier-Bataillon[41] ***Totenkopf***
SS-Nachschubdienste Totenkopf
SS-Wirtschafts-Bataillon Totenkopf
SS-Sanitäts-Dienste
SS-Nachrichten-Abteilung Totenkopf

To be able to exercise more control and influence over the unoccupied part of France (known as Vichy France) one had, on the other hand, to prevent a potential Allied invasion, so Hitler ordered *Unternehmen Anton* [Operation Anton]. As part of the occupation of southern France, which was launched November 11, 1942, the operational elements of *SS-Panzergrenadier-Division Totenkopf* crossed the Line of Demarcation in Angouleme and marched to Limoges. By way of Tulle, more units reached the region around Montepellier, on the Mediterranean.

After U.S. forces landed in North Africa on November 8, 1942, and the French troops stationed there quickly ceased any resistance, Hitler had doubts about the loyalty of the remaining French forces in France. Therefore, he then ordered, on November 19, 1942, that the French Army and Air

37 On March 1, 1943, the Regiment was awarded the name "Theodor Eicke" by Hitler, in honor of the *Divisionskommandeur* who was killed February 26, 1943.

38 In June 1942, organization of a *Panzer-Abteilung* began in Weimar-Buchenwald, for which eventually a *I. Abteilung* was formed in Angouleme. Thus, the *Panzergrenadier-Division* had the equipment of a *Panzer-Division*!

39 Formed from the *Panzerabwehr-Kompanie Leiner* of *SS-Heimwehr Danzig* and *Reservisten*.

40 The *Sturmgeschütz-Abteilung* replaced the missing *Panzer-Abteilung*.

41 Formed from elements of the *SS-Pionier-Sturmbann* of the *SS-VT* and *Reservisten*.

Force be disarmed, and that measures be taken to prevent the Fleet at Toulon from being transferred to the enemy. Only the police should remain. While the Fleet sank itself, demobilization of the fighting forces was largely accomplished without difficulties.

Since the reorganization of *SS-Panzergrenadier-Division Totenkopf* could not be carried out thoroughly due to the preceding deployment, in early December 1942, *SS-Obergruppenführer* Eicke was given replacements for the scattered *Division* elements via attachments from the *326. Infanterie-Division*. On December 19, 1942, his formation was again fully assembled for further training at Angouleme. The commanded reorganization could only be partially carried out, since Hitler, on December 30, 1942, had already demanded it be sent to the hard-pressed Eastern Front, to the sector of the newly formed *SS-Panzer-Korps*.[42] Their strength at the moment:

Officers	Other Ranks	Total
556	20,600	21,156
2.6%	98.4%	100%

The formation was placed under command of the *SS-Panzer-Korps* and was to be operational in the East by January 8, 1943. At this time, almost half of the *Division* consisted of little-trained recruits – they had received no training yet as a formation. In addition to the lack of some 50% of its vehicles, the formation had neither enough drivers, nor enough signal and communications personnel. While the other two – those *SS-Divisionen* under command of the *SS-Panzer-Korps* – were already rolling in the direc-

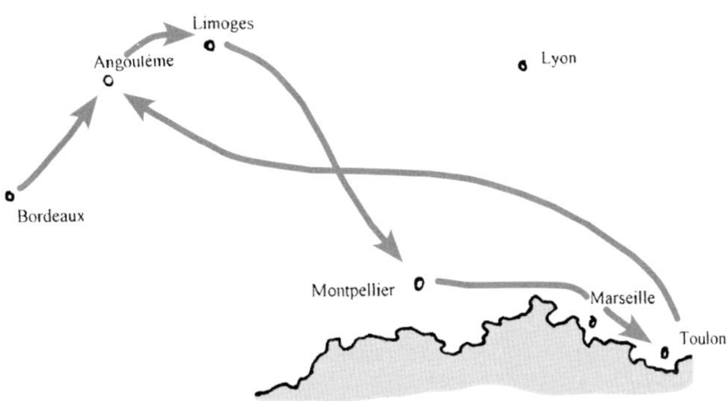

42 From there, the *Abteilung* moved temporarily at the end of March 1944 to the troop training grounds at Mailly le Camp in France. From Grafenwoehr, the *I. (Panther)/SS-Panzer-Regiment 3* joined the *Division* in Siedlice from July 25, 1944.

tion of Kharkov to *Heeresgruppe Süd*, *SS-Panzergrenadier-Division Totenkopf* was given a postponement until January 31, 1943. *SS-Oberscharführer* Wieninger reported to his wife about the impending redeployment to the Eastern Front on January 3, 1943:

> Now a not a very pleasant thing – I'll be writing to you maybe again from there, from where I just got back recently! So it may be, that this will happen with us already in 8-14 days, and so we can bury our hopes for another necessary short leave again! Oh well, we have learned all too well that they can't do without the SS there. But that we are needed so quickly again – we wouldn't have thought that! So then, back into it, we have now been allowed to live a few days among reasonable people, and that's enough for us for a long time!

On January 24, 1943, he continued:

> I have broken one of my teeth again. I could curse myself to death about it, now I can't eat almost anything, things look so bad with my teeth. And that cursed Russia is the only thing to blame – the 18 months there finished sent us all over the edge. If I now think of how good my teeth were, when I was just a young soldier, and how during every year of my term of service, one after the other is going *kaput*, I could cry. Now it's to the point where I no longer know how to get my food down! And when will there be another chance to get this straightened out?

With the *SS-Panzergrenadier-Divisionen Leibstandarte-SS Adolf Hitler* and *Das Reich* already in active service at Kharkov, *SS-Panzergrenadier-Division Totenkopf* reached the debarkation area at Kiev on February 6, 1943. Concentrating the formation, sent after the other formations on a land march, took from February 10-20, 1943, in the Poltava area (about 150 km southwest of Kharkov). On February 14, 1943, the *Division* received the command from *Armee-Abteilung Lanz* to redeploy the first troops to Valki (about 30 km southwest of Kharkov), and hold up the enemy forces there which were pushing forward to encircle Kharkov.

In the meantime, the situation developed dramatically. Contrary to the repeated orders of Hitler to defend Kharkov "to the last man," the commanding General of the SS-*Panzer-Korps*, *SS-Obergruppenführer* Hausser, decided to evacuate the city. It is interesting that he was not brought before a court martial for this by Hitler.

As a result, the two *Divisionen Leibstandarte* and *Das Reich* moved into new positions to the south, and the *SS-Schützen-Regiment Thule*, deployed at Valki, was placed under the command of the *Generalkommando z. b. V. Raus*. Starting February 20, 1943, *SS-Panzergrenadier-Division Totenkopf* finally marched out of the assembly area at Poltava to the front at Krasnograd-Karlovka.

In the sector of the *SS-Panzer-Korps*, the units were to push out from there into the area of Pavlograd, where they were to join up with elements of the *4. Panzer-Armee* advancing from the south. With these operations, they were to annihilate the enemy forces moving towards Saporoshje and prevent a potential encirclement of the formations stationed to the southeast (the *1. Panzer-Armee* and *Armee-Abteilung Hollidt*). For the German counter-offensive, which was to be launched on February 22, 1943, the *SS-Panzer-Korps* was placed under the command of the *4. Panzer-Armee*. While the *SS-Schützen-Regiment Thule*, as part of the *Generalkommandos z. b. V. Raus*, was engaged in an intense battle, the majority of *SS-Panzergrenadier-Division Totenkopf*, together with *SS-Panzergrenadier-Division Das Reich*, reached Pavlograd, where they turned northwards on February 25, 1943, to the Orelka-Losovaya line. The next day, *Divisionskommandeur*, *SS-Obergruppenführer*, and *General der Waffen-SS* Eicke was killed in action on a reconnaissance flight in a Fieseler Storch airplane. *SS-Brigadeführer* and *Waffen-SS Generalmajor* Simon took over leadership of the formation.

The German forces succeeded in steadily repulsing the enemy, and *SS-Panzergrenadier-Division Totenkopf* thrust forward, further northwards along the Orel, on March 1, 1943. The next day, the units, together with the *SS- Panzergrenadier-Division Das Reich*, met the first elements of the *SS-Panzergrenadier-Division Leibstandarte-SS Adolf Hitler*, which were pushing northwards. Together, in the next few days, the forces not only prevented the attempts of the enemy troops trapped southeast of Valki to break out, but also began to destroy them. During these operations, the onset of the thaw and lack of fuel created complications for the mobility of the formation's operational components:

41 *Panzer III*
11 *Panzer IV*
6 *Panzer VI*
6 *Befehlspanzer*
17 *Sturmgeschütze*

By March 5, 1943, the German counter-offensive south of Kharkov was considered complete. The next day, *SS-Panzergrenadier-Division Totenkopf* was concentrated in the area between Krasnograd and Valki, to stand by for the attack on Kharkov. By March 7, 1943, the troops had formed up in the area west of Kharkov. In this maneuver, the *Totenkopf Division* pushed on to Olschany, and eastwards from there. Making a 45-km long arc north of the city, they prevented the reinforcement of the Soviet troops in Kharkov, among other things. As the XXXVIII. *Panzer-Korps*, advancing from the south, reached the city on March 13, 1943, the enemy was trapped in Kharkov. The next day, the city was again in German hands.

After *SS-Schützen-Regiment Thule* was ordered back to the *Division*, they advanced, again fully manned, to the Donets at Chuguyev. From here, *SS-Panzergrenadier-Division Totenkopf* formed up in the sector of the *SS-Panzer-Korps* to attack northeast towards Belgorod-Volchansk. Following the successful capture of Belgorod, they were to mop up the area between the Donets and Kharkov that they had reached, finding any remaining enemy forces.

By March 21, 1943, the *Division* had moved in the area northwest of Volchansk, into defensive positions along the Donets. Four days later, it started a redeployment and relief of the *SS-Panzergrenadier-Division Das Reich* on both sides of Belgorod.

The casualties demonstrated the intensity of the fighting. From January 25 to March 31, 1943, *SS-Panzergrenadier-Division Totenkopf* lost over 2,700 men:

	Officers	**Other Ranks**	**Total**
Killed in action	49	644	693
Wounded	75	1,869	1,944
Missing	1	71	72

On April 19, 1943, *SS-Schützen-Regiment Thule* was disbanded, and an *SS-Kradschützen-Bataillon*, with two *Kradschützen* and one *Spähpanzerwagen-Kompanie*, was formed from the remnants. At the same time, the *Division* received some 5,000 replacements by the end of June 1943. These were mainly *Volksdeutsche* from southeastern Europe.

By late April 1943, preparation for the upcoming *Unternehmen Zitadelle* relief of *SS-Panzergrenadier-Division Totenkopf* by the *168. Infanterie-Division* was started, and the formation was concentrated to the northwest of Kharkov. There, and in the area southwest of Kharkov, where it moved in mid-May 1943, the replacements were given training, to the degree that was possible.

Janiak was awarded the *Panzerkampfabzeichen* [Panzer Combat Badge] in silver during the 3rd Battle for the Defense of Warsaw on 10/22/44.

The *SS-Kradschützen-Bataillon* was disbanded again on May 20, 1943, and the men were integrated into the *SS-Aufklärungs-Abteilung*. By June 1, 1943, the *Division* reported the following (*continued on p 150*):

The SS-Totenkopf-Division running a captured Soviet T-26 tank.

From 1943, the Panzer V "Panther" (here Ausf. A), with 7.5 cm KwK 42 L/70, was considered the best German tank.

Hans Janiak was called up to the SS-Nachr. Ers. Rgt. in May 1943; after his basic training, he served in *SS-Panzer-Regiment 3*.

In 1943, the *Waffen-SS* introduced camouflage fatigues for *Panzer* crews in the so-called plane tree pattern.

The Tiger II (Sonder-Kfz 182) was equipped with an 8.8 cm KwK 43 L/71. Length: 10.3 m; Width: 3.6 m; Height: 3 m; Weight: 68,000 kg; 5 man crew.

Officers	Unterführer	Enlisted Men	Total
586	2,964	16,567	19,999
2.9%	14.8%	82.9%	100%

It had, as operational equipment:

49 long *Panzer III*
7 short *Panzer IV*
26 long *Panzer IV*
10 long *Panzer VI*

In 1943, the Waffen-SS introduced camouflage fatigues for Panzer crews in the so-called plane tree pattern.

By the end of June 1943, the *Division* had moved from the refitting area at Kharkov to the region northwest of Belgorod. In the sector of the large formation redesignated as the *II. SS-Panzer-Korps*, *SS-Panzergrenadier-Division Totenkopf* moved into the starting positions for the German summer offensive at the *Kursker Bogen* [Kursk salient].

Unternehmen Zitadelle was launched on July 5, 1943; the Red Army had been expecting this operation. Even during the first day, the attacks were bogged down by heavy casualties; these were not only due to the bottomless mud caused by the rain, but also the echeloned-in-depth Soviet defense.

SS-Panzergrenadier-Division Totenkopf was deployed on the right flank of the *II. SS-Panzer-Korps*, and was soon engaged in heavy fighting with enemy tank forces, which wanted to attack the advancing German troops on their flanks. After successful defense operations, on July 8, 1943, elements of *SS-Panzer-Regiment 3*, *SS-Sturmgeschütz-Abteilung 3*, and *SS-Panzer-Aufklärungs-Abteilung 3* were sent to Lutschki, to provide a *Korpsreserve* for *SS-Panzergrenadier-Division Das Reich*.

The larger part of *SS-Panzergrenadier-Division Totenkopf* was relieved by the *167. Infanterie-Division* and followed the next day. On July 9, 1943, they formed up as the armored point for the *II. SS-Panzer-Korps*, to push across the Psel river. They succeeded in forming a bridgehead at Wassiljewka and Krasny Oktyabr, which was immediately attacked. In heavy fighting, the units attempted to battle their way forward towards Kursk, in order to join up there with the planned advance from the north by elements of the *9. Armee*, and thus encircle the enemy forces stationed to the west.

They should have kept to the planned operations, because on July 13, 1943, Hitler called off the offensive. The *4. Panzer-Armee* was about 40 km to the south, and the *9. Armee* in the north had advanced only about 20 km. They were still separated by more than 120 km. It was no longer possible for them to join forces at Kursk – far better, the *4. Panzer-Armee* should have made a thrust towards the *9. Armee* beyond Kursk, because, due to the time and the forces arrayed on the Soviet side, success appeared very questionable. In addition, the Red Army was pressing hard on the *2. Panzer-Armee*, to the north of the *9. Armee*, and formed up on July 17, 1943, against the *6. Armee* on the Mius, and against the *1. Panzer-Armee* on the middle Donets.

For *SS-Panzergrenadier-Division Totenkopf*, this meant that, during the night of July 17-18, 1943, it had to evacuate the bridgehead across the Psel, which had been so difficult to carve out, and to battle to maintain. *Unternehmen Zitadelle* had cost the *Division* the loss of almost 4,500 men; in about two weeks, it had lost the fighting strength of two *Regimenter*:

	Führer	**sonstige Dienstgrade**	**Gesamt**
Killed in action	30	654	684
Wounded	141	3,610	3,751
Missing	2	40	42

Through Kharkov, the formation followed the elements of the *SS-Panzer-Korps* already detached to the *6. Armee* to the assembly area east Stalino. When *SS-Panzergrenadier-Division Totenkopf* formed up in the *Korps* sector for a counterattack on July 30, 1943, the attack became bogged down in the face of a strong anti-tank front, as well as numerous minefields. The Red Army's extended in-depth defense positions caused extraordinarily high casualties during the frontal assaults. The enemy defense only collapsed when the German forces won some strategic heights. The enemy pulled back to the east bank of the Mius, almost in a rout. The front line was again stabilized. However, the German side's own casualties were again high for this successful operation. *SS-Panzergrenadier-Division Totenkopf* lost between July 30 and August 2, 1943:

	Führer	**sonstige Dienstgrade**	**Gesamt**
Killed in Action	14	205	219
Wounded	50	1,143	1,193
Missing	-	46	46

In barely four weeks, the formation thus lost about 6,000 men; as a result, it had to be reported as badly crippled.

After the *II. SS-Panzer-Korps* was transferred to Italy, *SS-Panzergrenadier-Division Totenkopf* was attached to the *XVII. Armee-Korps*, and initially remained in the positions along the Mius. As the Red Army again renewed its offensive at Kharkov, the *Division* was redeployed to Valki on August 5, 1943. From there, they moved to the *III. Panzer-Korps* sector defensive positions along the Maximovka-Krassnokutsky line. Deployed on the open west flank of the *III. Panzer-Korps*, the *Division* succeeded in crushing the enemy forces which had broken through during the intense fighting on August 14-16, 1943. This success was noted two days later in the *Wehrmachtbericht* [Armed Services radio report]:

> Also, in the area south and southwest of Belgorod, all Soviet attacks collapsed bloodily. 92 Soviet tanks were destroyed. *SS-Panzergren-adierDivision Totenkopf* especially distinguished itself in the offensive and defensive battles in this area.

From August 17-23, 1943 – now under the leadership of *XXXXVII. Panzer-Korps* – the formation took part in the thrust across the Merla to re-establish contact with the *XXIV. Panzer-Korps*. After intense fighting, they began to pull back in the Kolontajev marshes across the Merla on August 27, 1943. On September 1, 1943, *SS-Panzergrenadier-Division Totenkopf* reported a strength of:

	Führer	**Unterführer**	**Enlisted Men**	**Gesamt**
Actual	477	1,884	10,450	12,811
	3.7%	14.7%	81.6%	100%
Authorized	850	4,157	15,839	20,846
	4.1%	20%	75.9%	100%

The combat units especially had often lost over 50% of their total personnel. Through attachments of men from the rear services, such as bakers and butchers, it was possible to reinforce the units to some extent, at least temporarily.

The next few days again brought heavy Soviet attacks. During September 1-6, 1943, alone, the *Division* again lost nearly 1,000 men killed and wounded. By September 13, 1943, the first phase of the withdrawal – in a steady rain – to the area south of Kolontajev was completed. Since the natural obstacle of the Dnieper met the requirements for a new *HKL*, the dispatch of the *Division* began by September 20, 1943, first to the *8. Armee* at Poltava. From there, elements of the *I. /SS-Panzer-Regiment 3*, among others, were commanded to Grafenwöhr for retraining on the *Panzer V Panther*. Remaining under the leadership of the *XXXXVIII. Panzer-Korps* from September 23, 1943, the troops reached the bridgehead at Kremenchug. There, the *XI. Armee-Korps* took over leadership of the formations.[43]

Already by the evening of September 29, 1943, the bridgehead was abandoned, and they moved into positions across the Dnieper. While the adjacent troops were engaged in intense battles as the Soviets built a bridgehead, things remained quiet in front of the *SS-Panzergrenadier-Division Totenkopf* sector south of Kremenchug. When the enemy succeeded in breathing through at the *1. Panzer-Armee*, the *Division* was pulled out of its positions on October 18, 1943, and redeployed to the south as a *Korpsreserve*.

The 3. SS-Panzer-Division Totenkopf

On October 21, 1943, Adolf Hitler ordered that the two new *SS-Panzer-Korps* should not be organized as each one *Panze*r and one *Panzergrenadier-Division*, but as two Panzer-*Divisionen*. Accordingly, the *SS-Divisionen Hitlerjugend* and *Totenkopf* were to be organized into *Panzer-Divisionen*. For *SS-Panzergrenadier-Division Totenkopf*, this only meant that it would be renamed as an SS-*Panzer-Division* – it had already been organized in this formation since 1942. At the same time, the *Waffen-SS Divsionen* and *Regimenter* were serially numbered. The formation was now designated the *3. SS-Panzer-Division Totenkopf*; the two *Panzergrenadier-Regimenter* were given the numbering:

> ***SS-Panzergrenadier-Regiment 5***
> ***SS-Panzergrenadier-Regiment 6 Theodor Eicke.***

43 The *SS* and *Polizeikampfgruppe von Gottberg* consisted of the *SS-Polizei-Regimenter 2, 17,* and *22*, as well as *Polizei-Schützen-Regiment 31* [Police Rifle Regiment]. For *Flak*, the *I. /SS-Flak-Abteilung Kommandostab Reichsführer-SS*, and as artillery, the *Artillerie-Brigade 704* were placed under its command.

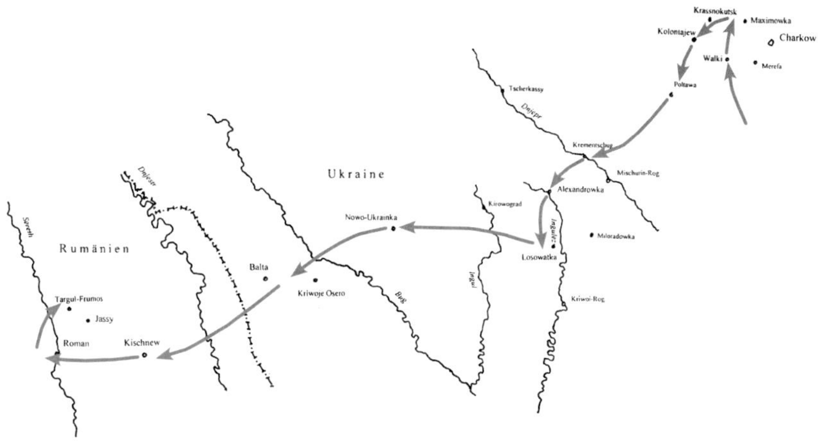

Placed under command of the *XXXX. Panzer-Korps*, the units formed up on October 22, 1943, near Alexandrovka, for a counter-strike across the Ingulez river. The attack was to be carried out on the northern flank of the enemy forces, which had broken through near the *1. Panzer-Armee* in the direction of Krivoy Rog. The limited German forces made success impossible, and the Red Army reached Krivoy-Rog on October 24, 1943. After being replenished with more formations, four days later, another – this time more successful – attempt was made to re-establish contact between the *8. Armee* and the *1. Panzer-Armee*.

Finally, *3. SS-Panzer-Division Totenkopf* moved into positions south of Petrovo on the Ingulez in early November 1943, to be concentrated from there southwards, starting on November 8, 1943, near Losowatka, as a reserve for the *1. Panzer-Armee*.

When the Red Army again took the offensive on November 14, 1943, the *3. SS-Panzer-Division* was engaged in intense defensive battles. In the period from July 5 to November 22, 1943, the formation had the following total casualties:

Officers	**Unterführer**	**Enlisted Men**	**Total**
438	1,618	10,807	12,863

In the same period it received, through replacements and convalescents, as well as by including the lightly wounded who had remained with the active units, the following:

Officers	Unterführer	Enlisted Men	Total
212	946	4,431	5,589

Thus, there was little compensation for the 7,274 casualties. The *Division* had only about 25% of its *Sollstärke*. Until March 10, 1944, the formation was engaged repeatedly in heavy fighting northwest of Krivoy-Rog.

The *3. SS-Panzer-Division,* severely decimated, was commanded by the *8. Armee* to redeploy through Novo Ukrainka across the Bug, to the region between Balta and Krivoe Ozero, in order to be at the disposal of the *VII. Armee-Korps*. After the last transport train arrived on March 20, 1944, it was again engaged in extremely intense defensive fighting until April 1, 1944. Then, the formation marched in the *8. Armee* sector through Kishinev to Romania, to the region west of Roman.

Arriving here in mid-April 1944, the *Division* was only refitted after consultations with Himmler. In addition to nearly 1,500 men on leave who were assembled on the Heidelager *SS* troop training grounds, the *16. SS-Panzergrenadier-Division Reichsführer-SS* was to detach 4,500 members to it.

Awaiting the expected Soviet May 1, 1944, offensive, *3. SS-Panzer-Division* advanced into the area west of Târgu-Frumos. Placed under command of the *LVII. Panzer-Korps*, the operational elements of the *Division* were engaged in defensive battles around the German Sereth bridgehead at Târgu-Frumos beginning May 2, 1944. In four days of ferocious fighting, the German-Romanian troops succeeded in repelling the attack and inflicting heavy casualties on the enemy forces. While the units positioned in the *HKL* were involved in repeated skirmishes, training of the incoming replacements – a total of about 6,000 men – was expedited, including in *SS-Feldersatz-Bataillon 3* [Field Replacement Battalion].

In mid-June 1944, the *Division* was concentrated to the southeast of Târgu-Frumos, to be available as an *Eingreifreserve* [task force] for *Armeegruppe Wöhler*. A few days later, *SS-Sturmgeschütz-Abteilung 3*, with one *Pak-* and two *Sturmgeschütz-Kompanien*, was reclassified there as the *SS-Panzerjäger-Abteilung 3*.

When, on July 7, 1944, the *OKH* ordered *3. SS-Panzer-Division* to transfer by rail to *Heeresgruppe Mitte* [Army Group Center] at Brest (a distance of over 800 km as the crow flies), this ended its nearly 18-month deployment under the command of *Armeegruppe Wöhler (8. Armee)*. Two days later, the *Division* boarded some 60 trains, and the journey began through Romania, Hungary, and Slovakia to Bialystok, and from there to

Grodno. Starting July 15, 1944, the formation was concentrated – under its new *Divisionskommandeur*, *SS-Oberführer* Becker – southwest of Grodno. Placed under command of the *4. Armee*, the first arriving units initially scoured the assembly area for Armia Krajowa (the Polish Home Army) insurgents. On July 18, 1944, it was placed under command of *Generalkommando von Gottberg*.[44] Since the Police units, without training or weapons, were not prepared for major battle after the previous heavy withdrawal fighting, the Red Army advance southeast of Grodno, across the Niemen river, brought the deployment of the first elements of the *3. SS Panzer-Division* to a standstill. Counterattacks towards the north were intended to relieve the German troops in the area of Augustów and re-close the gap in the front. For this mission, the formation made a thrust west of Grodno towards the *5. Panzer-Division*, formed up from the northward-stationed *XXXIX. Panzer-Korps*. On July 20, 1944, the *3. SS-Panzer-Division* reported the following:

	Actual	Operational	Under repair	In delivery
Panzer IV	28	17	3	8
Panzer V	68	-	-	68
Panzer VI	10	9	1	-
Sturmgeschütze	47	36	8	3
schwere Pak	24	17	7	-

In a few intensely combatted days of battle, the *Division* lost about 50% of its *Panzer* – excluding the *I. /SS-Panzer- Regiment 3 Panzer V*, which were still in transport – and had again lost over 1,000 men killed in action and wounded already.

Although the gap had not been closed, by pulling the *HKL* back to new positions, it was possible to stabilize the situation at the *4. Armee*. On July 24, 1944, *3. SS-Panzer-Division* was therefore pulled from the Grodno region and moved to Siedlce. Placed under command of *Gruppe von Roman (2. Armee)*, it was immediately engaged in fierce defensive battles on a front towards the south. The formation was also to attempt to establish contact with the *Fallschirm-Panzer-Grenadier-Division Hermann Göring* (reconstituted *9. Armee*), which was pushing from the west from the Warsaw bridgehead.

44 In *SS-Feldersatz-Bataillon 3* [Field Replacement Battalion], and already directly in the individual troop units, the former *Wehrmacht* members – according to their capabilities – were partly trained for combat by the turn of the year 1944-45.

The positions remained in the area west of Siedlce from Stanislawów to the northeast until mid-August 1944. Then, *SS-Oberführer* Becker led his *Division* in the sector of the *IV. SS Panzer-Korps* in *Unternehmen Brückenschlag* [Operation Bridging the Gap] to the Warsaw bridgehead. There, the formation moved into positions for the first battle for the defense of Warsaw, northeast of the million-population city and to the east of Radzymin. On August 17, 1944, *SS-Panzer-Regiment 3* reported:

I. Abteilung*: 40 *Panzer V* and 4 *Panzer IV
II. Abteilung*: 31 *Panzer VI* and *Panzer IV
***III. Abteilung*: 33 *Sturmgeschütze* (formed from *SS-Pz. Jäg. Abt. 3*)**

The Red Army was sometimes attacking the German positions several times each day, with a vast deployment of materiel and men and enormous casualties. In the most extreme defensive battles, the formation was able to fend off the Soviet attacks, but while the enemy always had new reserves to deploy, the German troops were bled dry. The *3. SS-Panzer-Division Totenkopf* alone lost over 5,000 men killed, wounded, and missing between July 16 and August 21 1944! On August 24, 1944, the *Division* reported an actual strength of 12,291 men and a combat strength of 4,419 men, but these included just 649 *Grenadiere* [infantry riflemen].

The Germans had to pull their *HKL* back even further to prevent a collapse of the entire front. In this operation, the *IV. SS-Panzer-Korps* was to occupy positions in the Vistula-Bug-Narev line by September 15, 1944. *3. SS-Panzer-Division* took over the area east of Jablonna. When it reached the Narev, the Red Army on their side initially took the offensive on September 20, 1944.

The *Division* used this time to incorporate some 5,000 replacements. Besides *Marine-Artilleristen*, the *Luftwaffe* alone provided the following:[45]

Führer	Unterführer	Enlisted Men	Total
12	944	3,360	4,316

On October 10, 1944, the Red Army, after heavy artillery preparation, formed up for the third major attack on Warsaw. The German positions were completely destroyed by thousands of shells. They were able to throw the enemy back in intense close combat through a counterthrust. As the first attacks abated somewhat on October 16, 1944, the Red Army had only made limited territorial gains. On October 25, 1944, *AOK 9* surprisingly ordered the withdrawal of the *IV. SS-Panzer-Korps* to the west bank of the Vistula, thus yielding ground to the enemy without a fight and making it easier for them to build their Vistula bridgeheads. On October 28, 1944, the third defensive battle for Warsaw ended. When *Heeresgruppe Mitte* perceived that the Soviet attacks in the sector of the *IV. SS-Panzer-Korps* had ended, on November 24, 1944, it ordered the *Korps* to become an operational reserve to support the *2. Armee* and had it replaced by *Infanterie* units.

For the *3. SS-Panzer-Division*, this entailed a march to the area Nasielsk-Nowe Miasto-Płońsk [German: Plöhnen], about 30 km to the northwest. Here, on December 25-6, 1944, they were given the command to transfer the entire *IV. SS-Panzer-Korps* to the *6. Armee (Heeresgruppe Süd)*. There, the Red Army had just surrounded the Hungarian capital. In 77 transport trains, the *3. SS-Panzer-Division* moved to Hungary and concentrated in Komárom [German: Komorn].

45 Since the fighting around Warsaw, together with the *I. /SS-Freiwilligen-Panzergrenadier-Regiment* 46 *Danmark*, this already involved the newly formed units of *11. SS-Freiwilligen-Panzergrenadier-Division Nordland* sent to the *IV. SS-Panzer-Korps*.

Kommandeur of *3. SS-Panzer-Division Totenkopf*, *SS-Brigadeführer* Helmuth Becker (right) in early 1945, together with the commanding General of the *IV. SS-Panzer-Korps*, *SS-Obergruppenführer Gille* (left).

By January 2, 1945, the first elements of the *IV. SS-Panzer-Korps* were already taking part in *Unternehmen Konrad* [Operation Konrad] and were concentrated in the Vertes mountains. The *3. SS-Panzer-Division* pushed forward from Naszály to Bajót. Moving through heavy snow, the men then reached Baja, where there were severe back-and-forth battles with Soviet infantry and tank forces.

The mission to reach the Danube, moving through Zsambek to Tordas and Érd, south of Budapest, could not be fulfilled. The units were stalled by the numerous Soviet anti-tank lines of defense, dug-in tanks, and constant counter-attacks, even before they reached Mány and Zsambek. When the attack towards Budapest foundered, it was initially abandoned on January 8, 1945, and the formations regrouped.

Forced onto the defensive, *3. SS-Panzer-Division* formed up for *Unternehmen Konrad 2* on January 9, 1945, in an easterly direction to Pilisvörösvár. In tough battles, elements of the *IV. SS-Panzer-Korps* were able to fight forward to 17 km from Budapest. On January 13, 1945, Hitler inexplicably called off the *Nordlösung* [Northern solution] to relieve Budapest. Instead, the *IV. SS-Panzer-Korps* was to be redeployed south into the Székesfehérvár area, and there carry out the so-called *Südlösung* [Southern solution]. On January 14-15, 1945, its replacement by the *3. Kavallerie-Brigade* began, and it redeployed to the some 100-km distant assembly area to prepare for *Unternehmen Konrad 3*.

On January 18, 1945, the *3. SS-Panzer-Division* formed up from the area of Berhida (southwest of Székesfehérvár) to attack Tacz. The large number of anti-tank weapons and obstacles impeded the advance. Even after they overcame these barriers, the enemy continued to attack, often rashly. In fierce fighting, the units were able to reach Baracska by way of Seregelyes. Meanwhile, the Red Army had succeeded in building a strong defensive front between the Danube and Lake Velence. As a result, the Germans again abandoned their goal of advancing to Budapest on January 25, 1945. Instead, they should only have pushed forward to the northwest, to turn the enemy's flank and then swing in to Budapest.

In extremely heavy fighting, they were deployed at Pettend with, among others, the *I. /SS-Freiwilligen-Panzergrenadier-Regiment 23 Norge* under their command.[46]

The attack was re-launched the very next day, and, after fierce Soviet counterattacks, the formation pulled back from January 27, 1945, to the

46 This actually belonged to the 11.-Freiwilligen-Panzergrenadier-Division Nordland.

initial positions. Again it was regrouped, and a thrust to the area of Psz. [manor] Szabolcs to the east was planned. This could no longer be carried out. Instead, the battle-weary troops were already having problems just preventing an enemy breakthrough between Lake Velence and the Vertes mountains.

On January 31, 1945, *3. SS-Panzer-Division Totenkopf* reported their losses since June 22, 1941:

	Führer	**sonstige Dienstgrade**	**Total**
Killed in action:	453	16,616	17,069
Wounded:	1,058	35,358	36,416
Missing:	24	2,291	2,315

Thus, the formation, with a total of some 55,000 casualties, had lost nearly three times its entire membership!

Although already engaged in intense defensive battles, the *OKW* reported on February 1, 1945, even more about the relief of Budapest on the *Wehrmachtbericht*:

> In the hard offensive and defensive battles between Lake Velence and the Danube, the *SS-Panzer-Division Totenkopf*, under the leadership of *SS-Brigadeführer* and *Generalmajor der Waffen-SS* Helmut Becker, in heavy fighting against the constantly reinforced Soviet forces, has advanced far, by some 95 kilometers. In defense against enemy attempts to regain the ground, it destroyed during the past days 110 of 131 attacking tanks, mostly in close combat using *Panzerfaust* ["armored fist," anti-tank weapon]. This tried and true Eastern Division, in the fighting in Hungary since January 1, 1945, has captured or destroyed 387 tanks, 792 guns, and 832 trucks.

On February 2, 1945, the German forces began their retreat, and the *3. SS-Panzer-Division* reached Székesfehérvár. The attempt to relieve Budapest had failed, and was finally abandoned. While the German leadership was planning for *Unternehmen Frühlingserwachen* [Operation Spring Awakening] and had pulled the *6. SS-Panzer-Armee* from the West for this operation, it remained quiet on the *3. SS-Panzer-Division* front, except for both sides' reconnaissance patrols. During the period February 1-28, 1945, about three *Division* members were killed in action each day – these figures confirm that things were quiet, and the time was used to enhance the positions and carry out the training and integration of replacements. Thus, by March 1, 1945, the formation had reached an actual strength that was even higher than its authorized strength:

Officers	Unterführer	Enlisted Men	Total
488	4,157	14,708	19,353
2.5%	21.5%	76%	100%

In contrast, this was the authorized strength:

Officers	Unterführer	Enlisted Men	Total
593	3,888	12,944	17,425
3.4%	22.3%	74.3%	100%

For heavy weapons, however, *3. SS-Panzer-Division* had only the equipment of a *Panzer-Bataillon*:

Panzer IV **16**
Panzer V **8**
Panzer VI **7**
***Sturmgeschütze* 17**
Art.-Batterien* 5 *leichte* and 5 *schwere
Mobility was reported as 80%.

While the *6. SS-Panzer-Armee*, suffering heavy casualties, attempted to break through to the south, things remained quiet for the *3. SS-Panzer-Division* in the area north of Székesfehérvár. On March 16, 1945, the Red Army formed up for its Vienna Offensive. At first, the German side was able to seal off the breaches resulting from the very strong artillery barrages.

However, critical situations developed with the Hungarian formations under German command. When the Hungarian *2. Panzer-Division* pulled itself out, this left the *3. SS-Panzer-Division*'s left wing exposed. The situation became ever more critical for the *Division*. *Alarmeinheiten* [Emergency alert units] made up of rear services personnel were deployed to secure the northern flank. To prevent the front from collapsing north of Székesfehérvár, the *I. SS-Panzer-Korps* of the *6. SS-Panzer-Armee* was ordered to pull out of the action and redeploy to the sector of *Armee-Gruppe Balck* on March 16, 1945.

After fierce fighting, the very next day *3. SS-Panzer-Division Totenkopf* got the command to pull out. Even while receiving replacements, the individual units repeatedly lost contact with each other in the chaotic retreat. The losses in men and materiel were enormous. Some of the bloodiest battles were fought at Söréd and Mor.

Although the *I. SS-Panzer-Korps* was trying to stabilize the situation, there was no way to make any coordinated interventions on the muddy roads, which were also often clogged with refugees. In this situation, it was impossible to carry out the counterattacks ordered to repel the enemy to the east.

On March 21, 1945, the remnants of *3. SS-Panzer-Division* were placed under command of the *I. SS-Panzer-Korps* near Csatka (about 30 km north of Veszprem). Most of the heavy weapons and vehicles were already lost due to lack of fuel or through enemy action; the entire formation was only operational in quickly assembled battle groups. In these conditions, the Red Army was repeatedly able to break through the weak lines and attack the German troops on their flanks and in the rear.

The attempts to form a resistance in the *Klara-Stellung* [Klara postion], near Zircz, were overtaken by events, even before all units had streamed back to the position. The many commands from superior authorities could do nothing to change the fact that the troops had nothing more to deploy against the Soviet onslaught. In the *I. SS-Panzer-Korps* sector, this meant that the enemy was able to advance on Papa. On March 25, 1945, *3. SS-Panzer-Division* was still some 15 km east of the city. The very next day, the Red Army occupied Papa after a short fight. The German troops retreated to the northwest, back to the Rába bridgehead at Marczaltö (the so-called *Susanne Stellung*).

After marching nearly 70 km further to the northwest, the men reached the area of Sopron. Here, *3. SS-Panzer-Division* withdrew from the command of *I. SS-Panzer-Korps* on March 31, 1945. While the *1.* and *12. SS-Panzer-Divisionen* marched westwards to Vienna Neustadt, the formation pulled back northwards through the Leitha mountains to Schwechat, about 50 km away. Here it was placed under command of the *II. SS-Panzer-Korps*.

Moving through Schwechat, the troops reached Vienna, about 20 km away, on April 6, 1945; immediately, violent house-to-house fighting broke out. The *3. SS- Panzer-Division* units were deployed in south Vienna near the South and East Railway Stations, which are close to each other, and the Swiss Garden.

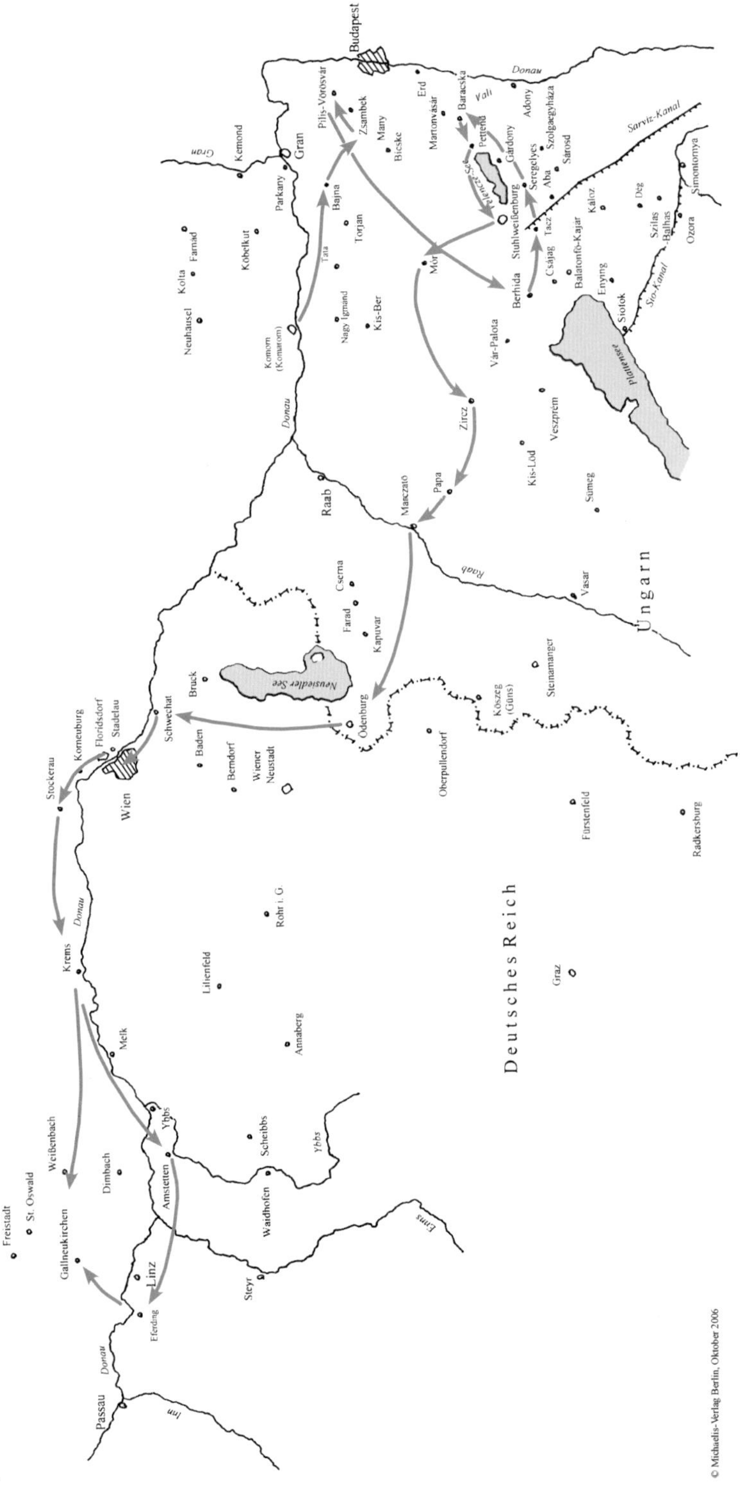
Budapest
Donau
Gran
Kemond
Parkany
Pilis-Vörösvár
Zsambek
Many
Bicske
Erd
Martonvásár
Baracska
Vali
Pettend
Gárdony
Adony
Szolgaegyháza
Sárosd
Seregelyes
Aba
Sarviz-Kanal
Velencze-See
Stuhlweißenburg
Tacz
Csájag
Berhida
Balatonfo-Kajar
Káloz
Enying
Deg
Szilas-Balhas
Ozora
Simontornya
Siófok
Sio-Kanal
Plattensee
Mór
Bajna
Torjan
Tata
Nagy Igmand
Kis-Ber
Komorn (Komarom)
Kobelkut
Farnad
Kolta
Neuhäusel
Vár-Palota
Zircz
Veszprem
Kis-Lod
Papa
Marczalto
Raab
Sümeg
Vasar
Ungarn
Cserna
Farad
Kapuvar
Neusiedler See
Bruck
Ödenburg
Köszeg (Güns)
Steinamanger
Schwechat
Floridsdorf
Stadelau
Korneuburg
Stockerau
Wien
Baden
Berndorf
Wiener Neustadt
Oberpullendorf
Fürstenfeld
Radkersburg
Rohr i. G.
Krems
Lilienfeld
Graz
Deutsches Reich
Melk
Annaberg
Ybbs
Scheibbs
Weißenbach
Dimbach
Amstetten
Waidhofen
St. Oswald
Freistadt
Gallneukirchen
Linz
Steyr
Enns
Eferding
Passau
Inn
© Michaelis-Verlag Berlin, Oktober 2006

By April 9, 1945, the battle groups had been pushed back towards the northeast, to the north bank of the Danube Canal, where they moved into lines in the Prater. Shortly thereafter, the Red Army crossed the Danube Canal in inflatable boats; the defenders retreated to the North Railway Station. On April 12, 1945, the last units moved across the Floridsdorf Bridge to the north bank of the Danube. Fighting continued south of Stadlau, to Kaisermühlen. During the march northwest to the *Division* assembly area at Stockerau, elements of the battered *3. SS-Panzer-Division* were deployed to constrict the Soviet bridgehead at Korneuburg. At Stockerau, the units were to be brought back to authorized strength with attachments from various *SS-Ausbildungs-* and *Ersatzeinheiten* [Training and Replacement units], and be supplied with the lacking materiel (especially guns and tanks).

As early as April 18, 1945, the first units were ordered to move westwards, to the area between Stockerau and Krems. There, they were to prevent the enemy from crossing the Danube. Once they had lost the majority of their heavy weapons, most of the members found themselves deployed as *Infanterie* (including from *SS-Panzer-Regiment 3*).

On April 25, 1945, the *Division* reported a strength of:

Officers	Unterführer	Enlisted Men	Total
332	2,592	5,819	8,743
3.8%	29.7%	66.5%	100%

In just about seven weeks, the formation had lost a full 50% of its personnel. Lacking materiel resources, the units were only capable of infantry operations. The men had nothing more to use against a massive enemy attack using artillery support and tanks.

While the Red Army halted further advances, the U.S. Army quickly pushed on to Austria. On May 4, 1945, *3. SS-Panzer-Division* was ordered to move into a strong-point type of front towards the west. While the majority of the troops held the Danube front to the south, several units moved some 60 km west and secured the Danube-Dimbach-Weißenbach-St. Oswald-Freistadt line. The next day, they fought their first battles with U.S. troops before the security line at Zel; there were more at Königswiesen.

On May 7, 1945, the *II. SS-Panzer-Korps* ordered its troops to surrender their positions during the evening, reach the Enns through Amstetten, and enter American captivity. After approximately 75% of the *Division* had been assembled near Gallneukirchen, the U.S. Army handed the men over to the Red Army on May 14, 1945.

This ended the deployment of an *SS* formation whose first members were generally previously deployed as concentration camp guards. Taking the brunt of attack and defense again and again, and reinforced with several thousand members of the *Luftwaffe* and *Kriegsmarine*, during nearly six years of war, almost 20,000 *Division* members were killed in action. About 40,000 were wounded, and some 3,000 were registered as missing.

5.

SS-PANZER-DIVISION WIKING

The SS-Division (mot.) Wiking

When the *OKW* informed the *Waffen-SS* on September 6, 1940, that there were 15,718 German volunteers of the age group born in 1920, a few days later, Adolf Hitler commanded the formation of the ***SS-Division (mot.) Germania***.[47]

The number of men still required to attain the authorized strength of about 20,000 men were to be come from volunteers from the Netherlands and Flanders, as well as Denmark and Norway.

There had already been a call-up for Danes and Norwegians in late April 1940 to raise the *SS-Standarte Nordland* [Northland], in the wake of *Unternehmen Weserübung* [Operation Exercise on the Weser] – the invasion of Denmark and Norway. The call-up for Dutch and Flemish men to raise *SS-Standarte Westland* was launched in August 1940.

The attempt to form an additional motorized *Division* was leading to difficulties even before the Russian campaign. As the *KTB/OKW* [*Kriegstagebuch des Oberkommmando*: *OKW* War Diary] noted November 8, 1940:

47 Initially it was planned to name the *SS-Verfügungs-Division* the *1. Regiment Deutschland*, and the new *Division* the *2. Regiment Germania.*

> On being informed by the Ob. d H. [*Oberbefehlshaber des Heeres*: Army commander in chief] that, because of the formation a fourth tripartite *SS-Division (mot.)*, ordered by the Führer to be done by the spring of 1941, equipping two of the new 10 mot. *Divisionen* to be formed, or four *Divisionen* [of the] *12. Welle* [12th wave, way of ordering German Infantry Divisions] with vehicles, would be delayed by approximately two months, until the end of May 1941, the Führer decided that there can be no delay allowed in establishing the 10 mot. *Divisionen* by the organization of the fourth *SS-Division*, and the *Divisionen 12. Welle*, as much as it cannot be complete until April 1, 1941, are to be organized so that they are of limited operational capacity. The fourth *SS-Division*, which should be furnished with Kfz. by April 1, 1941, from the accumulation of motor vehicles from production, to a level which ensures its deployment in the field deployment.

This formation, to be made up of three-quarters Reich Germans and one quarter of "incoming personnel from congeneric countries (Norway, Denmark, Holland)" was also called the *Nordische Division* [Nordic Division]. Detailed by the *SS-Standarte Germania* of the *SS-Verfügungs-Division*, it was to be distributed as follows:[48]

Divisionstabb	**Munich**
SS-Standarte Westland (I.-III. Sturmbann)	**Munich**
***SS-Standarte Germania* (ditto)**	**Altomünster**
***SS-Standarte Nordland* (ditto)**	**Vienna**
SS-Artillerie-Standarte	**Dachau**
SS-Nachrichten-Abteilung	**Nuremberg**
SS-Aufklärungs-Abteilung	**Munich**
SS-Panzerjäger-Abteilung	**Aischach**
SS-Pionier-Bataillon	**Allershausen**
SS-Nachschub-Dienste	
SS-Sanitäts-Dienste	

On December 21, 1940, Hitler decreed that the formation be renamed:
SS-Division (mot.) Wiking
As *Kommandeur*, he appointed *SS-Brigadeführer* Steiner.

The influx of "Germanic" volunteers remained far below expectations. Of the desired total of some 5,000 foreigners, by mid-January 1941, only 600 Dutch and 100 Flemish men had registered for *SS-Standarte Westland*, and around 200 Danes and 250 Norwegians for *SS-Regiment Nordland*.

48 The designations of *Standarte/Regiment* were at times used simultaneously by the different military services.

SS-Standarte Westland was posted in Munich.

Training on the *schwere Maschinengewehr*.

SS-Standarte Germania in Hamburg-Langenhorn.

As a result, Hitler gave permission on February 22, 1941, for the *SS-Hauptamt* to call for recruiting Finnish volunteers. Although not of "Germanic" origin, the Finns were at least northern Europeans. These men ultimately made up around half of *III./SS-Standarte Nordland.* Thus, at the beginning of 1941, there were only slightly more than 2,000 northern and western European volunteers in a *Division* of 20,000 men.

By the end of March 1941, the *Division* was sent to the Heuberg troop training grounds for training as a military unit. From April 1, 1941, the *Division* was integrated into the *Heer* and placed under command of *Heeresgruppe C.*

The unit was transported by rail in early June 1941 to the area north of Breslau [now Wroclow, Poland], and deployed in the sector of the *XIV Armee-Korps (mot.)* of *Panzergruppe 1* for the forthcoming Eastern campaign. On June 18, 1941, the troop units moved into the sector southeast of Lublin. One week after the start of *Unternehmen Barbarossa*, the formation was ordered through Zamosc to Lviv, and marched from there to the 120-km distant Tarnopol, where they encountered their first battles.

Fierce fighting developed in early July 1941 while crossing the Zbruch, the former border river between Poland and Ukraine, near Santanov and Husiatyn. During the day of July 7, 1941, *SS-Division Wiking*, moving through streaming rain and on muddy roads, was able to reach the Bug near Proskurov. On July 16, 1941, there was heavy fighting in Tarashcha. While some *Division* elements marched southwards in the sector of the *XIV Armee-Korps (mot.)* to take part in crushing the enemy forces in the Uman pocket, the majority were placed under command of the I*II. Armee-Korps (mot.)* on July 29, 1941, and positioned along the Ros river, up to the town of Kaniv on the Dnieper. From here, the units followed the retreating enemy troops south of the Dnieper to Smila, where there was heavy fighting on August 6, 1941. Just two weeks later, the *Division* was stationed in Dnepropetrovsk, 250 km further eastwards. In just two months, the units had covered over 1,000 km.

Deployed in the Dnjepropetrovsk bridgehead, it fought extremely fierce defensive battles during the period up to September 28, 1941. In early October 1941, the units formed up for the thrust on Pavlograd. The muddy season started as the autumn rains began, with the result that the *Division* – since October 10, 1941, back under the command of the *XIV Armee-Korps (mot.)* – was virtually without supplies until the end of the month. In early November 1941, *Panzergruppe 1* crossed the Mius to Rostov. Former *SS-Funker* [radio operator] Hans Karl Erlewein (*I./SS-Standarte Westland*) wrote to his parents during these days:

> Now, you can hear something from me again. I'm doing fine so far. The only complaints are the really bad diarrhea, but everyone has it. It comes from the greasy food. We have been stationed for several days in a Russian village. Our huts are crawling with lice. My body is completely bitten and pricked by lice and bedbugs.
>
> The Russians are now always falling back/giving way. We hope that this campaign will end soon. ...
>
> When a Russian sometimes shoots harder at us with his "Ari" [slang for artillery], we only think it's for the best, because we know then that the Russians are getting a move on, they're going to scram, just as fast as they can! A few days ago we saw a Stuka [dive bomber] attack by 12 German planes on a Russian village, where there were tanks and a lot of artillery. You should have seen how the Russians got out of there fast as the first ones came down in.

After fierce fighting and strong counterattacks, *Panzergruppe 1* moved back over the Mius and into winter positions. By this time, *SS-Division Wiking* casualties were around 50% from death, injury, and frostbite among its troops who had been in combat since July 1, 1941. The *Regimenter* were quartered in the region from north of Uspenskaya, to Alexeyevka in the south. It was difficult to erect field positions in the frozen-hard ground.

The Soviets again launched heavy attacks in December. In addition to those wounded by enemy fire, there were significant casualties due to frostbitten noses, ears, feet, and arms. A collection station was set up in Uspenskaya for outpatient treatment of patients suffering from frostbite. Günther Adam remembers:

> The forward assault came to an end. After we got to Shakhty, the situation – the lack of supplies and the winter – forced us to retreat. Back then I was as an *SS-Sturmmann Richtkreisunterführer (R 1)* [stormtooper aiming circle NCO 1st rank], and as VB [*Vorgeschobener Beobachter*: Forward Observer] had to maintain contact with the *Bataillonskommandeur*. The order to retreat to the Mius position reached us in the command post. Withdrawals began that same night, and everyone there at the time knows what it took to start the vehicles in this cold, and to painfully force our way through the snow.
>
> After several days, we got near the town of Sovietika. Here we were to construct a new position, and we beat our way into the ground with mines and hand grenades. But we made it and built our bunker, which did not deserve any such name. It protected us only against the worst cold. Also the weather had become clearer. During the day the sun shone, but there was crackling frost.

In the
Caucasus.

Grendiere and 5 cm Pak waiting for a Soviet counterattack.

Repairing an Opel Blitz 3t.

Hans-Karl
Erlewein.

SS-Untersturmführer
Thiessen.

VW-Schwimmwagen
[amphibious vehicles]
(Sdr. Kfz. 166).

We had to hold our own sector. Ivan also got there fast, but did not press us decisively. We could quickly repel his small forays.

On November 30, 1941, we were to be replaced by a *Heeres-Einheit* [Army unit]. We had already pulled our two *leichte Infanteriegeschütze* back about 300 m when the relief was called off and an overall change of position ordered.

On the morning of December 1, 1941, we were attacked by very strong forces. We now had to evacuate our position and get on the guns. The platoon troops I was Führerfor took over *Infanterie* protection for our comrades on the guns.

The open area where we lay was covered with small straw stacks, which were powdered with snow and gave us cover. At dawn, a roaring mass of men came towards us. At the same time it started to snow. Our guns fired, direct shelling. We could see the devastating effect, but the enemy pulled himself together again. We were all under the heaviest infantry fire. We suffered our first casualties. Then our guns went silent, because we ran out of ammunition. A gun was blown up. *SS-Sturmmann* Hurny ran to the other and threw a hand grenade into the barrel. When it detonated he collapsed. This was all happening about 30 m from me. I could see that *SS-Hauptsturmführer* Dietsche was lying next to a gun and firing with his rifle. Around him were some silent bodies. Only now, after our guns were silent, could I tell how it sprayed and whistled around us. Since we had already shot off everything, we looked for ammunition on our fallen comrades.

The driving snow was thicker, and at least gave us some cover. Then we saw an *SS-Führer* running a few meters from us; we knew him by his cap, as we thought. Werner jumped up in the hail of fire and ran after him to ask him for a compression bandage. Then I saw how the supposed Führer turned around, a shot flashed, and Werner buckled. But he rose again, and with a few steps he was beside the supposed *SS-Führer* and struck him on the head with his carbine. Now I could not stay still any longer and ran to Werner, who was waiting for me. Next to him lay a Russian officer. His *Tellermütze* [flat cap] had led us to the mistake that we had an *SS-Führer* before us. But now it was back in the hail of fire. It was useless to take cover. We only noticed the tracer bullets being shot over us. Werner had been shot in the stomach, it seemed, for the blood gushed out from under his belt. With my right hand, which held my 08, I held my wounded left arm tight. Blood was also oozing from my camouflage jacket. We plodded to the *Bataillon* command post.

Suddenly, out of blowing snow came the hum of motors, and barking firings from 2 cm guns. Was Ivan coming now even with tanks? No, no, in front of us out of the snow appeared *Panzerspäh-*

> *wagen*, with the *Balkenkreuz* [Iron Cross national military insignia]. We waved and had the luck to be recognized, because they were firing in our direction. The first eight-wheeler pulled up beside us. A bearded *Oberstleutnant* [lieutenant colonel] asked what it looked like in front of us, threw us bandage packs, and wished us "Break a leg." As I learned later, his name was *Oberstleutnant* Höfer.

In February 1942, the *Finnen-Bataillon* [Finnish battalion] reached the *Division* and replaced the first 400 Finnish volunteers, who returned to Finland after their one-year tour of duty was over. Nearly 100 Norwegians left the *Division* at the same time, as their tours of duty ran out – they had no interest in serving any longer. Due to its recent losses and the lack of replacements, one *Batallion* each was disbanded in both *SS-Regimenter Westland* and *Nordland*.

A small *Kampfgruppe* was set up in January 1942, which was sent to the hard-pressed *III. Panzer-Korps* stationed to the north. During its winter offensive, the Red Army had broken some 100 km into the German lines there, near Isjum. After about eight weeks, the *Alarmeinheit* was returned to the *Division*. An *SS-Panzer-Abteilung* reached the formation at the same time; as a result, it had practically the same organization as a *Panzergrenadier-Division*.

SS-Funker [radio operator] Hans Karl Erlewein, who had been wounded, described the unusual calm on the front on April 27, 1942, in a letter to his mother:

> Now I'm finally back where I belong. Last night we arrived at the *Kompanie*. First, the *Bataillonskommandeur* greeted us. He had immediately recognized me, when I said my name. He has been promoted to *SS-Sturmbannführer* and won the *Deutsches Kreuz* in gold. The trip went without any disturbances, only once did we have to use the flak. The front is three km away, and tonight we move forwards. Believe me, I'm telling the complete truth; you can't hear a single shot, all day and all night long. The front is as quiet as things are for you at home, and it will probably be that way a few more weeks.

After over six months in the Mius position, *SS-Division Wiking* was relieved on July 16, 1942, and marched to the *LVII. Panzer-Korps*, northwest of Tanganrog. Five days later, the attack on Rostov began. On July 23, 1942, the *Division* helped capture Rostov, and shortly after crossed the Don towards the south. By August 5, 1942, the formations had covered almost 250 km with hardly any fighting, and the men were repeatedly able to see

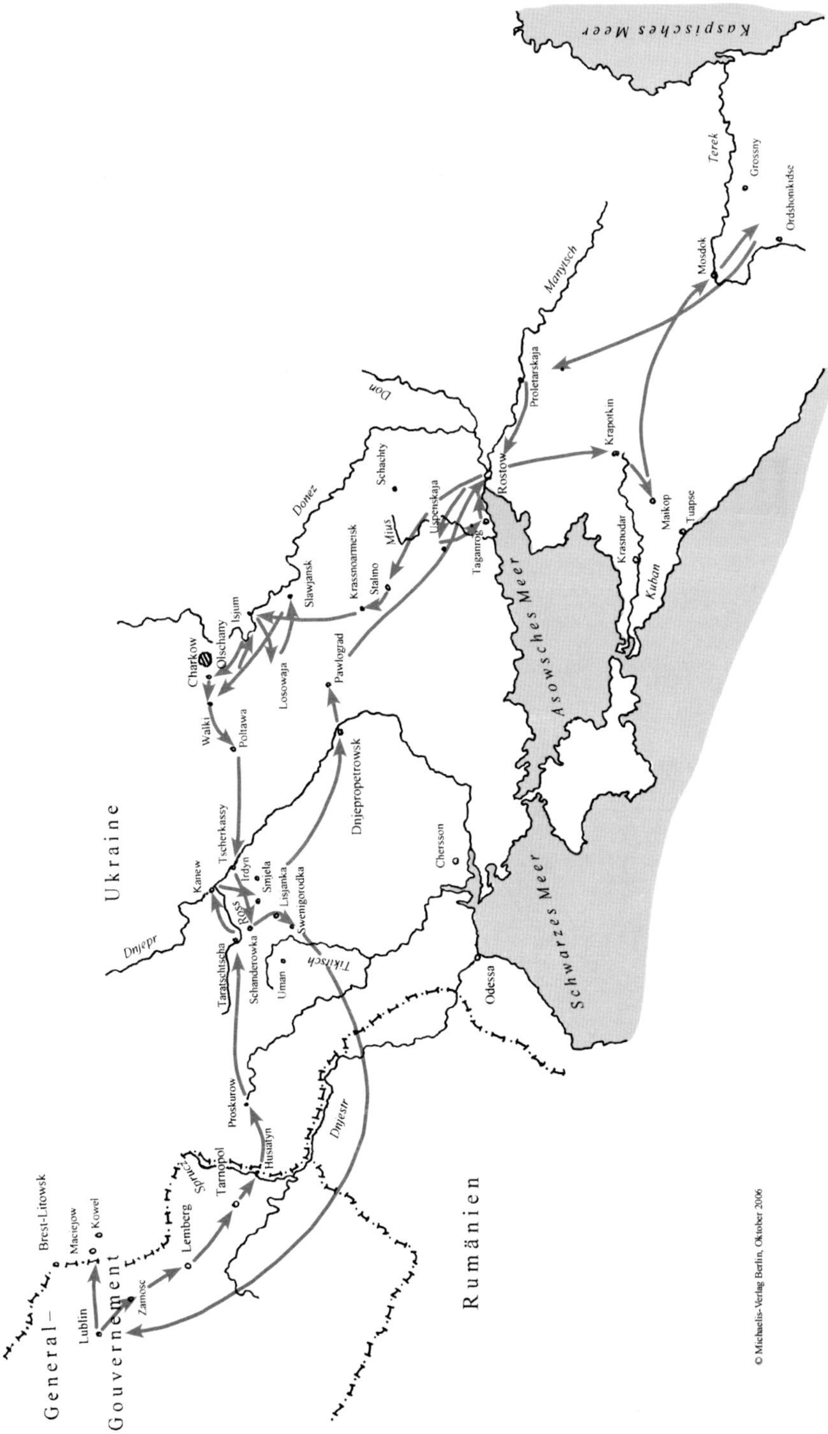
Kaspisches Meer
Terek
Grossny
Ordshonikidse
Mosdok
Manytsch
Proletarskaja
Don
Krapotkin
Maikop
Tuapse
Krasnodar
Kuban
Rostow
Schachty
Donez
Uspenskaja
Taganrog
Mius
Krassnoarmeisk
Stalino
Slawjansk
Isjum
Olschany
Charkow
Losowaja
Pawlograd
Asowsches Meer
Walki
Poltawa
Dnjepropetrowsk
Ukraine
Tscherkassy
Kanew
Irdyn
Smjela
Lisjanka
Swenigorodka
Chersson
Dnjepr
Ross
Taratschtscha
Schanderowka
Uman
Tikitsch
Schwarzes Meer
Odessa
Proskurow
Husiatyn
Tarnopol
Dnjestr
Strypa
Lemberg
Brest-Litowsk
Maciejow
Kowel
Zamosc
Lublin
General-
Gouvernement
Rumänien

camel caravans. Fierce battles only began at the Kuban river. *SS-Regiment Nordland* was assigned to occupy Krapotkin, while *SS-Regiment Germania* was to take Grigoripolitskaya. Finally concentrated around Grigoripolitskaya, *SS-Division Wiking* crossed the Kuban to the Laba river. On August 9, 1942, the formation crossed the river to the west, near Petropavlovskaya. The next day, the first part of the *Division* crossed the Belaya river at Velikoje. On August 14, 1942, the units succeeded in occupying the Chadyshenskaja oil region.

Since the motorized *Division* would not be able to make an advance on Tuapse – on the Black Sea, about 100 km away as the crow flies – through the Caucasus Mountains, the formation initially held back, and was reinforced when *SS-Regiment Westland* was sent after it. Former *SS-Sturmmann* Günter Adam remembers:

> The *Divisionsstab* was moved to Maikop. Again we drove past fields of melons, tomatoes, sunflowers, and especially vineyards. At every stop some of us stood guard, while the others gathered up the fruit. We were especially taken with the big green watermelons. We had gorgeous, sunny weather; the temperature rose to over 30 degrees. However, our mosquito nets were very uncomfortable, as the heat built up underneath them. Every day, we took a tablet of atabrine for malaria (in summer 1941 we had to take quinine, which was a terribly bitter medicine, and the tablets crumbled in your mouth).

After the *XXXXIV. Jäger-Korps* [Rifle Corps] was moved into the front, on September 19, 1942, *SS-Division Wiking* was detached from the *LVIII. Panzer-Korps* and sent by way of Maykop to the *LII. Armee-Korps (1. Panzer-Armee)*, which was about 350 km away in the area of Mozdok, on the Terek river.

On September 27, 1942, the *Division* attacked Malgobek from the area south of Mozdok, in order to advance from there to Grossny. On October 5, 1942, they succeeded in taking Malgobek after heavy fighting.

Panzer III Ausf. K **of** ***SS-Pz. Gren. Div. Wiking*.**

Order to fire.

Schwere 21 cm Mörser 18
[mortar].

The SS-Panzergrenadier-Division Wiking

As the Red Army succeeded in encircling the *13. Panzer-Division* elements to the south, and between Ordzhonikidze and Gisel to the west, the formation – designated since November 9, 1942, as *SS-Panzergrenadier-Division Wiking* – was redeployed to the *III. Panzer-Korps*. Since the *Division* had already been organized as a motorized *Division* and already had a *Panzer-Abteilung*, this new name did not entail any fundamental regrouping of the *SS-Panzergrenadier-Division*. The *III. (gepanzerte)/SS-Panzergrenadier-Regiment Germania* was newly reorganized in France, and first transferred to the *Division* in 1944.

On November 16, 1942, the units formed up for the successful relief of the *13. Panzer-Division*, and were finally transported together with *Heer* units into positions west of Gisel. After the *6. Armee* was encircled at Stanlingrad on November 22, 1942, on Christmas 1942, *SS-Panzergrenadier-Division Wiking* was ordered to join the *4. Panzer Armee*, which had been given the mission to relieve the *6. Armee*.

After being transported and marching over some 500 km, the first sections arrived on December 27, 1942, north of Proletarskaya (about 175 km east of Rostov). Placed under command of the *LVII. Panzer-Korps*, they were immediately engaged in fierce defensive battles – it was inconceivable that it would be possible to rescue the *6. Armee*. In January 1943, the Germans created a line on the Manych river at Proletarskaya, which at least allowed them to temporarily repulse the Soviet tank attacks.

After the Red Army got across the river, the German forces pulled back to Rostov. Since the Soviet troops wanted to encircle the Germans before they got to the Don, the retreat at times resembled a rout. However, *SS-Panzergrenadier-Division Wiking* was able to reach Rostov on February 5, 1943, after a march of some 175 km under constant enemy harassment. Here it was detached from the *LVII. Panzer-Korps (4. Panzer Armee)* and transferred to the *III. Panzer-Korps (1. Panzer Armee)* in the Stalino region, about 180 km to the northwest. There, they were to stabilize the front west of the Donets, further to the north.

However, as the Red Army managed to take large areas to the west, and this way encircle *Heeresgruppe Don* by a strike west of Stalino southwards to the Black Sea, *SS-Panzergrenadier-Division Wiking* was ordered to the area of Krasnoarmeysk. By February 10, 1943, they were fighting the elements of the Soviet 4th Guards Tank Corps stationed there. *SS-Panzergrenadier-Division Wiking* formed up for a counterattack on February 18, 1943. Due to the surprisingly bad Soviet leadership and the enemy's shortage of fuel, the Germans crushed the enemy Tank Corps at Krasnoarmeysk-Grischino.

Now placed under command of the *XXXX. Panzer-Korps*, the *Division* took part in the German counter-operations, which succeeded in retaking the region up to the Donets. In early March 1943, the formation moved into positions between Isjum and Protopokovka on the Donets.

With effect from March 18, 1943, *SS-Panzergrenadier-Regiment Nordland* was detached from *SS-Panzergrenadier-Division Wiking* to form the cadre of the newly-established *SS-Panzergrenadier-Division Nordland*. The *III. (finn*: Finnish)/*SS-Panzergrenadier Regiment Nordland* was discharged to Finland and disbanded in Hanko on July 11, 1943.

In mid-April 1943, the remaining elements of the *Division* were sent for refitting in the area of Losovaya (about 80 km southwest of Isjum). In addition to replacements from the homeland, the formation was also reinforced here by the Estonian *SS-Panzergrenadier-Battalion Narva*. One month later, *SS-Panzergrenadier-Division Wiking* was pulled back to the Donets front to form an *Armee-Reserve* at Slavyansk (about 45 km southeast of Isjum).

Placed under command of the *XXIV. Panzer-Korps*, on July 5, 1943, it was transferred to the region north of Valki (about 50 km west of Kharkov) as a reserve for *Armee-Abteilung Kempf*, in preparation for *Unternehmen Zitadelle*. The *Divisionskommando* had already received the order by July 16, 1943, to pull back towards Isjum, and just two days later, the first units launched an attack on the Soviet bridgehead over the Donets. Without effective heavy weapons support the operation was unsuccessful. The *Division* was at least able to repel strong enemy attacks from the bridgehead. On July 19, 1943, *SS-Panzergrenadier-Battalion Narva* faced dramatic battles, as nearly 100 Soviet tanks overran the Estonian *SS* volunteers' positions. By concentrating all their forces, it was possible to repel this attack.

The Red Army shifted its main concentration point and attacked to the southeast of Isjum, in the direction of Slavyansk, in early August 1943. Again, the German troops were at first able to stop the Soviet advance in fierce defensive battles. Attempts to throw the enemy back over the Donets failed, however, after heavy casualties due to the enemy's superiority in heavy weapons.

On August 5, 1943, *SS-Panzergrenadier-Division Wiking* was withdrawn from active service and marched on August 11, 1943, to the region of Kharkov. The next day, the units reached Olshany (about 20 km west of Kharkov) and were placed under the command of the *III. Panzer-Korps (8. Armee)*. The first skirmishes the next day escalated by August 18-19, 1943, into extremely heavy offensive and defensive battles. In this fighting, *SS-*

The retreat from the East began in early 1943.

SS-Panzergrenadier-Division Wiking **fought on the Donets front in spring 1943.**

Panzergrenadier-Division Wiking alone destroyed 84 enemy tanks. However, due to the Red Army's enormous materiel superiority, this meant only a short break in the attacks.

At the end of August 1943, the Soviet forces re-launched their attacks. The units retreated and tried unsuccessfully to form a new defensive front at Valki (about 50 km west of Kharkov). The *Division* reached the Dnieper by way of Poltava after almost 300 km of constant rear guard defensive fighting, crossing it on September 27, 1943, at Cherkassy.

Just a few days later, the Red Army succeeded in crossing the river – which contains many islands – at a number of different places and building bridgeheads at points, including the mouth of the Ros (about 30 km north of Cherkassy). In heavy fighting, forces, including *SS-Panzergrenadier-Regiment Westland*, were at least able to force the enemy partly off the western bank back to the islands in the river, or even completely back to the eastern bank.

Finally, *SS-Panzergrenadier-Division Wiking* took over about 50 km of the *HKL* between Kanev and Cherkassy. In addition to the sometimes great difficulty in constructing defensive positions, they faced repeated actions against the partisans operating in the rear area.

The 5. SS-Panzer-Division Wiking

This *SS* formation was, in context of the simultaneous serialization of the *Waffen-SS* units, renamed the ***5. SS Panzer-Division Wiking*** on October 22, 1943. While the Division units were given an additional "5," the two *Panzergrenadier-Regimenter* were numbered as follows:

> ***SS-Panzergrenadier-Regiment* 9**
> ***Germania SS-Panzergrenadier-Regiment* 10 *Westland***

The former *SS-Panzer-Abteilung Wiking* became the *I.* Abteilung, as part of the organization of *SS-Panzer-Regiment 5*. In early January 1944, they had barely 30 tanks. The *II. Abteilung*, which was to be equipped with *Panzer V Panther* tanks, was only attached to the *Division* in the summer of 1944.

On the Dnieper, the Red Army succeeded on November 13, 1943, in building a bridgehead at Cherkassy and, after fierce fighting, a month later conquered this tenaciously defended city The Soviet bridgehead across the Dnepr was thus extended by more than 20 km to Smela. The *5. SS Panzer-Division* – now under the command of the *XI. Armee-Korps* – positions now ran from south of Kanev, along the Dnieper towards Cherkassy, and turned towards the southwest to Smela.

On December 31, 1943, the Division reported a strength of:

Officers	**Unterführer**	**Enlisted Men**	**Total**
430	2,748	11,469	14,647
2.9%	18.8%	78.3%	100%

These figures include the *II./SS-Panzer-Regiment 5* and *III. (gep. [gepanzert] /SS Panzergrenadier Regiment 9 Germania*, which were not stationed on the front, so that some 12,500 men were on active duty. This represented about 70% of the authorized strength of 18,000 men.

Because of Hitler's order to hold the positions on the Dnieper, the Red Army offensive launched on January 25, 1944, was able to encircle the *XI.* and *XXXXII. Armee-Korps* within Zvenigorodka-Kanev-Cherkassy by January 28, 1944.

The *5. SS Panzer-Division Wiking* initially formed thin barrier lines with the rear guard troops in the southwestern part of the pocket. There was especially fierce fighting near Olshana beginning January 28, 1944. *Division Versorgungseinheiten* [supply units] defended the town; losing it would have caused the collapse of the pocket. Reinforced by elements of *SS-Panzer-Pionier-Bataillon 5* and *SS-Panzergrenadier-Battalion Narva*, as well as of *I./SS-Panzer-Regiment 5*, the Germans were able to hold the positions until February 5, 1944.

Two days later, the German relief attempt began. For this, *SS-Panzer-grenadier- Regiment 9 Germania* was ordered on February 9, 1944, to push forward into the area of Shenderovka, already occupied by the enemy, to incorporate the troops of the *III. Panzer-Korps*. Up until February 15, 1944, the German relief force tried to fight its way from the west into the encircled troops. In the mud and heavy anti-aircraft fire, however, they could not achieve this goal.

Taking cover in foxholes, trenches, and grenade craters.

Members of the *5. SS-Panzer-Division Wiking* fighting under the command of *SS-Gruppenführer* Gille in the Kovel area, late March to early May 1944.

On February 16, 1944, the more than 50,000 besieged soldiers, with Hitler's approval, formed up to break out to the southwest, towards Lysianka. East of Shenderovka, *I./SS Panzer Regiment 5*'s last tank secured the cohesion of the *57.* and *88. Infanterie Divisionen*, which were deployed as a rear guard. The greater part of the *5. SS-Panzer-Division* – mostly consolidated into battle groups – formed the left, and therefore southern, flank for the breakthrough.

Under massive Soviet artillery and tank fire, as well as continuous air strikes, on February 17, 1944, about 34,000 men reached the German positions of the *III. Panzer-Korps* on the western bank of the Tikich river. Estonian *SS-Freiwillige* Jaan Valtin remembers:

> I belonged to a light battery of *SS-Panzer-Artillery Regiment 5*. Our final field emplacement was in the village of Shenderovka. Here we had fired only a few grenades; we had run out of ammunition. On February 16, 1944, we got orders to burn everything that was not essential and could be spared! That meant: our laundry, second uniforms, shoes, letters, books, etc., were all taken to a pile, doused with gasoline and set on fire. The afternoon passed and nothing happened. Finally, the order came at about 22 hours to change positions to the *Abteilung* command post. A few minutes later, our guns were already rolling towards the center of the village. With astonishment we noticed, that this time the telephone cable between the firing position and the observation post was just lying there, about 3.5 km long! We wrapped ourselves in the last remaining blankets and tried to sleep a bit, curled up on the prime mover. Suddenly loud commands rang out, the engines were started, and along with another battery, we drove out of the village. We halted a long time on a bridge – heavily laden horse wagons were causing a jam. It was beginning to get light as our four guns got over the bridge. Not far behind, the *3. Batterie* of our Regiment was in firing position. The gunners waved to us hesitantly. Then another halt – the gunners were called to the leader.
>
> The village in front of us was occupied by the Russians, and had to be fought free first. We waited. About one and a half hours later, a 3t prime mover with a 2 cm four-barrel flak gun mounted on it and two trucks with about 25 men drove past us to the front. After about 15 minutes we heard a few bursts of fire and a faint "hurray." A moment later we gunners were assembled, divided into two groups, and sent on both sides of the road to the village. When I fired my carbine at some Soviet vehicles in the village, I lost contact with my comrades and was alone with six or seven *Wehrmacht* men. I set off to find my battery. Together with a comrade, I reached a small village

with about 12 houses on both sides of the village street. Everywhere you could see groups of German soldiers, Hiwis [*Hilfswilliger*], horse-drawn carts and some riding horses. I discovered the prime movers of our battery and hurried over.

With the clusters of *Landsers* [German equivalent of "doughboys"] we drove on. Our prime mover started to skid and slammed into a big tree – that was the end of our ride. The chief gunner stuck a hand grenade into the engine compartment and immediately a black, oily pillar of smoke and fire sprang up. Along with the *Richtkanonier* [gun-pointer], I took out the bolt of our *Haubitze* and threw the pieces all over the place.

I lost contact again, and saw about 300 m away a lot of soldiers in small and large groups. In between were horse-drawn wagons, a few riders, and a *Küchenwagen* [field kitchen wagon]. Suddenly there was movement in the bunch of men, and they began to run; the driver whipped the horses and the riders started to gallop. Then I saw, from behind, that two Russian tanks were rolling through the crowd, and were shooting everyone down and running over them. Meanwhile, I ran under the cover of trees into a clearing. Here apparently a bigger group had rested before me. At least a dozen empty liquor and cordial bottles were lying around, next to cigarette boxes and shreds of papers. By a tree, I found a lot of officer's shoulder boards in a pile. Finally, again with others, I reached the little Gniloi Tikich river. From the right side they were calling "keep to the left" – that is, go downstream. Everyone turned in that direction. This way we reached an area full of bread bags, holsters, laundry bags, bullet pouches, and so on. Here I found a whole *Kommissbrot* [Army dark bread] in a bag. Since it was frozen I could not take a bite, so I had no choice but to tuck it under my arm and go on. I then tried to get across the river on a tree trunk. I fell into the water, but was able to save myself on the bank. Since I had lost my rifle, I looked for a new one and found one nearby. Around 2.5 km away, I saw the snow-covered roofs of some houses (Lysyanka). Since the snow was trampled down in this direction, I followed that way. A soldier was sitting on a tree, his head sunk on his chest. I stood beside him and said, "Come, *Kamerad*, we have to go on!" He was already dead.

A little later, my clothes had frozen from the outside. I felt as if I was wearing medieval armor. I could only move my arms and legs if they were stretched out. Just in front of the village, I came to a wider path and followed it. I then slid into an anti-tank ditch, but I could no longer get out by myself. Two *SS-SturmEnlisted Men* from the *Leibstandarte* rushed over to help me and pulled me out: one grabbing me on the left side, one on the right. The houses were all crowded and stank horribly. In the last house, some *Kameraden* took

> me in. They helped me undress and dry the uniform – I fell asleep. I was awake when someone shouted: "Everyone up! March forward. Clear the village!" The village street was full of soldiers. I joined them, and that is how we got out of the pocket!

The approximately 4,000 men remaining of the *5. SS Panzer-Divis*ion, without heavy weapons and vehicles, concentrated at Risino (about 25 km west of Zvenigorodka), and on February 25, 1944, were sent through Romania to the area east of Lublin for refitting.

Approximately 8,000 men had been killed, wounded, or had fallen into Soviet captivity. About three weeks later, on March 16, 1944, those who remained were transported to Kovel, about 140 km to the east. In the barracks there the formation was to be refitted, and at the same time become a reserve for the already nearby front.

When *SS-Gruppenführer* Gille reached Kovel by airplane, the *Division* men being transported by rail were stopped by partisans about 50 km away from Kovel, and they were forced into a time-consuming fight to free the tracks. Even before they reached the city, this important transport hub had been surrounded by Soviet troops. On March 17, 1944, Hitler declared it a *Fester Platz* [fortress, position which could not be given up] under the command of *SS-Gruppenführer* Gille.

By March 21, 1944, the German relief forces had assembled near Maciejow. In addition to elements of the *131. Infanterie-Division* and *Sturmgeschütz-Abteilung 190*, the newly formed *III. (gep.)/SS Panzergrenadier Regiment 9 Germania*, which had been brought up from France, and the newly formed *II. (Panther)/SS-Panzer-Regiment 5* were also part of the advancing forces. Other elements of *5. SS-Panzer-Division Wiking* – most of them only equipped with hand weapons – were used to secure the flanks.

The relief attempt began on March 29, 1944. In this operation, elements of *II./SS-Panzer-Regiment 5* succeeded, separately from the other troops, in pushing through towards Kovel the next day and reinforcing the trapped forces. When these forces proved insufficient to break the Soviet ring around Kovel, the *LVI. Panzer-Korps*, with the *4.* and *5. Panzer-Division*, were sent in.

On April 4, 1944, elements of the *5. SS-Panzer-Division* formed up, together with the two *Heer Panzer-Divisionen*, to again attempt to relieve Kovel. In heavy fighting, the troops were able to break through the numerous Soviet anti-tank defenses, entering the city from the north the next day. From here, the troops moved towards the west and southwest, to make contact with the *131. Infanterie-Division*. The fierce battle had relieved

Kovel! Until early May 1944, *Division* elements were deployed into the area of Kovel to further consolidate the front. Except for the newly-formed troop units, which were still under command of the *LVI. Panzer-Korps* in Kovel, the *Division* was ordered for a final refitting at the Heidelager *SS* troop training grounds.

Primarily due to temporary attachments of *Volksdeutsche* from south-eastern Europe, as well as men on leave and convalescents, the formation was able to report the following strength as of June 30, 1944:

Fuhrer	**Unterfuhrer**	**Manner**	**Gesamt**
435	3,066	13,847	17,348
2.9%	18.8%	78.3%	100%

In mid-July 1944, the formation was moved to the intensely embattled area of Bialowieza, 380 km distant (about 65 km south-east of Bialystok). This is where the units which had remained at the front (*III./SS-Panzergrenadier Regiment 9* and *II./ SS-Panzer-Regiment 5*) had been stationed since July 16, 1944, fighting against advancing enemy troops.

During the transport, the units were informed that they would be deployed in a new location, and thus, on July 19, 1944, they had already been moved to Kamieniec Litewski (about 38 km north of Brest-Litovsk), in the sector of the *XX. Arme-Korps (2. Armee)* along the Lesna river, into a bridgehead against the fast approaching enemy tank units.

The *5. SS Panzer-Division Wiking* was unable, however, to even partially stabilize the battered *Heeresgruppe Mitte* front. Instead, it was dragged into the almost chaotic retreat, and had to march the next almost two weeks about 160 km southwest. After crossing the Bug, the formation at the end of July 1944 – from now placed under the command of the newly deployed *IV. SS- Panzer-Korps (2. Armee)* – moved into positions near Stanislavov [Ivano-Frankivsk], with the front to the south and west. There was no continuous *HKL* to the *9. Armee* at Warsaw.

On August 3, 1944, the attack began on Okuniew to the west. This was to establish contact with the elements of *XXXIX. Panzer-Korps* which were advancing eastwards from the Warsaw area.

After successfully closing the gap in the front, the *5. SS Panzer-Division HKL* ran from Stanislavov about 10 km to the west. On August 10, 1944, *SS-Gruppenführer* Gille took over the *IV. SS-Panzer-Korps* (now *9. Armee*); *SS-Standartenführer* Muhlenkamp was then assigned command of the *5. SS-Panzer-Division.*

The retreat in summer 1944.

Mid-sized *Flamm-Panzerwagen* [tank flame throwers] (Sdr. Kfz. 251/16).

BMW R-75.

Panzer V Panther
Ausf. A.

Winter conditions on the Eastern Front often brought total exhaustion of men, animals, and machinery.

Mid-sized *Schützenpanzerwagen* (Sdr. Kfz. 251 Ausf. C).

© Michaelis-Verlag Berlin, Oktober 2006

As the front was shortened, during the night of August 12, 1944, the unit switched positions with the *3. SS- Panzer-Division* and went back to a position some 20 km to the north. The *5. SS-Panzer-Division* had at this time:

5 average strength *Panzergrenadier-Bataillone*[49]
6 *leichte Artillerie-Batterien* (30 *Feldhaubitzen* 10.5 cm)
4 *schwere Artillerie-Batterien* (18 *Feldhaubitzen* 15 cm)
11 *schwere Panzerabwehrkanonen* 7.5 cm
12 *Sturmgeschütze*
16 *Panzer IV*
21 *Panzer V Panther*

On August 14, 1944, after heavy artillery preparatory attacks, enemy troops succeeded in breaking through the boundary to the *3. SS-Panzer-Division*, deployed to the right side. Counterattacks were unsuccessful.

49 The combat strength of the *Panzergrenadiere* amounted to barely 2,000 men. *SS-Panzergrenadier* Battalion Narva, functioning as the *III. /SS-Panzergrenadier-Regiment Westland*, was detached from the formation and transferred to the *20. SS-Freiwilligen-Grenadier-Division* (*estnische Nr. 1*). *SS-Panzer-Aufklärungs-Abteilung 5* was in the homeland for refitting.

Four days later, the Battle of Warsaw began in a hurricane of Soviet artillery fire. In addition to further heavy fighting on the boundary to the *3. SS Panzer-Division*, critical situations also developed at the boundaries to the neighboring units to the left, which was at the same time the border to the *2. Armee XX. Armee-Korps*.

Because the *5. SS-Panzer-Division* forces were not sufficient to re-establish the line, *Grenadier-Brigade 1131* and others were marched to the left flank, where *SS-Panzergrenadier Regiment 10 Westland* was fighting. However, the units could not counter the massive Soviet attacks by up to seven Divisions at times. On August 24, 1944, the *Division* – stationed on the Radzymin-Niepont line (about 10 km south of Wyszkow) – reported that it had a combat strength of 2,065 men, with a *Tagesstärke* of 10,335 men. Thus, in barely two months the formation had lost almost exactly 7,000 men killed in action, wounded, and missing.

By September 6, 1944, the troops had to withdraw over the Narew river and moved into an approximately 12-km long *HKL* from Serock to Nieporent to the south, in the so-called *Nassen Dreieck* ["wet or watery triangle"]. The formation, which was classified as having "only a limited defensive capability," still had over 9 *Artillerie-Batterien* with a total of 35 *Haubitzen*.[50]

To increase combat strength, the newly formed *III./SS Panzergrenadier Regiment 10 Westland*, manned by Ukrainians and about 1,000 members of the *Luftwaffe* – with no infantry experience – who had been assigned to the *Waffen-SS*, were sent to the *5. SS-Panzer-Division*. The very heavy and bloody fighting at first subsided on September 25, 1944.

On October 2, 1944, the *5. SS-Panzer-Division* reported the following battle strength:

I. /SS-Panzergrenadier-Regiment 9	**193 men**
II./SS-Panzergrenadier- Regiment 9	**396 men**
III./SS-Panzergrenadier-Regiment 9	**176 men**
I. / SS Panzer Grenadier Regiment 10	**527 men**
II. */SS-Panzergrenadier- Regiment 10*	**332 men**
III. */SS-Panzergrenadier- Regiment 10*	**548 men**
SS-Panzer-Pionier-Bataillon 5	**384 men**
***SS-Panzer-Aufklärungs-Abteilung* 5**	**325 men**

50 The term *Nasses Dreieck* ["Wet or watery triangle"] refers to the very marshy region between the Bug and Vistula rivers. The triangle was enclosed to the east by the *HKL*.

Medical treatment for a wounded soldier.

Panzer V Panther Ausf. A of the *II./SS-Pz. Rgt 5*.

German war cemetery at Modlin.

The combat strength was therefore about 5,000 men; the *Tagesstärke* some 10,000 men. On October 10, 1944, the Red Army again took the offensive, launching heavy attacks on and breaches of the German *HKL* by October 28, 1944. Costly German counter-attacks were able to prevent further collapse of the front, with the units (under the command of *SS-Standartenführer* Ullrich) withdrawing to a position approximately 12 km further west.

Since every enemy attack and *Feuerüberfall* [sudden concentration of fire], as well as the fire attack and categorically launched counterattacks, were decimating the German units, which were without replacements and supplies, the Soviets, with their immense numerical superiority, were able to steadily win ground.

On November 16, 1944, the remnants of the Ukrainian *SS* volunteers *III./SS Panzergrenadier Regiment 10* were released back to the *14. Waffen Grenadier Division* of the *SS* (*galizische Nr. 1* [Galician No. 1]). As replacements, the newly formed *I. Bataillone* of *SS-Panzergrenadier-Regimenter 23 Norge* and *24 Danmark* were sent to the *5. SS-Panzer-Division*. In addition, more *Luftwaffe* members were attached to the *Division*.[51]

As the Hungarian capital was encircled by the Red Army on Christmas 1944, the *IV. SS-Panzer-Korps* was given orders to transfer to *Heeresgruppe Süd*. Because the *Generalkommando* and the *3. SS-Panzer-Division* had already been taken out of action on December 25, 1944, near Modlin, the *5. SS-Panzer-Division* briefly joined the *XXXVI. Panzer-Korps*.

Shortly afterwards, the units were loaded up for transport to Győr, to *Armeegruppe Balck*. From there, they marched about 50 km to the east to the initial positions in front of Tata. As the command for the attack to relieve Budapest (approximately 60 km away) was issued on January 1, 1945, of a total of 87 transport trains, only 28 – although most of these were carrying combat troops – had arrived.

In the mountainous and forested terrain, the German forces were initially able to take Tata, but the difficult terrain meant that *SS-Panzer-Artillery-Regiment 5* could only provide limited support. To the cheers of the Hungarian population, *SS-Panzergrenadier- Regiment 9 Germania* and *I. / SS-Panzergrenadier-Regiment 23 Norge* occupied Tarján on January 3, 1945. After the remainder of the *Division* reached Hungary, both *Panzergrenadier-Regimenter* attacked together and were able to reach Bicske on January 5, 1945. The occupation and a thrust on to Martonvasar foundered due to the strong enemy opposition, and as a result, the attack was abandoned. *Unternehmen Konrad* – the first relief attempt for Budapest – had failed.

51 This actually belonged to the *11.-Freiwilligen-Panzergrenadier-Division Nordland*.

Heeresgruppe Süd re-disposed itself and planned *Konrad 2*. For this operation, *SS-Panzergrenadier-Regiment 10 Westland* was initially to change position on January 10, 1945, to the area south of Esztergom [German: Gran] and move through the Pilis mountains to again form up to relieve Budapest. After taking Piliszentkereszt, the commanding General of *IV. SS-Panzer-Korps*, *SS-Obergruppenführer* Gille, also ordered *SS-Panzergrenadier Regiment 9 Germania* to move to the new attack area, to exploit this success.

When the deployed elements of the *5. SS-Panzer-Division* had approached about 17 km towards Budapest, Hitler, disregarding the situation, ordered on January 12, 1945, that the attack be ended! The next day, the *I./ SS-Panzergrenadier Regiment 24 Danmark* of the *6. Panzer-Division* and the *I./SS-Panzergrenadier Regiment 23 Norge* were, together with *I./SS-Panzergrenadier Regiment 9 Germania*, placed under command of the *3. Kavallerie-Brigade*. In the *IV. SS-Panzer-Korps* sector, the *5. SS-Panzer-Division* moved some 80 km to the southwest to the area of Csajag, on Lake Balaton.[52]

From here, on January 18, 1945, the formation was to participate in the so-called *Süd-Lösung* for the relief of Budapest (*Unternehmen Konrad 3*). After heavy fighting, the units were able to break into the Soviet *HKL* in Balatonfökajar. The next day, the troops crossed the Sárvíz canal, east of the some 20-km distant Kalóz, and turned north towards Sárosd, about 16 km away. From here, the *5. SS-Panzer-Division* pushed forward to the northeast, and on January 23, 1945, reached the Danube at Adony. The distance to Budapest was still about 45 km. Finally, elements of the *Division* reached the Vali river. Due to the in-depth defense, as well as the constantly changing orders from *Armee-Gruppe Balck*, the advance was stalled. The units had to go into the defensive between Baracska and Adony.

The Soviet offensive was launched January 29, 1945; by the next day it had already forced deep breaches in the *5. SS-Panzer-Division HKL*. The formation – under command of the *III. Panzer-Korps* – began pulling out of the Gardony-Szolgaeghyaza line February 1 , 1945. Since there was no continuous front any more, the enemy was also able to advance westward towards Seregelyes. During February 4-5, 1945, the formation moved into the *Margarethe-Stellung* [Margareta position], in the area before Székesfehérvár.

52 The two *Regimenter* then took part, separate from the *5. SS-Panzer-Division Wiking*, in the fighting around Székesfehérvár in the sector of the *1. Panzer-Division*. On January 23, 1945, they were placed under tactical command of *SS-Panzer-Division Totenkopf*.

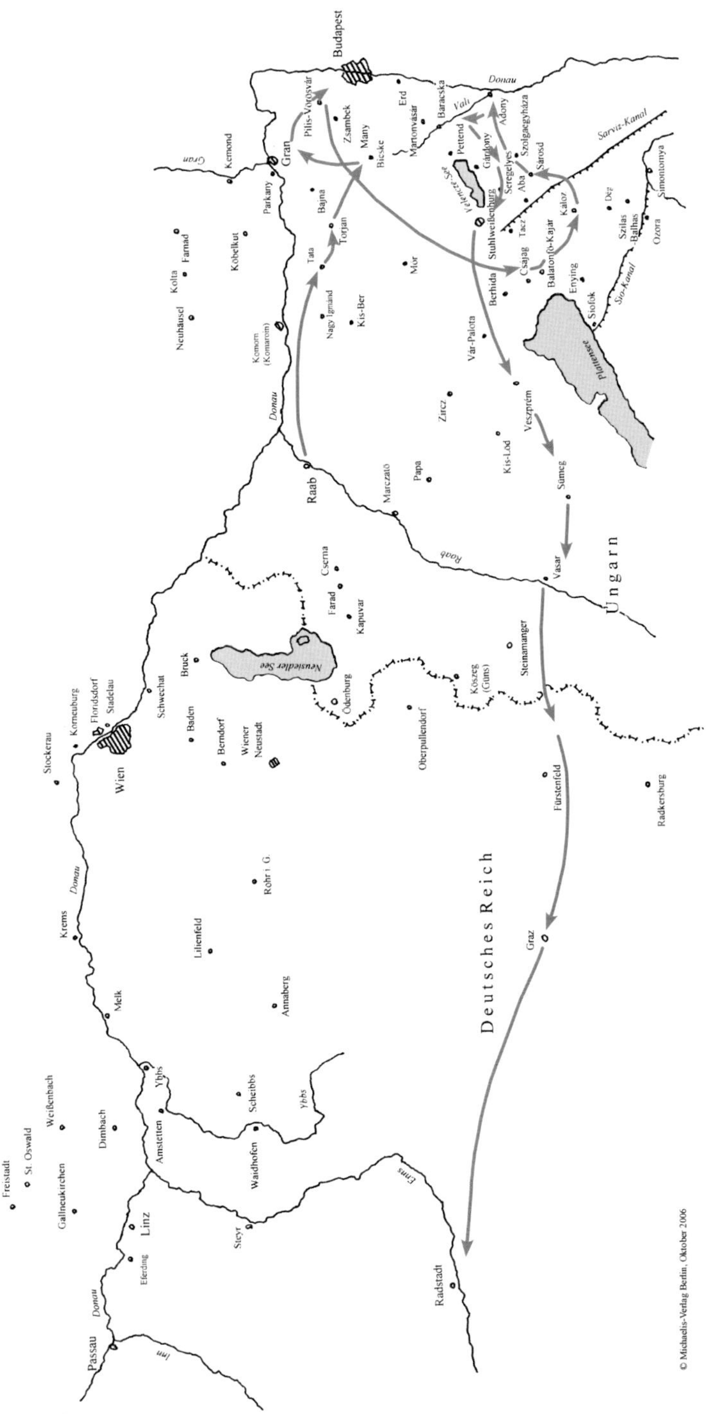
Budapest
Donau
Gran
Kemond
Parkany
Pilis-Vorosvár
Zsambek
Many
Bicske
Erd
Martonvasár
Baracska
Adony
Pettend
Gárdony
Velencze-See
Seregelyes
Szolgaegyháza
Sarvíz-Kanal
Sárosd
Aba
Stuhlweißenburg
Tacz
Kaloz
Balatonfö-Kajár
Csajág
Berhida
Enying
Siófok
Sio-Kanal
Szilas
Balhas
Ozora
Simontornya
Deg
Bajna
Torjan
Tata
Kobelkut
Farnad
Kolta
Neuhäusel
Komorn (Komarom)
Nagy Igmánd
Kis-Ber
Mor
Vár-Palota
Veszprém
Plattensee
Zircz
Kis-Lod
Sümeg
Papa
Marczató
Raab
Vasar
Ungarn
Cserna
Farad
Kapuvar
Neusiedler See
Bruck
Ödenburg
Köszeg (Güns)
Steinamanger
Oberpullendorf
Fürstenfeld
Radkersburg
Wien
Schwechat
Stadelau
Floridsdorf
Korneuburg
Stockerau
Baden
Berndorf
Wiener Neustadt
Rohr i. G.
Lilienfeld
Annaberg
Krems
Melk
Ybbs
Scheibbs
Weißenbach
Dimbach
St. Oswald
Freistadt
Gallneukirchen
Amstetten
Waidhofen
Enns
Linz
Steyr
Eferding
Passau
Inn
Radstadt
Graz
Deutsches Reich
© Michaelis-Verlag Berlin, Oktober 2006

The *5. SS-Panzer-Division* – called a *Kampfgruppe* after February 6, 1945, due to its small numbers – was again under the command of the *IV. SS-Panzer-Korps* four days later. On February 22, 1945, after about two weeks of quiet on the front, it was transferred to the area on both sides of Székesfehérvár. After the *Kampfgruppe* was again brought up to strength, primarily with *Luftwaffe* and *Kriegsmarine* members, it was again designated the *5. SS Panzer-Division* after February 27, 1945.

On March 16, 1945, the pause on the front ended. After a heavy barrage, the Red Army attacked at Székesfehérvár. While the adjacent *3. SS Panzer-Division* was pressed westwards, the *5. SS Panzer-Division* was at first able to hold its positions. On March 10, 1945, it had – although barely 50% mobile:

4 *Panzer IV*
13 *Panzer V Panther*
8 *Sturmgeschütze*
6 *leichte Artillerie-Batterien*
4 *schwere Artillerie-Batterien*

Thus, the *Panzer-Regiment* had the strength of three weak companies, with no fuel. As encirclement of the city loomed on March 21, 1945, *SS-Oberführer* Ullrich decided to pull his units out against the orders of Hitler. Marching northwest of Lake Balaton, the *Division* lost nearly all its armored vehicles and heavy weapons because it had no fuel.

Without any *HKL* and almost in disarray, the exhausted units tried to get to the West. On March 24, 1945, a rear defensive line was briefly set up around Vészprem. Behind this, the units which had been decimated in recent days were to be refitted with replacements. The commander of *SS-Panzer-Nachrichten-Abteilung 5*, *SS-Sturmbannführer* Schmeißer, remembers:

> The new replacements now came from *Heimatverbänden* [homeland units], which had been set up in the cities as the *Sicherheits- und Hilfsdienst (SHD)* [Security and Assistance Services], to be deployed during air raids and fires; even young *Flakhelfer* [anti-aircraft helpers] were included. For us, at the time, they were children or old men between 50 and 60 years old. In *SS-Panzer-Nachrichten-Abteilung 5*, they were used for the supply train, because they had absolutely no combat experience. The freed-up men were assigned to battle groups.

This did nothing to prevent not only the rapid advance of the Red Army, which by March 29, 1945, had pushed back the remnants of the *5. SS-Panzer-Division*, after fighting at Sümeg in the Rába bridgehead, to Vasvár (Eisenburg), but neither to provide any restoration of deployment capability. The soldiers had marched some 130 km in about a week.

Then came the command to move to the *Reichsschutzstellung* [Reich line of defense] in the area of Fürstenfeld, about 60 km to the southeast. After renewed heavy fighting, the first units broke loose on May 7, 1945, to reach the 160-km distant line of demarcation on the Enns.

By way of Graz-Radstadt, the troops arrived in the Kleinarl Tal [valley] and went into American captivity. This ended the nearly four-year deployment of the *5. SS-Panzer-Division Wiking*. The formation had experienced the rapid and often almost uncontested advances into the Caucasus, and the fierce and extremely bloody fighting in retreat battles beginning in late 1942. By March 1945, its military operations had almost liquidated the *Division*. It is interesting to note that the propaganda stating the formation consisted of "Germanic" volunteers was not correct. In 1945, not even 5% of the members were northern or western European volunteers.

SS Brigadeführer Bittrich (left) commanded SS-Division Hohenstaufen from its formation until July 1944.

Silvester Stadler – here still as an SS-Obersturmbannführer – led the Division until the end of the war.

9.

SS-PANZER-DIVISION HOHENSTAUFEN

The SS-Panzergrenadier-Division 9

On Dec. 19, 1942, Adolf Hitler, anticipating the invasion of France, ordered the formation of a central reserve in Normandy, in two new *SS-Divisionen* in the sector of the *Oberbefehlshaber West*. They were to be motorized units that could move rapidly in case of a large-scale Allied landing; the enemy troops were to be destroyed on the land.

In response, the *SS-FHA* issued an order on January 8, 1943, to raise two *SS-Panzergrenadier-Divisionen* of volunteers of the age group born in 1924-25. The first of these was ***SS-Panzergrenadier-Division 9***, which, starting January 1943, was to be led by *SS-Brigadeführer* Bittrich, and organized at the French Mailly le Camp troop training grounds (about 35 km east of Sezanne) in the following formation:

DIVISIONSSTAB
SS-Panzer--Grenadier-Regiment 1 (I.-III Batallion.)
SS-Panzer--Grenadier-Regiment 2 (I.-III. (gp.) Battalion)
SS-Kradschützen-Regiment 9
SS-Panzer-Regiment 9[53]

53 Formation of the *Panzer-Regiment* was delayed continually by the lack of equipment. Initially, only the *II. Abteilung (Panzer IV)* could be set up. The *I. Abteilung (Panzer V)* was only formed at the end of 1944. Since there were hardly even any *Panzer IV* hardly available, a *Panzer-Abteilung – de facto* the *II.* – was formed with 42 *Sturmgeschütze* and three *Panzerbefehlswagen* [armored command cars] as an intermediate formation.

SS-Panzerjäger-Abteilung 9
SS-Sturmgeschütz-Abteilung 9[54]
SS-Artillerie-Regiment 9
SS-Flak-Abteilung 9
SS-Pionier-Bataillon 9
SS-Nachrichten-Abteilung 9
SS-Sanitäts-Abteilung 9
SS-Wirtschafts-Bataillon 9
SS-Nachschub-Truppen 9
***SS-Instandsetzungs-Abteilung 9* [Maintenance]**

Since the plan was for the formation to include a *Panzer-Regiment*, the structure of the units already resembled that of a *Panzer-Division*. In addition to surplus weapons from the *6. SS-Gebirgs-Division Nord*, the new formation was primarily equipped with captured Soviet guns and anti-tank canons. The enlisted men consisted of *RAD* [*Reichsarbeitsdienst*] volunteers, so that the *Waffen-SS Werbe-* [recruitment] and *Musterungskommissionen* [registration, physical examination commissions] exercised psychological pressure on the young men. Individual *SS-Truppenteile* [troop units] were attached in their entirety to the new *Division*; for example, the *SS-Polizei-Grenadier-Ausbildungs- und Ersatz-Bataillon*, [*SS* Police Grenadier Training and Replacement battalion], primarily made up of Alsatians, was ordered to the *Division*.

In early March 1943, the formation was transferred to the *15. Armee* sector between Lillers-Cassel-Houthuist-Kortryk-Armentieres, so that it would be on hand near the coast in case of an enemy invasion. Certainly, the *Division* was still not in operational condition at this time.[55]

In the middle of the month, the formation was given the name Hohenstaufen. Later, at the end of March 1943, when individual training within the units was considered complete, training began in groups and platoons. To do this, they were to gain access to the larger framework at the troop training grounds Maria ter Heide near Brasschaet (about 10 km northeast of Antwerp) and Beverloo near Pael (about 20 km northwest of Hasselt).[56]

4 According to the *K.St.N.* [*Kriegsstärkenachweisung*: Wartime charts of official composition of German military units], no *Sturmgeschütz-Abteilung* was provided in a *Panzergrenadier Division*. It was formed temporarily as a replacement for an operational *Panzer-Regiment*. When the *Sturmgeschütz-Abteilung* was disbanded at the turn of the year 1943-44, the majority of the enlisted men, as well as the guns, were ordered to the *Panzer-Regiment*.

55 This place was about 7 km north of the well-known city Langemarck.

56 The name Hohenstaufen did not honor only one individual, as the *10. SS-Panzergrenadier-Division Frundsberg* or the *17th SS-Panzergrenadier-Division Götz von Berlichingen* did, but an entire lineage that helped to shape the history of Germany for centuries.

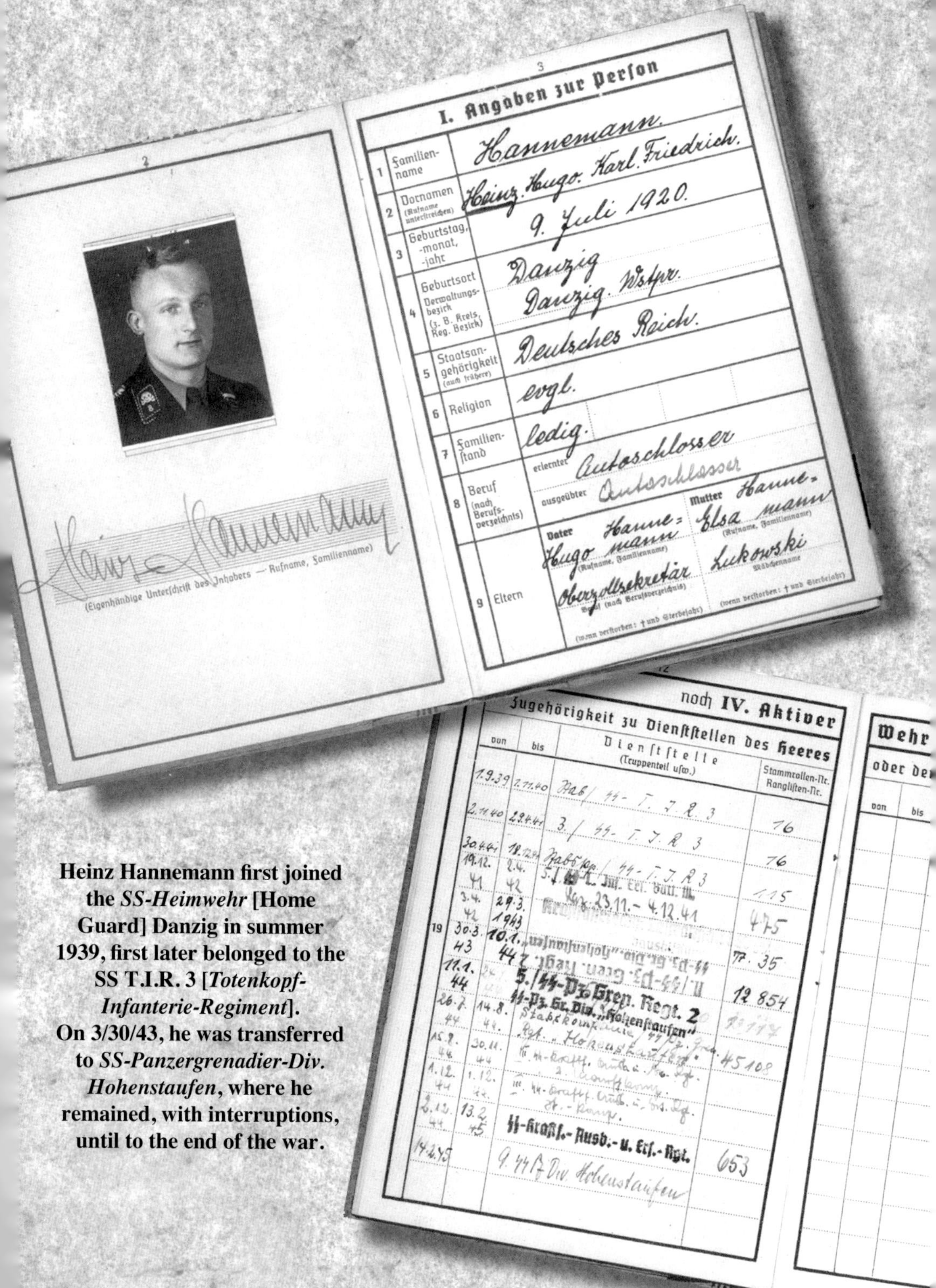

Heinz Hannemann first joined the *SS-Heimwehr* [Home Guard] Danzig in summer 1939, first later belonged to the SS T.I.R. 3 [*Totenkopf-Infanterie-Regiment*]. On 3/30/43, he was transferred to *SS-Panzergrenadier-Div. Hohenstaufen*, where he remained, with interruptions, until to the end of the war.

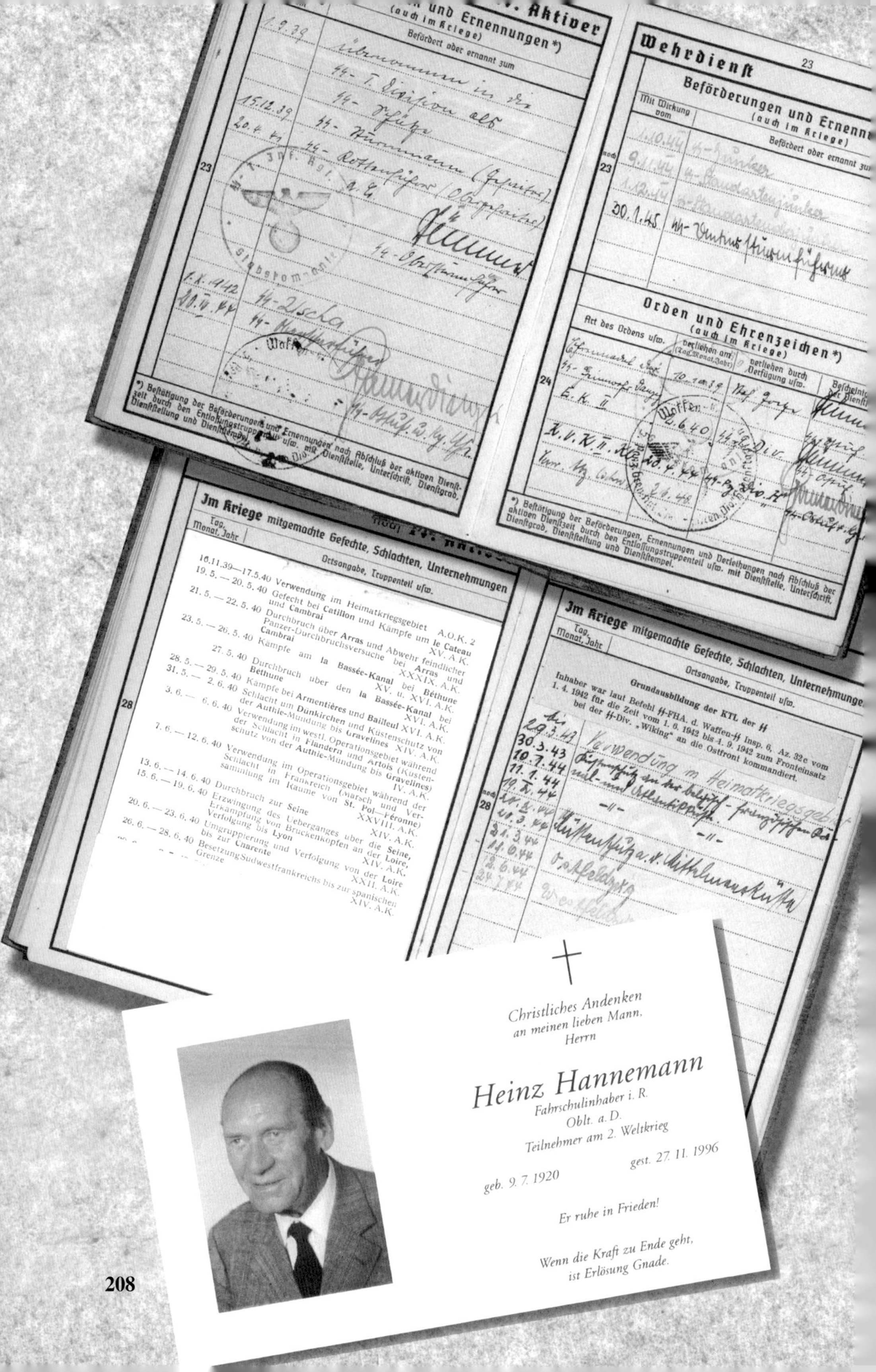
und Ernennungen*) Aktiver
(auch im Kriege)
Befördert oder ernannt zum
Wehrdienst
23
Beförderungen und Ernenn
(auch im Kriege)
Mit Wirkung vom
Befördert oder ernannt zum
Orden und Ehrenzeichen*)
(auch im Kriege)
Art des Ordens usw.
verliehen am (Tag, Monat, Jahr)
verliehen durch Verfügung usw.
*) Bestätigung der Beförderungen und Ernennungen nach Abschluß der aktiven Dienstzeit durch den Entlassungstruppenteil usw. mit Dienststelle, Unterschrift, Dienstgrad, Dienststellung und Dienststempel.
*) Bestätigung der Beförderungen, Ernennungen und Verleihungen nach Abschluß der aktiven Dienstzeit durch den Entlassungstruppenteil usw. mit Dienststelle, Unterschrift, Dienstgrad, Dienststellung und Dienststempel.
Im Kriege mitgemachte Gefechte, Schlachten, Unternehmungen
Tag, Monat, Jahr
Ortsangabe, Truppenteil usw.
16.11.39—17.5.40 Verwendung im Heimatkriegsgebiet A.O.K. 2
19. 5. — 20. 5. 40 Gefecht bei Catillon und Kämpfe um le Cateau und Cambrai XV. A.K.
21. 5. — 22. 5. 40 Durchbruch über Arras und Abwehr feindlicher Panzer-Durchbruchsversuche bei Arras und Cambrai XXXIX. A.K.
23. 5. — 26. 5. 40 Kämpfe am la Bassée-Kanal bei Béthune XV. u. XVI. A.K.
27. 5. 40 Durchbruch über den la Bassée-Kanal bei Béthune XVI. A.K.
28. 5. — 29. 5. 40 Kämpfe bei Armentières und Bailleul XVI. A.K.
31. 5. — 2. 6. 40 Schlacht um Dünkirchen und Küstenschutz von der Authie-Mündung bis Gravelines XIV. A.K.
3. 6. — 6. 6. 40 Verwendung im westl. Operationsgebiet während der Schlacht in Flandern und Artois (Küstenschutz von der Authie-Mündung bis Gravelines) IV. A.K.
7. 6. — 12. 6. 40 Verwendung im Operationsgebiet während der Schlacht in Frankreich (Marsch und Versammlung im Raume von St. Pol—Péronne) XXVIII. A.K.
13. 6. — 14. 6. 40 Durchbruch zur Seine XIV. A.K.
15. 6. — 19. 6. 40 Erzwingung des Ueberganges über die Seine, Erkämpfung von Brückenköpfen an der Loire, Verfolgung bis Lyon XIV. A.K.
20. 6. — 23. 6. 40 Umgruppierung und Verfolgung von der Loire bis zur Charente XXII. A.K.
26. 6. — 28. 6. 40 Besetzung Südwestfrankreichs bis zur spanischen Grenze XIV. A.K.
Im Kriege mitgemachte Gefechte, Schlachten, Unternehmungen
Tag, Monat, Jahr
Ortsangabe, Truppenteil usw.
Grundausbildung der KTL der ǁ
Inhaber war laut Befehl ǁ-FHA. d. Waffen-ǁ Insp. 6, Az. 32c vom 1. 4. 1942 für die Zeit vom 1. 6. 1942 bis 4. 9. 1942 zum Fronteinsatz bei der ǁ-Div. „Wiking" an die Ostfront kommandiert.
Christliches Andenken
an meinen lieben Mann,
Herrn
Heinz Hannemann
Fahrschulinhaber i. R.
Oblt. a. D.
Teilnehmer am 2. Weltkrieg
geb. 9. 7. 1920
gest. 27. 11. 1996
Er ruhe in Frieden!
Wenn die Kraft zu Ende geht,
ist Erlösung Gnade.

On May 26, 1943, the *Schnelle Regiment* (*SS-Kradschützen-Regiment 9*) was reclassified as *SS-Panzer-Aufklärungs-Abteilung 9*. *SS-Panzerjäger-Abteilung 9* was again disbanded due to lack of *Panzerabwehrkanonen* and only re-formed in the summer of 1944. In June 1943, the *9. SS-Panzergrenadier-Division Hohenstaufen*, with a strength of 19,319 men, was transported to the region of Amiens. Training as a *Batallion* formation was to be carried forward at the troop training grounds there, and the *Division* was to achieve full operational readiness by July 1, 1943. This meant that only about six months of training was estimated for this motorized formation. Due to the lack of weapons and other materiel equipment (including *Panzer* and *Schützenpanzerwagen*), training could not be carried out on schedule.

Only on August 17, 1943, did the *OB West* announce the allocation of motorized vehicles to the *9.* and *10. SS-Panzergrenadier-Division*. The command was then revised, so that the available vehicles were to be supplied exclusively to *9. SS-Panzergrenadier-Dvision Hohenstaufen*. When, however, it then had to re-allocate the equipment to the *14. Panzer-Division* at the beginning of October 1943, the *OKW* announced on October 11, 1943, that the *9. SS-Panzergrenadier-Division* was to be outfitted immediately from captured Italian supplies.

The 9. SS-Panzer-Division Hohenstaufen

Four days later, as part of the simultaneous numbering of *Waffen-SS-Divisionen* and *Regimenter*, it was announced that the formation would be renamed: **9. SS-Panzer- Division Hohenstaufen.**

The two *SS-Panzergrenadier- Regimenter* were given the numbers 19 and 20.

Since the reclassification of the better-manned *Panzergrenadier-Division* into a *Panzer-Division* – such as by reducing the *Artillerie* from four to three *Abteilungen* – would free up personnel, just 1,400 *Division* members were attached to the *16.* and *17. SS-Panzergrenadier-Division*en, for example. On December 31, 1943, the *Division* reported a strength of:

Officers	Unterführer	Enlisted Men	Total
466	2,587	15,181	18,234
2.6%	14.2%	83.2%	100%
614	3,923	13,260	17,797
3.5%	22.1%	74.4%	100%

After more attacments, this was the *Tagesstärke* on February 1, 1944:

	Officers	Unterführer	Enlisted Men	Total
Actual	466	2,577	14,369	17,412
Authorized	2.7%	14.8%	82.5%	100%

This corresponds to the *Sollstärke* in numbers, but the formation still lacked some 1,500 *Führer* and *Unterführer*.

On February 18, 1944, the *19. Armee* was redeployed to the region of Orange-Salon-Nimes-Montpellier. The coast of southern France was only sparsely occupied by German troops to guard against a landing of Allied forces, and this situation was even further weakened by the transfer of the *715. Infanterie-Division* to the Nettuno front in Italy. Although still not sufficiently equipped with heavy weapons and vehicles, the *OKW KTW* [*Kriegstagebuch*] noted that *AOK 19* now had "a fully battle-ready *Panzerverband* as a reserve." One can see how misinformed the higher command headquarters' administrative offices were in planning the deployment and assignment of troops under their command. In southern France, repeated operations were also carried out against the so-called terrorists. Günter Adam remembers one such operation:

> We were given a deployment order against terrorists in the mountains. It was a difficult march on the mountain roads in thick fog, and we moved with activated night vision devices. When we reached our destination at night, we first had to occupy the police station. It was known that the police often made common cause with the terrorists. This was even supposed to be a terrorist stronghold. Every moment we expected to get shot. Around the small market place, a few windows were lit up – one of them was the police station. *SS-Untersturmführer* Lohausen and I rushed into the guard house, as we thought, but behind the door there was only a staircase going upstairs. When we stormed

up this, we realized our mistake; we had gone into a guesthouse, and the police station was the side door. However, things stayed quiet. The action was a washout. On the outskirts of town, we went into some empty barracks and spent the night dozing and shivering with cold, because it had also started to snow outside. We were sure we were right in the middle of a wasp's nest and waited for some surprises, but all was quiet. When day dawned and the sun came up, everything was peaceful. The inhabitants were standing in the street and waiting for the bus that would take them to work. No trace of hostility. When we stopped in a small town, people even came to our vehicles and gave us wine and almonds.

Areas of deployment and security sectors in the West 1943-44.

On March 26, 1944, the *9. SS-Panzer-Division* was ordered to the *II. SS-Panzer-Korps* sector on the Eastern Front. The *Korps'* mission was to restore contact between the *4.* and almost-encircled *1. Panzer-Armee* between Tarnopol and Kamenez-Podolsk. This deployment counteracted the original reason it was formed, which was to operate as a central reserve for the expected invasion.

Transported by rail along the route Lyon-Besancon-Belfort-Strasbourg-Karlsruhe, Germany-Nuremberg-Plauen-Neisse-Hindenburg-Krakow, they reached Lviv at the beginning of April 1944 and disembarked there. In motorized march, the units moved in heavy snowfall to the area of Rohatyn (about 60 km southeast of Lviv), and were there placed under the command of the *4. Panzer-Armee* for immediate active service. *SS-Panzer-Aufklärungs-Abteilung 9* marched from Rohatyn, initially further southwards to Stanislas, but were ordered back to Rohatyn on April 7, 1944, to follow from there the *9. SS-Panzer-Division*, which was concentrating at Brzezany.

The next day, *I./SS-Panzergrenadier-Regiment 19* joined with *I./SS-Panzer-Artillery Regiment 9* and *II./SS-Panzer-Regiment 9* in the successful attack on the Soviet bridgehead over the Strypa at Zlotniki (about 40 km southeast of Brzezany). On April 9, 1944, the entire *Division* was placed under command of the *XXXXVIII. Panzer-Korps*, and were to take part from the assembly area at Brzezany in the relief operation across the Strypa for the German troops trapped since March 24, 1944, in Tarnopol.

In the bottomless mud caused by the onset of spring, initially the *I./SS-Panzergrenadier-Regiment 1*, with *II./SS-Panzergrenadier-Regiment 20* and elements of *II./SS-Panzer-Regiment 9*, formed up on April 11, 1944, for the attack, and were able to push forward across the Strypa to Horodyszcze. The fighting around this village, and the effort to build a bridgehead over the Wosuszka river, went on until April 14, 1944. *SS-Panzer-Regiment 9* had on that day the following:

31 *Panzer IV*
27 *Sturmgeschütze III*

After the bridgehead had been established, the real relief attack on Tarnopol began. They succeeded on April 16, 1944, in advancing to Zagrobelo, however, from there they were only able to move about 50 soldiers from Tarnopol. The actual success of the operation, therefore, was just destruction of considerable enemy forces during the about 10 km-deep attack. Günter Adam remembers:

> It was about April 13, 1944, when we got orders to occupy Hill 367 at Horodyszcze. That was the infantry part of the company, meaning with no *Pak-*, *Flak-*, or *Infanteriegeschütz-Zug* [infantry howitzer platoon]. I was then *Kompanie-Truppführer* [squad leader] for *SS-Hauptsturmführer* Günter von Brocke, and had to search, in the darkness, for the place to cross over the Strypa and make contact with the comrades waiting for us. By the light of a rising flare, I saw right in front of me a VW with a crew. When I got nearer to the car, I saw that the car was charred, and so were the three comrades sitting in it ...
>
> Finally, a little further on, I saw the expected signallers. While avoiding making any noise, the *Kompanie* was briefed and got underway. After we crossed the river, we had to go up a steep slope and then over an open plain, which seemed endless to us. Despite all our precautions, Ivan noticed that something was up with us and attacked. He certainly had the idea that he had run into a relief mission. But this time he had bad luck! The ditch, the old Russian position, was now doubly occupied, and he was repelled at great cost, but then again came against our trenches. Our comrades were from the *II./SS-Panzergrenadier-Regiment 20* and suffered large casualties. The fallen *Kommandeur*, *SS-Sturmbannführer* Frank, lay in a bunker; he would get the *Ritterkreuz* after his death. The position was not exactly comfortable. Our *Sani* [*Sanitäter*: medical orderly], Anton Schulte, has done superhuman work under fire, but unfortunately the Grim Reaper got a big harvest. Many a comrade from the old days left us

forever. I would like to mention all the names, but they have also escaped me. Ammunition and food became scarce. There was no support, neither artillery nor air support. Therefore, the leader decided to send a messenger to the rear. It was to be our young comrade, *SS-Sturmmann* Petersen, just 18 years old, and this in the bright morning. I volunteered to undertake this run for Peters, which at first the leader didn't want, but then let himself be convinced that two men would have a better chance to get help. Under heavy fire cover from the *Kompanie*, we ran out and reached our second trench quite fast. The open flat area in front of us had only been about 500 meters wide, but it seemed endless to us. Despite the hard bombardment, we got through, and we were able to recover under the steep slope. After some searching, we found our forward Division command post in a ruined farmhouse, reinforced to give some makeshift cover. It was occupied by our esteemed Ia [Ia (*1. Generalstabsoffizier*): 1st General Staff Officer in the tactical detachment of a Division HQ], *SS-Sturmbannführer* Harzer, who had the *Division-Begleit-Kompanie* [Escort Company]. We described the situation on the hill, and asked the accessory *Kommandeur* of the *Artillerie-Regiment* for artillery support. He asked rather incredulously what the *Begleit-Kompanie* would want with such support, but Harzer made it clear that the *Kompanie* was within range of enemy hand grenades. They said there would be help, which did come a bit later. Then it was back to the *Kompanie*. This time without fire cover, because the comrades knew nothing about our coming. Now all the weapons were being fired at Peters and me. The nastiest were the *Granatwerfer* [light mortars]. They pinned us down on the ground and under the smallest cover. Since we could not get back this way, we decided to split up. One of us would be sure to get through. But the fire did not subside. For over an hour I could only gain a little ground, and assuming that Petersen had long ago reached the *Kompanie*, and in order not to disgrace myself, I stormed off in a zigzag. The *Kompanie* got the message from my shouting and now gave me fire cover, and after a renewed spurt, I dove into our trench. Petersen had not yet gotten there! The *Kompanie* was now watching out for him, and by his shouts we spotted him. Under our strong cover fire, he arrived safely with us. For us, *Unternehmen* Tarnopol was almost over. As far as I can remember, 40 comrades were killed and as many wounded. We cleared out of our position after a few days and went back across the Strypa. Spring weather had set in, and it was muddy. On the eastern bank, two Panthers were stuck in the mud and could not be gotten out of the place. With tears in their eyes, the crews had to blow up their Panzers and leave the bank. Our decimated *Kompanie* withdrew to Brzezany on April 20, 1944.

Günter Adam as a member of *Division-Sicherungs-Kompanie* [Division Security Company] *9*.

Members of the *Div. Sicherungs-Kp. 9* in a Steyer 1500 A 1.

BMW R-12.

Repairing a *Sturmgeschütz III* with 7.5 cm *Sturmkanone* [assault canon] *L/48*.

Almost all *Kampfwagen* except for the (*Jagd-*) Panzer V and VI, could be transported this flatbed trailer (*Sdr.Kfz. 116*)

***Stabsscharführer* [staff sergeant] of the *Werkstatt-Kompanie/SS-Pz.* [machine shop company] *Rgt. 9*.**

The heavy 18 t *Zug-Kraftwagen* [halftrack or prime mover] (*Sdr. Kfz. 9*) could pull a flat bed trailer of up to 35 t total weight.

Ford V 8/300
Maultier
["Mule"].

Train transport from France to the Eastern Front, including to the unsuccessful attempt to relieve Tarnapol.

(left) Zündapp [blasting machine] KS 750...

(right) Panzer IV Ausf. II.

Members of *SS-Panzer-Regiment 9* in the Ukraine.

Herbert Golbs. He was later awarded the gold *Nahkampfspange* as a member of *SS-Panzergrenadier Regiment 19*.

9. *SS-Panzer-Division Hohenstaufen* was taken out of active service and concentrated in the region of Brzezany-Podhajce on April 20, 1944, to be at the disposal of *Heeresgruppe Nordukraine*. A week later, the formation was again placed under command of the *II. SS-Panzer-Korps*, which in early May initially ordered the combating of Soviet partisans in the cantonment area. *SS-Panzer-Aufklärungs-Abteilung 9* was deployed in the area of Sokal for this mission.

On June 2, 1944, the *SS-FHA* announced that the *Panzer-Divsionen* would be reorganized as *Panzer-Division 44* [Type 1944]. As part of this reclassification, a new *SS-Panzerjäger-Abteilung 9* was formed in Rastenburg at the *SS-Panzerjäger-Ausbildungs-und Ersatz-Abteilung*.

The *9. SS-Panzer-Division* (strength: about 17,500 men) reported the following at that time:

	Authorized	Actualaltual
Panzer III	12	4
Panzer IV	58	41
Sturmgeschütze	40	38
Schützenpanzerwagen	335	259
schwere Pak 7.5 cm	25	24

On June 11, 1944, the movement order came for redeployment back to the Western Front. The *Division* had originally been formed in early 1943, to defend against the invasion which had begun there five days earlier. A total of 216 soldiers had been killed in the fighting in Galicia and some 650 were wounded. Another 90 were missing and believed to have been captured.

Fourteen days later, the larger part of the *9. SS-Panzer- Division Hohenstaufen* was concentrated in the area of Alencon (about 90 km southeast of Caen), and marched through Argentan-Falaise to the front. Three days later, the units marched into the assembly area at Haut des Forges. The subsequent attack, as part of the German counteroffensive, quickly bogged down in the heavy barrage from the Naval artillery and waves of fighter-bomber attacks and had to be abandoned.

Briefly reinforced by *SS-Kampfgruppe Weidinger* of the *2. SS-Panzer-Division Das Reich*, *9. SS-Panzer-Division Hohenstaufen* repeated its unsuccessful attacks. On June 30, 1944, the *Divisionskommando* reported a strength of:

	Officers	Unterführer	Enlisted Men	Total
Actual	433	2,539	12,926	15,898
	2.7%	16.0%	81.3%	100%
Authorized	635	4,415	14,439	19,489
	3.3%	22.7%	74.0%	100%

By July 1, 1944, the units had to report 1,145 killed in action, wounded, and missing.

On July 8, 1944, *9. SS-Panzer-Division Hohenstaufen* was relieved by the *277. Volksgrenadier-Division*, and took up a position east of Evrecy under the command of the *10. SS-Panzer-Division* as a contingency reserve. There was already heavy fighting by July 11, 1944, at Hill 112, at Maltot and Éterville.

Decimated by the high casualties, by mid-July 1944, one *Bataillon* each of the two *Panzergrenadier-Regimenter* was disbanded and the men distributed among the two remaining ones. On July 23, 1944, there was another reclassification, and the *III. (gp.)/SS-Panzergrenadier-Regiment 20* was placed under command of *SS-Panzer-Regiment 9*. The three remaining *Bataillone* were reconstituted into the *SS-Panzergrenadier- Regiment Hohenstaufen*. *SS-Panzer-Regiment 9* reported on this day as operational:

Panzer IV	**22**
Panzer V	**10**
Sturmgeschütze	**13**

Facing the British-Canadian offensive in the Caen area, the units were moved to the right bank of the Orne, in the Clinchamps-St. Laurent-de Condel region. Already on July 25, 1944, the two existing *Kampfgruppen – SS-Panzergrenadier-Regiment Hohenstaufen* and *gepanzerte Gruppe Meyer* – were given the mission of recapturing the May-Tilly line. Even the most intense fighting against an enemy with far greater superiority of materiel and personnel brought only short-term success. The units assigned completely used up their replacements in a matter of days.

One week later, the remains of the *Division* were again withdrawn from active service and set in march to another flash point about 40 km to the southwest, in the area of Montchauvet-Chenedolle. There, British forces had pushed through into the boundary between the *7. Armee* and *5. Panzer-Armee*, in the direction of Vire. As had been the situation since June 29,

1944, the mission was only able to delay the further advance of the Allied troops; it was impossible to stop or even to push them back, whatever the effort made, because of the enemy's superiority.

Once the British troops succeeded in breaking through the left wing of the *9. SS-Panzer- Division* at Chenedolle (about 10 km east of Vire) in early August 1944, elements of the *10. SS-Panzer-Division Frundsberg* were given the mission to again stabilize the situation. While elements of the *5. Panzer-Armee*, as part of *Unternehmens Lüttich* [Operation Liege], were to advance on Avranches, the *SS* formations were still engaged in defensive fighting near Chenedolle.

On August 13, 1944, the *Division* received the command, along with the other units of the *II. SS-Panzer-Korps*, to move to the region north of Argentan, to the *5. Panzer-Armee*, in order to stop the advance of American troops pushing forward to the north there. It became apparent that the Falaise pocket was being set up.

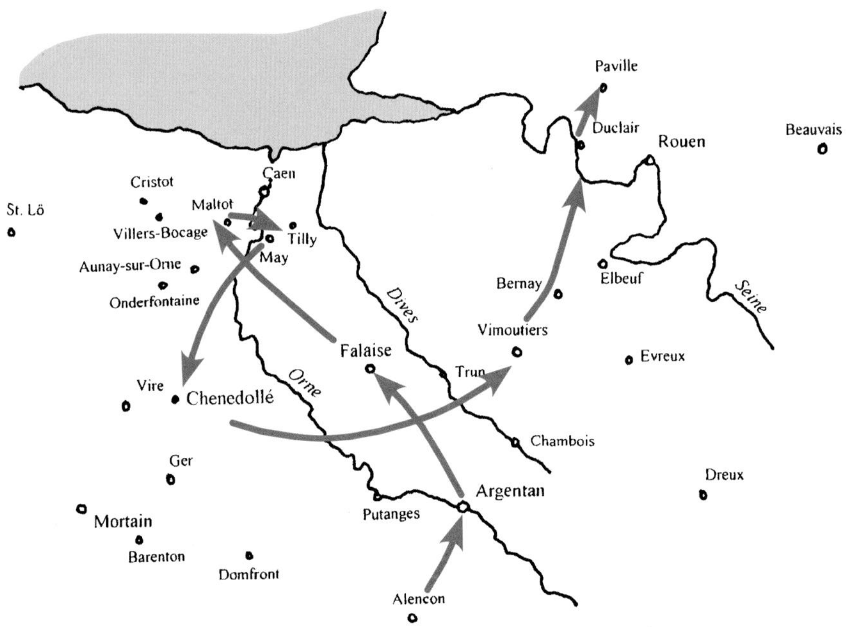

Fuel shortages and constant air attacks delayed the move towards Vimoutiers (about 20 km northeast of Argentan). On crowded roads and byways, the columns also remained stuck in front of the bridges in the general retreat of the *7. Armee* and *5. Panzer-Armee* across the Orne. Mostly marching on foot and on vehicles of other formations, the men tried to cross the Dives near Trun on August 18, 1944. The result was that the remains of the *9. SS-Panzer-Division* got into fierce battles with the Canadian units attacking from the north. Günter Adam remembers:

> In the bushes we met a *Schützenpanzer* of *SS-Sanitäts-Abteilung 9* and helped the comrades with loading some wounded. Infantry fire showed us that it was high time to get out of there. We collected the ammunition from the wounded and set off on foot. After some time, we came across one of our Panthers which was securing the place. The *Kommandant* – an *SS-Oberscharführer* – was sitting in the open turret hatch, quietly eating breakfast. We let him know we were there, and he gave us some cans of meat, fish, and some bread. Suddenly he shouted: "Look out, Amis [Americans] – thick ahead of us" – and reversed. We again came under fire and got out of there fast. Again, the sounds of battle and tank noises around us. Around noon we met our *SS-Panzer-Aufklärungs-Abteilung 9*. We tried to dig in anticipation of the usual fire attacks, but were in a place where the subsoil was downright chalk cliffs. Without hoes and spades there was no way to dig into the earth. Thus, we only had shallow depressions that we covered with planks and brush wood.
>
> In the evening, our driver arrived with supplies and ammunition. The enemy sent in patrols only at night, which we recognized and forced back. The next morning I was called to *SS-Hauptsturmführer* Gräbner. He was – in contrast to normal – "*scheißfreundlich*" [lit. shit friendly/just palsy-walsy] to me, and let me know that he had orders to pull the *Aufklärungs-Abteilung* back. My *Kradschützen-Zug* was supposed to cover the start of the march. He wished me and my platoon "all the best as POWs" and disappeared!
>
> Left on our own, we held our position with no enemy contact. It was as if there weren't any of the enemy anymore. After we had held the position for 24 hours, I decided to also abandon it. On August 16, 1944, we found our own *Divisions-Sicherungs-Kompanie* again and were greeted with big hellos as "prodigal sons." The next day I was commissioned to explore the gap in the front at Trun.

In any case, all the units still managed, together with the remnants of the *2. SS-Panzer-Division Das Reich*, to reach Vimoutiers, while to the west, the German forces were surrounded. After reorganization of the approximately 6,000 men who remained after the 75 km-long retreat from Chenedolle to Vimoutiers, the *9. SS-Panzer-Division Hohenstaufen* formed up on August 20, 1944, as the northern flank protection for the *2. SS-Panzer-Division Das Reich,* to relieve the Falaise pocket. Of the approximately 80,000 trapped German soldiers, some 50,000 were taken as Allied prisoners of war, about 10,000 were killed in action, and only about a quarter reached their own lines. By comparison, at Stalingrad 18 months earlier, about 90,000 German soldiers surrendered.

The *5. Panzer-Armee* reported the next day that the *9 SS-Panzer-Division* had a combat strength of about 460 *Grenadieren*, 20-25 *Panzer*, and 20 *Artilleriegeschütze*. That was the strength of one *Grenadier-Bataillon*, two *Panzer-Kompanien*, and five *Artillerie-Batterien*. In total, there were, including other *Division* troops, such as remnants of the *SS-Panzer-Pionier Battalion 9*, about 2,500 to 3,000 men in active service. The rest belonged to rear services, such as the *SS-Wirtschafts-Bataillon 9* [food supply battalion].

During the German retreat, the units crossed the Seine near Duclair (about 12 km west of Rouen) on August 30, 1944, and concentrated near Paville (about 10 km north of Duclair). While part of the *Division* was sent to the area of Hasselt for refitting, the *1. Generalstabsoffizier*, *SS-Obersturmbannführer* Harzer, formed an approximately 3,500-man strong *Kampfgruppe*, which was ordered to the area of Cambrai and consisted of the following:

1 *Bataillon/SS-Panzergrenadier-Regiment 19*
1 *Bataillon/SS-Panzergrenadier-Regiment 20*
Remnants of *SS-Panzer-Aufklärungs-Abteilung 9*
1 *Abteilung/SS-Panzer-Artillerie-Regiment 9*
SS-Flak-Abteilung 9
2 *Nachschub-Kompanien*
1 *Pionier-Kompanie*
1 mixed *Nachrichten-Kompanie* and various *Wirtschafts-Einheiten*

they were to cover the city to the west, in the sector of the *LXXXI. Armee-Korps*. There was already serious fighting with attacking American armored units by September 2, 1944.

The rest of the *Division* concentrated on September 5, 1944, in the area east of the Meuse at Sittard (about 30 km northwest of Aachen), and marched to the about 110 km-distant area around Arnhem. *SS-Kampfgruppe Harzer* also arrived here in the next few days, from the area of Cambrai. A *Panzergrenadier-Bataillon* remained at Valkenburg (about 20 km northwest of Aachen), and was later placed under command of the *10. SS-Panzer-Division Frundsberg*.

SS-Sturmbannführer Otto Meyer was given command of *SS-Panzer Regiment 9*. On 1/14/42, he was, as a member of the *SS-Regiment (mot.) Deutschland*, awarded with the *Deutsches Kreuz* in gold, and received the *Ritterkreuz* for the mission before Tarnopol on 6/2/1944. He was posthumously awarded the *Eichenlaub* [Oak Leaf Cluster] for destruction of a British Guards Tank Division south of Caen on 9/30/44. Meyer fell on 8/28/44 at Duclair.

zugleich Personalausweis
Nr. 25
für
SS-Schütze
(Dienstgrad)
den
ab 1. 9. 1943 SS-Sturmmann
(Datum) (neuer Dienstgrad)
ab 30. 1. 1944 SS-Rottenführer
ab 1. 3. 1945 SS-Unterscharführer
Kurt Gmelch
(Vor- und Zuname)
Beschriftung und Nummer der Erkennungsmarke 04600
Blutgruppe A
Blutgruppe
Gasmaskengröße 2
Wehrnummer Altenburg Thür. 09/310/1
K 167 SS-Vordruckverlag W. F. Mayr, Miesbach 17884

geb. am 13.3.09 in Frohburg i. Sachsen
(Ort, Kreis, Verw.-Bezirk)
Religion evgl. Stand, Beruf Kraftfahrer u. landwirtschaftl. Arbeiter
Personalbeschreibung:
Größe 1.77
Gestalt muskulös
Gesicht oval
Haar blond
Bart keine
Augen graublau
Besondere Kennzeichen (z. B. Brillenträger):
Narbe im Genick
Schuhzeuglänge 44
Schuhzeugweite
(Vor- u. Zuname, eigenhändige Unterschrift des Inhabers)
Die Richtigkeit der nicht umrandeten Angaben auf Seite 1 und 2 und der eigenhändigen Unterschrift des Inhabers bescheinigt
Debica, den 1. März 1943
40. SS-Rekr.-Depot
(Ausfertigender Truppenteil, Dienststelle)
(Dienststempel)
SS-Ostuf. u. Kp. Fhr.
(Eigenh. Unterschrift, Dienstgrad u. Dienststellg. d. Vorges.)
Waffen-SS
SS-Rekr. Depot Debica
2
Bescheinigungen
über die Richtigkeit der Zusätze und Berichtigungen auf Seite 1 und 2
Lfd. Nr.
Art der Änderung
auf Seite
Datum
Truppenteil
Unterschrift
Dienstgrad und Dienststellung
Der Sanitäts-Unteroffizier Gmelch
wurde am 9.5.45. entlassen, aus der
3

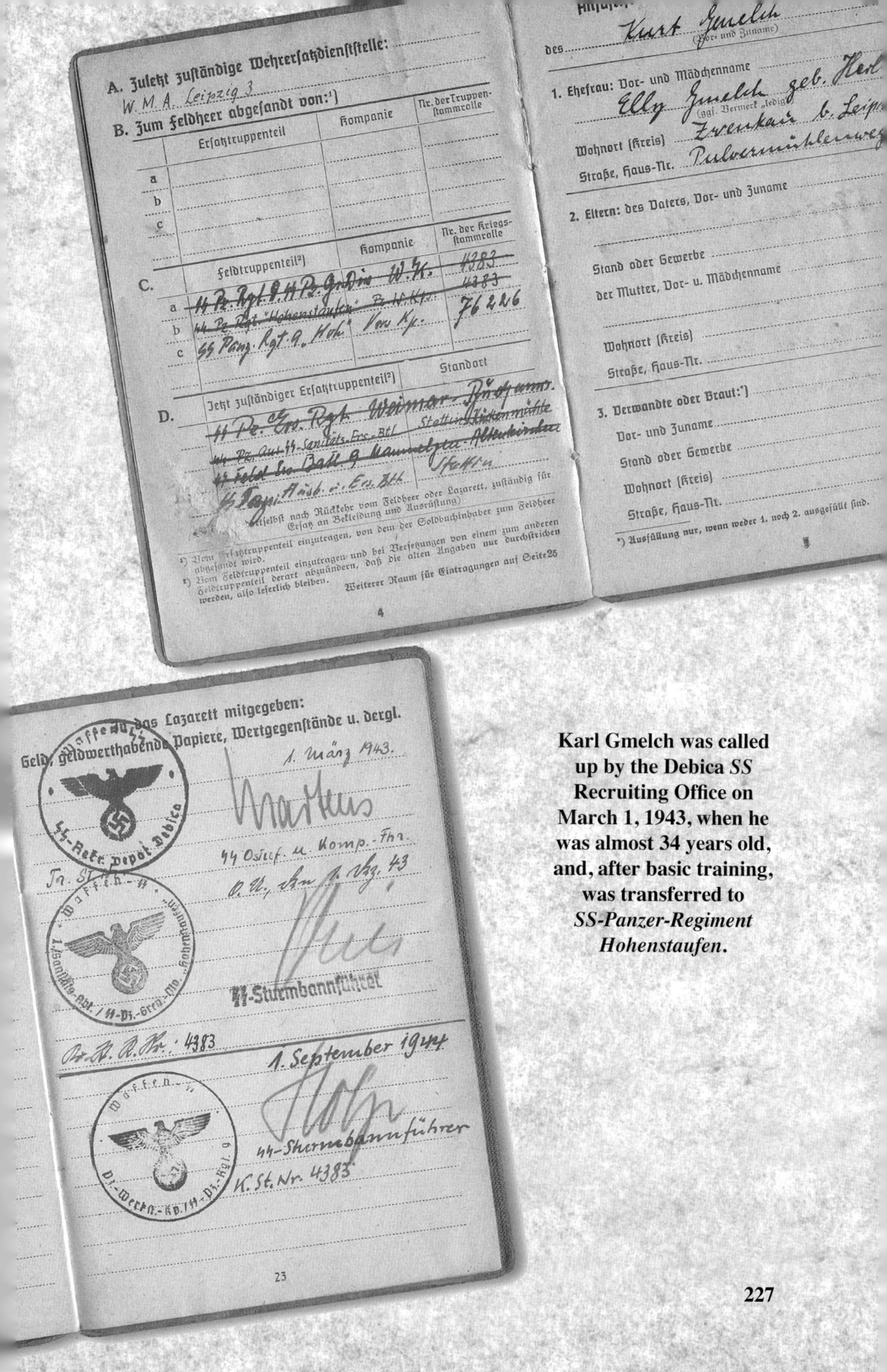

Karl Gmelch was called up by the Debica *SS* Recruiting Office on March 1, 1943, when he was almost 34 years old, and, after basic training, was transferred to *SS-Panzer-Regiment Hohenstaufen*.

On September 10, 1944, the *II. SS-Panzer-Korps* ordered that the *10. SS-Panzer-Division Frundsberg* be refitted near the front, as well as reorganization of *9. SS-Panzer-Division Hohenstaufen* at Altenkirchen-Siegen. To carry this out, the command was issued to transfer a *Panzergrenadier-Bataillon* and *Artillerie-Abteilung*, as well as large amounts of weapons and equipment to *10. SS-Panzer-Division*.

Two days later, it was redeployed to Germany. When the Western Allies' airborne Operation Market Garden was launched on September 17, 1944, there were still about 2,500 *Division* members in the area northwest of Arnhem. The troops were immediately concentrated near Velp, and then formed up to counter the British paratroopers who had landed east of Oosterbeek, and in part in the western districts of Arnhem. This led to heavy fighting around the bridge over the Lower Rhine.

A special procedure occurred on September 22, 1944, near Oosterbeek. After German-British negotiations, the *9. SS-Panzer-Division* took over the maintenance of about 1,200 wounded British soldiers.

While American troops were able to capture the bridges over the Meus at Grave, and that over the Waal at Nijmegen, the remnants of the *II. SS-Panzer-Korps* denied success to the British units. On September 26, 1944, the last enemy resistance at Arnhem collapsed. With nearly 8,000 British paratroopers killed in action or taken prisoner, the German forces had achieved their final successful operation in World War II. Karl Schneider remembers:

> I was born July 19, 1925, in Rheinbischofsheim (Kehl District), and on October 5, 1942, I was sent to the RAD [*Reichsarbeitsdienst]-Feld-Abteilung K 1/322* (*Feldpostnummer* [field post number] 19 573) at Lubeln, in the Westmark [western region of Nazi Germany; the town is now Longeville-les-St-Avold in Lorraine, France.] After active service in southern France (Camargue/Gulf of Biscaye) and the Saar region, in April 1943 I was discharged at Karlsruhe. I was then conscripted to the *4./Grenadier-Ausbildungs-und Ersatz-Bataillon 111*. In December 1943, we were sent to the Eastern Front, to the area south of Mogilev. Here I was assigned to the *4./Grenadier-Regiment 111* of the *35. Infanterie-Division* (Fisch Division). At first, we fought east of the Dnieper and, from the beginning of January 1994, in the Pripyat marshes (about 30 km south of Bobruisk).
>
> On March 2, 1944, I was wounded by shrapnel in the left leg and foot, and was first sent to the base hospital in Minsk, then to the Thorn field hospital, and finally to the general reserve hospital in Brussels. From there, in mid-June 1944, I got to the *Genesenden-Kompanie* [convalescent company] of the *Grenadier-Ersatz-Battalion 111* at Vlissingen Walcheren.
>
> As the Allies were advancing from Normandy, our *Kompanie* (Leader: *Oberleutnant* Gebauer) was also deployed in early August 1944 with other troops against the British armored spearheads which had pushed forward west of Antwerp. In this process, our *Kompanie* was totally wiped out at Bevernfast.

> I got another shrapnel wound there on August 3, 1944, in my left knee. During the retreat across the Scheldt, we were taken in as "stragglers" by members of the *SS-Panzer Grenadier-Ausbildungs-und Ersatz-Bataillon 4* on August 26, 1944, when we were crossing the Waal by ferry at Gorinchem/Holland; they constructed a rear position in Gorinchem and had their command post in the nearby sugar factory.
>
> Without further ado, the grade *Obergefreiter* [corporal] was crossed out in my pay book and replaced by *SS-Rottenführer* [SS-corporal]. It was that simple to become a "member of the Waffen-SS!" As a trained driver of *Schützenpanzerwagen*, trucks, and cars, I was ultimately assigned to the *SS-Sanitäts-Abteilung 9 Hohenstaufen.*

SS-Kampfgruppe Harz was gradually pulled out of the sector and ordered to the refitting area of the *9. SS-Panzer-Division Hohenstaufen* in the Westerwald, where the process began to reinforce the unit with materiel and personnel. The vehicles supplied, however, were of every possible different make, and they quickly broke down due to lack of spare parts. With the attachment of *Luftwaffe*, and sometimes the *Marine* members to the *Division,* it at least attained 70% of the authorized strength of about 18,000 men.

On October 17, 1944, the formation was redeployed to the Münster-Hamm-Paderborn-Gutersloh region; two weeks later, still under command of the *Befehlshaber* of the *Ersatzheere* [Commander of the Replacement Army], it was transferred to the Euskirchen-Münstereifel-Neuenahr area.

On December 10, 1944, the Division reported the following:

	Authorized	**Actual**
Panzer IV	30	39
Panzer V Panther	60	35
Sturmgeschütze	28	49
schwere Pak 7.5 cm	28	25
leichte Feldhaubitzen	-	24
schwere Feldhaubitzen	-	14
10 cm Kanonen	-	6

Karl Schneider

zugleich Personalausweis
Nr.
für
(Dienstgrad)
(neuer Dienstgrad)
(Datum)
44-Oberscharführer
44-Hauptscharführer
(Vor- und Zuname)
Erkennungsmarke
Blutgruppe
Blutgruppe B
Gasmaskengröße
Wehrnummer
Geb. am
(Ort, Kreis, Verw.-Bezirk)
Stand, Beruf
Religion
Personalbeschreibung:
Gestalt
Größe
Haar
Gesicht
Augen
Bart
Besondere Kennzeichen (z. B. Brillenträger):
Schuhzeugweite
Schuhzeuglänge
Heinz Haber
(Vor- u. Zuname, eigenhändige Unterschrift des Inhabers)
Die Richtigkeit der nicht umrandeten Angaben auf Seite 1 und 2 und
der eigenhändigen Unterschrift des Inhabers bescheinigt
den
(Ausfertigender Truppenteil, Dienststelle)
(Eigenh. Unterschrift, Dienstgrad u. Dienststelle d. Vorges.)
Kompanie Steinert
2
Lfd. Nr.
Art der Änderung
auf Seite
Datum
Truppenteil
Unterschrift
Dienstgrad und Dienststellung

~~In das Lazarett mitgegeben:~~

~~Geld, geldwerthabende Papiere, Wertgegenstände u. dergl.~~

Waffen-SS 9. SS-Panzer-Regiment SS-Panzer-Gren.-Div.

23. Febr. 1943

i. V. Aßbauer

SS-Untersturmführer u. Regiments-Adjutant

K. St. Nr. 4282

Waffen-SS 9. Panzer-Grenadier-Div. SS-Pz. Werkstatt-Kompanie

1. Dezember 1943

SS-Hauptsturmführer u. Kompanieführer

K. St. Nr. 4282

Waffen-SS Pz.-Werkst. Pz.-Rgt. 9

1. September 1944

SS-Sturmbannführer

K. St. Nr. 4282

15

Heinz Haber joined the *1. SS-Totenkopf-Standarte Oberbayern* [Upper Bavaria] April 4, 1938, and from there was transferred in June 1939 to the *SS-Heimwehr Danzig*. In mid-October 1939, he was inducted in *SS-Totenkopf-Infanterie-Regiment 3*. After being wounded, he was eventually attached to the *SS-Panzerjäger-Abteilung-Nord*, and after a course at the *SS-Kraftfahrtechnischen Lehranstalt* [Motor Transport Technical School], Haber was transferred to *SS-Panzer Regiment Hohenstaufen*.

Bescheinigung

Dem SS-Unterscharführer (Dienstgrad) Haber, Heinz (Name)

wird hiermit bescheinigt, daß er am Kraftfahrzeug mit Holzgaserzeuger und Mercedes-Benz Kohlegaserzeuger und in dessen Betrieb ausgebildet ist.

Berechtigt zur Erweiterung des Führerscheins,
gem. Kraftf. techn. Anhang z. d. Verordnungsblättern der Waffen-SS 1942, Blatt 13.

Berlin, den 14. Januar 1943.

SS-Hauptsturmführer
und Lehrgangsleiter

Kommandoamt der Waffen-SS (Dienstsiegel)

A.Nr 108280. A 5. 6. 7. 42: 300. K.-Nr 0/1467.

Thus, the formation was well-equipped, but despite this, its capability was severely limited by lack of fuel. Through further arrivals of personnel replacements, the *Division* reached an even higher actual than authorized strength:

	Officers	Unterführer	Enlisted Men	Total
Actual	434	3,251	15,920	19,605
	2.2%	16,6%	81.2%	100%
Authorized	614	3,923	13,260	17,797
	3.5%	22.0%	74.5%	100%

The reinforcement in numbers, with men from the *Luftwaffe* and *Kriegsmarine* who had little combat experience, along with members of the numerous *Waffen-SS* agencies, did not result in any qualitative improvement. The three-month refitting and training of the troops in Germany also did nothing to change the lack of motivation.

Advanced into the Stadtkyll-Jünkerath-Blankenheim region on December 17, 1944, *9. SS-Panzer-Division Hohenstaufen* lined up the next day at Schoenberg, going by way of Losheim. Initially with elements stationed in the battle around St. Vith, the formation was placed under command of the *I. SS-Panzer-Korps* on December 19, 1944; it was, by pushing forward through Recht, supposed to relieve *SS-Kampfgruppe Peiper* of the *1. SS-Panzer-Division* at La Gleize.

However, even as *SS-Panzergrenadier-Regiment 19* reached the mountainous area of Bra-Villettes on December 25, 1944, the trapped *SS-Kampfgruppe* Peiper had already been wiped out. Enemy resistance in this sector of the front made it impossible to advance, so the formation was regrouped, and the *9. SS-Panzer-Division* redeployed at the end of December 1944 to the area north of Bastogne.

Here, beginning January 3, 1945, the formation and other troops were supposed to occupy the town, which had been heavily embattled for several days. Due to high losses of men and materiel the attacks had to be abandoned, after achieving no success. Three days later, *Heer Infanterie* forces again began to relieve the *9. SS-Panzer-Division*.

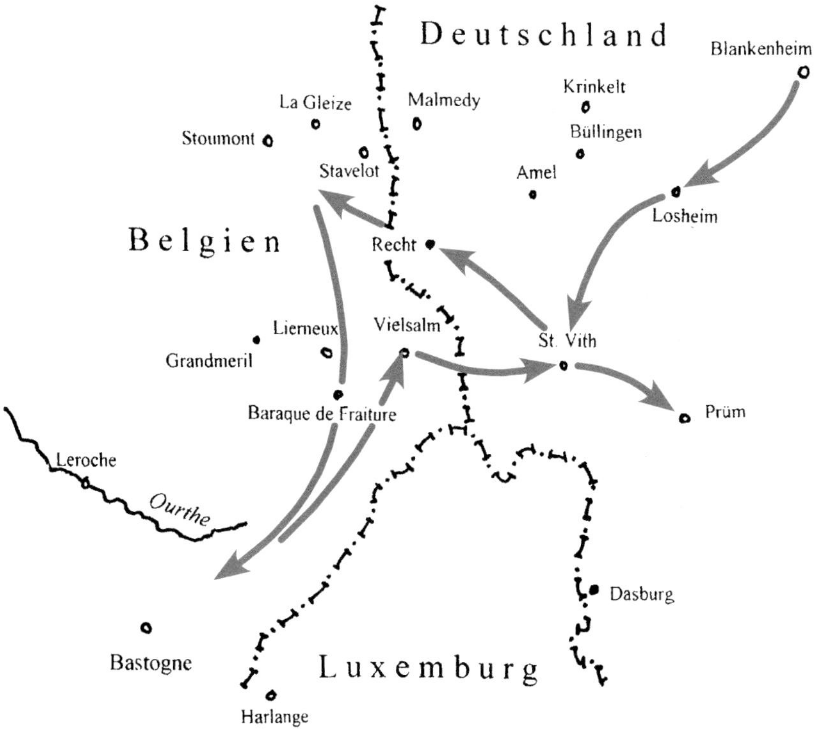

Initially ordered to the sector of the *6. Panzer-Armee* as *Heeresgruppenreserve* [Army Group reserve] in the 35 km-distant area of Vielsalm, the troop units had to be repeatedly deployed to support the beleaguered front. Pushed back to St. Vith, the *9. SS-Panzer-Division Hohenstaufen* was finally pulled out of the front January 23, 1945, and initially concentrated near Prüm (about 25 km southeast of St. Vith). Four days later, it was transferred to the refitting area Mayen (about 25 km west of Koblenz).

With new transfers of replacements from the *Luftwaffe* and *Waffen-SS*, the *Division* had again attained, by the end of January 1945:

Officers	Unterführer	Enlisted Men	Total
444	3,261	15,757	19,462
2.3%	16,8%	80.9%	100%
614	3,923	13,260	17,797
3.5%	22.0%	74.5%	100%

This high level in personnel strength no longer had any effect on operational capability. Replenished with older age groups, *Volksdeutsche*, and foreigners of the *SS-Ausbildungs-und Ersatzeinheiten* units, the formation's fighting power declined steadily, and this was not only due to the lack of ammunition, weapons, and supplies.

By February 9, 1945, transfer had begun to send units to Hungary for the planned German *Plattensee-Offensive*. Placed under command of the *II. SS-Panzer-Korps* (*6. SS-Panzer-Armee*), the troop units first marched from the disembarkation station at Györ towards Kisber.

On March 3, 1945, the *Division* reported an armory of:

Panzer IV	**19**
Panzer V Panther	**24**
Sturmgeschütze	**16**
Jagdpanzer IV	**17**
Jagdpanzer V	**10**
Flak-Panzer IV	**4**
***schwere Pak* 7.5 cm**	**15**

Two days later, the units moved into starting positions in the area of Seregélyes (about 15 km southeast of Székesfehérvár) for *Unternehmen Frühlingserwachen*. In heavy snowfall, the next day the troop units moved in the bottomless mud in the direction of Sarosd, but they could only report small gains in territory. Instead, they soon faced ferocious enemy counterattacks and had to pull their positions back.

On March 17, 1945, the *9. SS-Panzer-Division* reported a *Tagesstärke* of 10,820 men and a combat strength of 4,614 men. How they arrived at these figures is inexplicable! It is certain that the formation had not lost nearly 10,000 men since the end of January 1945. One possibility is that it was reclassified as a *Panzer-Division* 45 [Type 1945], which was ordered in the meantime: this had a lower authorized strength than a *Panzer-Division* [Type 19] 44.[57]

Two days later, relief of the *9. SS-Panzer-Division* by *Heer* elements began, and it was concentrated in the sector of *II. SS-Panzer-Korps*, southwest of Székesfehérvár. While elements of the *Division* were to be sent to the *IV. SS-Panzer-Korps* at Székesfehérvár, on March 20, 1945, the units still deployed in the area of Aba-Sarosd were engaged in heavy defensive fighting.

57 See Appendix: Order of Battle.

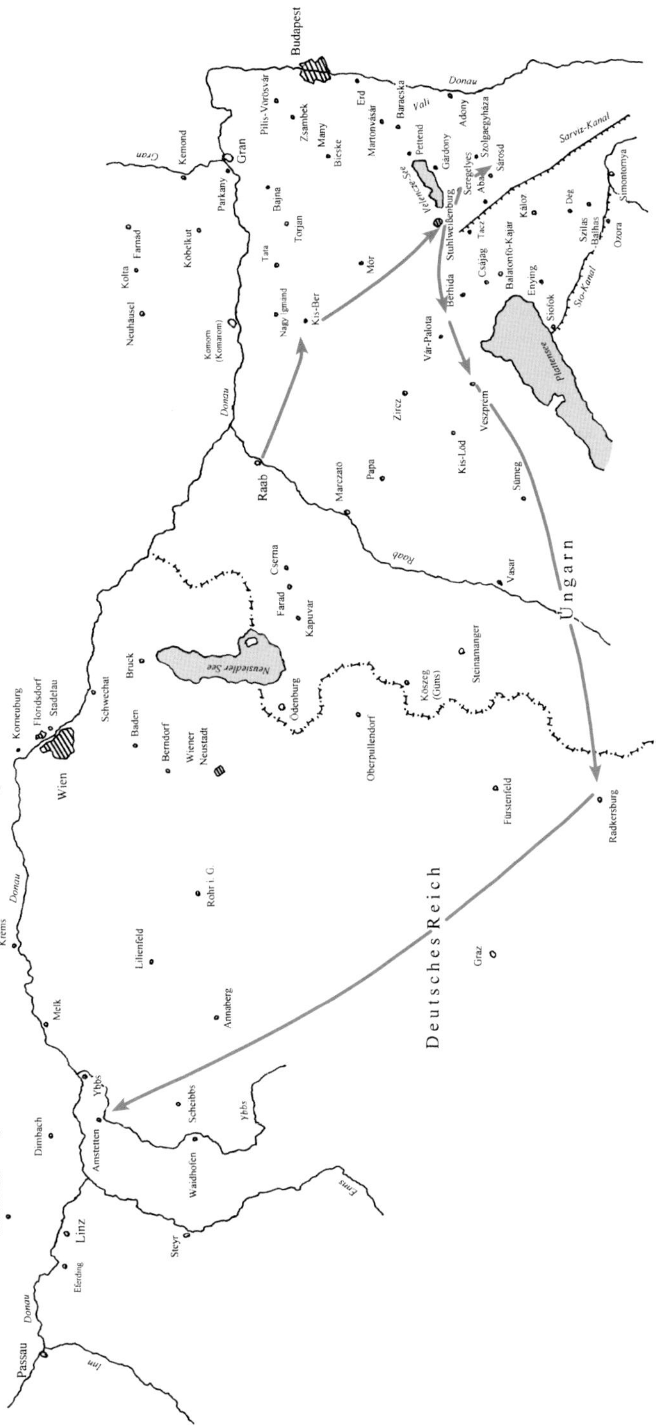
Budapest
Donau
Gran
Kemond
Parkany
Pilis-Vörösvár
Zsambek
Many
Bicske
Erd
Martonvásár
Baracska
Vali
Pettend
Gárdony
Adony
Szolgaegyháza
Sárosd
Sarviz-Kanal
Velence-See
Seregelyes
Aba
Stuhlweißenburg
Tacz
Csájág
Balatonfő-Kajar
Káloz
Deg
Szilas
Balhas
Simontornya
Ozora
Sio-Kanal
Siofok
Enying
Berhida
Vár-Palota
Plattensee
Veszprem
Zircz
Mor
Bajna
Torjan
Tata
Nagy Igmand
Kis-Ber
Kolta
Farnad
Köbelkut
Neuhäusel
Komorn (Komarom)
Raab
Marczato
Papa
Kis-Lód
Sümeg
Vasar
Ungarn
Cserna
Farad
Kapuvar
Neusiedler See
Bruck
Schwechat
Odenburg
Steinamanger
Köszeg (Güns)
Oberpullendorf
Stockerau
Korneuburg
Floridsdorf
Stadelau
Wien
Baden
Berndorf
Wiener Neustadt
Fürstenfeld
Radkersburg
Deutsches Reich
Graz
Krems
Rohr i. G.
Lilienfeld
Annaberg
Melk
Ybbs
Scheibbs
Weißenbach
St. Oswald
Freistadt
Dimbach
Amstetten
Waidhofen
Gallneukirchen
Linz
Steyr
Enns
Eferding
Passau
Inn

The situation deteriorated rapidly due to the major Soviet offensive. In a chaotic retreat, by March 22, 1945, the *9. SS-Panzer-Division*, now placed under command of the I. *Kavallerie-Korps* [1st Cavalry Corps], was already about 30 km to the northwest, near Berhida-Ösi-Varpolata (about 20 km west of Székesfehérvár).

After the battles at Veszprem, *9. SS-Panzer-Division* was actually to march north, to close the gap there between the *6. Armee* and *6. Panzer-Armee* up to Kisbér. In the confusing situation and extremely violent fighting, there ultimately was a fierce dispute between *Divisionskommandeur SS-Oberführer* Stadler and the *6. Armee Oberbefehlshaber*.

Moving through the Zala region, the units pulled back on April 7, 1945, to the *Reichsschutzstellung*. Deployed at Radkersburg, the *Division* was now under command of the *XXII. Gebirgs-Korps* [Mountain Corps]. In the relatively quiet period until the end of April 1945, the *Division* was again replenished with replacements. It now functioned mainly as a collection point for scattered and broken *Wehrmacht* troop units. On April 28, 1945, the order came to move to the area of Amstetten, about 180 km away. From there, the units reached the Enns on May 8, 1945, and went into American captivity.

This was the end of the *9. SS-Panzer-Division Hohenstaufen*'s deployment. Initially formed with about 20,000 *RAD* members, the heavy casualties in Normandy were compensated with foreigners and *Volksdeutsche*, as well as members of the *Kriegsmarine* and *Luftwaffe*, who had little or no motivation. Thus, the *Division*'s general character was a higher number of personnel, but at the same time, due to the lack of trained *Führer* and *Unterführer*, limited operational capability. It was well-equipped with vehicles, *Panzer*, and heavy weapons, but this was made relative by the extreme lack of fuel.

10.

SS-PANZER-DIVISION FRUNDSBERG

The 10. SS-Panzergrenadier-Division Karl der Große [Charlemagne]

The ***SS-Panzer-Grenadier-Division 10*** was the second *SS-Division* that Hitler ordered December 19, 1942, to be formed as a central reserve for the *Oberbefehlshaber* West theatre of operations.

Under the command of *SS-Brigadeführer* Debes, the initial mustering of recruits enlisted from the RAD began in February 1943, at the approximately 80 x 80 km area for its initial organization between Bordeaux-Limoges-La Rochelle in the *1. Armee* sector. The plan was for the Division to be organized as follows:

	QUARTERS:
DIVISIONSSTAB	**ANGOULÊME**
SS-Panzer-Grenadier-Regiment 1	**Saintes**
SS-Panzer-Grenadier-Regiment 2	**Barbezieux**
SS-Kradschützen-Regiment 10	**Rouillac**
SS-Panzer-Regiment 10	**Aigre**
SS-Panzerjäger-Abteilung 10	**La Braconne**
SS-Sturmgeschütz-Abteilung 10	**La Braconne**
SS-Artillerie-Regiment 10	**Jarnac**
SS-Flak-Abteilung 10	**Angoulême**
SS-Pionier-Bataillon 10	**Nersac**
SS-Nachrichten-Abteilung 10	**Angoulême**

SS-Sanitäts-Abteilung 10	**Angoulême**
SS-Wirtschafts-Bataillon 10	**Angoulême**
SS-Nachschub-Truppen 10	**Angoulême**
SS-Instandsetzungs-Abteilung	

Formation of the *Panzer-Regiment* was repeatedly delayed due to the lack of equipment. Initially, it was only possible to train the *II. Abteilung* on *Panzer IV* tanks. *Panzer V*s could only be supplied to the *I. Abteilung* by late 1944. Since even the delivery of *Panzer IV*s was difficult, the *II. Abteilung* was first to be set up in an intermediate organization, with 42 *Sturmgeschütze* and three *Befehlswagen* [command vehicles] *Panzer III.*

Although the formation, which was given the additional name ***Karl der Große*** [Charlemagne] on March 1, 1943, had difficulties in equipping the units with materiel, it already had the formal structure of a *Panzer-Division.*[58]

In June 1943, the *OKW Organisations-Stab z. b. V.* [organizational Staff *zur besonderen Verwendung*: for special deployment] set a new *Kfz-Soll* [motor vehicle authorized allowance] for all *Kriegsstärkenachweisungen (KStN)* [chart of a unit's theoretical organization and composition]. According to these specifications, by means of reorganization and refitting, initially only 75% of the previous authorized allowance amounts were to be allocated. In fact, these formations generally did not even receive 50% of the previous authorized amounts. In addition, all the *West-Divisionen* were limited to just 21 *schweren Panzerabwehrkanonen.* The *Pak* made available as a result were consigned to the *65.*, *284.*, and *715. Infanterie-Divisionen.*

In July 1943, the *10. SS-Panzergrenadier-Division Karl der Große*, with a strength of just 20,000 men, moved into an area east of Biarritz, also about 80 x 80 km in size. The *SS-Kradschützen-Regiment* – also called a *Schnelles Regiment* – was disbanded, and an *SS-Panzer-Aufklärungs-Abteilung* was trained instead

By August 2, 1943, the *OKW* informed the *OB West* that the *10. SS-Panzergrenadier Division* was to be deployed for *Unternehmen Siegfried* [Operation Siegfried] – occupation of the southern coast of France, to protect against enemy landings. The Division was sent by rail by way of Pau-Toulouse-Narbonne to *Armeegruppe Felber* in the area north of Marseille.

58 *Karl der Große* [Charlemagne] was born April 2, 742, and became King of the Franks in 768. In 773-774, he conquered Lombardy, and subjugated and Christianized the Saxons in several campaigns (772-804). In 788, Bavaria became part of the Frankish Empire, followed in 795-796 by the submission of the Avars. In 800, Charlemagne was crowned Holy Roman Emperor by Pope Leo II. In 30 years of fighting, he succeeded in expanding the boundaries of the Frankish empire to such an extent that it became the most important empire of the Western Middle Ages. He showed formidable rigor in all educational and cultural work. In 782, in Verden alone, he had 4,500 hostages executed at one time. Charlemagne died January 28, 814.

Training was continued during the next few weeks in southern France, and there was an effort to bring the unit's equipment up to the authorized strength. On August 17, 1943, the *OB West* announced the allocation of motor vehicles to the *9.* and *10. SS-Panzer-Grenadier-Divisionen.* The command, however, was amended, so that the existing motor vehicles would only be supplied to the *9. SS-Panzergrenadier-Division Hohenstaufen.* Thus, there was initially no change in the *10. SS-Panzergrenadier- Division*'s precarious motor vehicle situation. Only on October 11, 1943, did the *KTB/OKW* announce that the *10. SS-Panzergrenadier-Division* would also be immediately equipped with captured Italian materiel. This way, the motorized formations remaining in the West could be made mobile again as soon as possible.

On October 19, 1943, *II./SS-Panzer Grenadier Regiment 2* was detached from the *Division* structure and sent to the heavily embattled *Kampfgruppe/SS-Panzergrenadier-Division Das Reich* on the Eastern Front.

Deployment and Secured Regions in the West 1943-44.

The first *Kommanduer* of *10. SS-Division Frundsberg*, *SS-Brigadeführer* Debes (2nd from left), and his successor, *SS-Brigadeführer* Treuenfeld (2nd from right), at the *Division* change of command in autumn 1943.

Lothar Deves at a *HIAG Suchdienst [Hilfsgemeinschaft auf Gegenseitigkeit der Angehörigen der ehemaligen Waffen-SS*: Mutual Help Association of Former *Waffen-SS* Members tracing service] meeting in Hameln, 1959.

SS-Soldbuch
zugleich Personalausweis
Nr. 856
für
den SS-Grenadier
(Dienstgrad)
ab 1. 2. 1945 (Datum) SS-Sturmmann (neuer Dienstgrad)
ab
ab
Adam Kirchner
(Vor- und Zuname)
Beschriftung und Nummer der Erkennungsmarke F.E.B. 10/856
Blutgruppe
Gasmaskengröße
Wehrnummer
K 167 SS-Vordruckverlag W. F. Mayr, Miesbach 1978

geb. am 7. 1. 25. in (Ort, Kreis, Verw.-Bezirk)
Ungarn
Religion r.-k. Stand, Beruf Taglöhner
Personalbeschreibung:
Größe 1,70 Gestalt
Gesicht oval Haar
Bart
Augen
Besondere Kennzeichen (z. B. Brillenträger):
Gehört.
Schuhzeuglänge 43. Schuhzeugweite 7.
Kirchner Adam.
(Vor- u. Zuname, eigenhändige Unterschrift des Inhabers)
Die Richtigkeit der nicht umrandeten Angaben auf Seite 1 und 2 und der eigenhändigen Unterschrift des Inhabers bescheinigt
den 14 NOV. 1943
SS-Feld-Ersatz-Bataillon 10
(Ausfertigender Truppenteil, Dienststelle)
Obersturmführer und Adjutant
(Eigenh. Unterschrift, Dienstgrad u. Dienststellg. d. Vorges.)
(Dienststempel)
2

Bescheinigungen
über die Richtigkeit der Zusätze und Berichtigungen auf Seite 1 und 2
Lfd. Nr. | Art der Änderung | auf Seite | Datum | Truppenteil | Unterschrift | Dienstgrad und Dienststellung
1 | Beförderung | 1 | 30.1.45 | | |
3

Along with about 2,500 more *Volksdeutsche* from Hungary, 18-year-old Adam Kirchner was sent to the *10. SS-Panzergrenadier-Division* in 1943. By this time, it did not matter to the Waffen-SS that he was deaf!

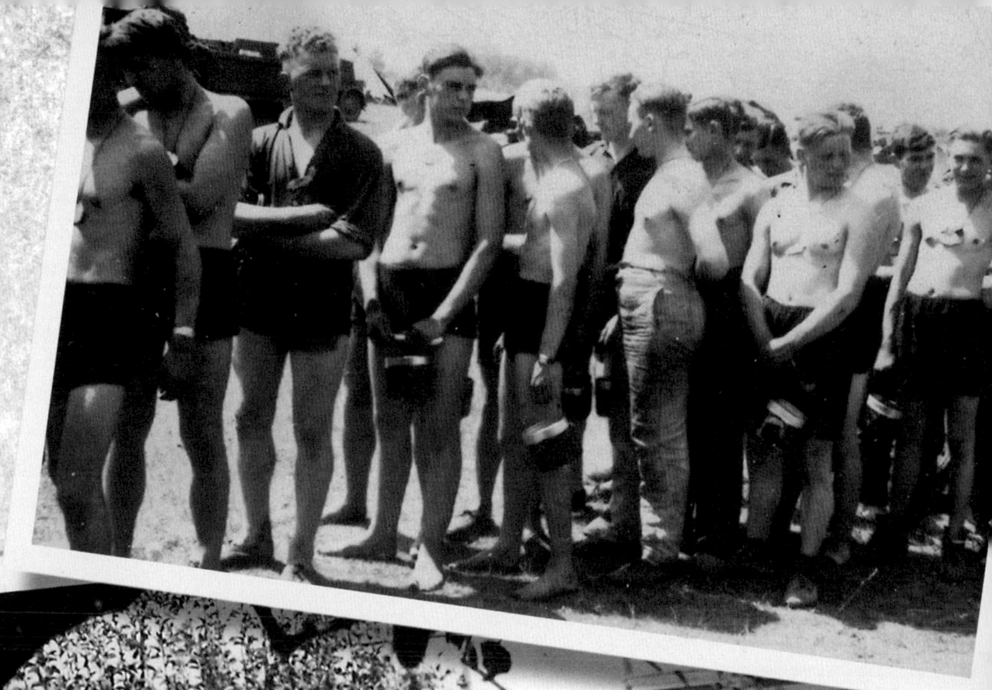

Mannschaften and *Führer* of *SS-Pionier-Batallion 10*.

Sturmgeschütz III and members of
SS-Sturmgeschütz-Abteilung 10.

15 cm
Feldhaubitze
18.

10.5 cm
Feldhaubitze
18.

Training in France.

The 10. SS-Panzer-Division Frundsberg

On October 26, 1943, Adolf Hitler ordered, as part of the simultaneous serial numbering of the *Waffen-SS Divisionen* and *Regimenter*, that the formation be renamed the: **SS-Panzer-Division Frundsberg.**[59]

The two *SS-Panzergrenadier-Regimenter* were given the numbers 21 and 22. Since the *Division* had been allocated a *Panzer-Division* since the *Kriegsstärkenachweisung* was established, no further heavy units were to be formed. Rather, the formation – which had been moved into the region between Dives and Seine – even got a new, lower *Sollstärke*. The surplus of about 1,500 men was commandeered for the reorganization of the *Waffen-SS*. The *KTB/OKW* recorded in this regard on November 12, 1943:

> The *OKW* declares itself to be in agreement with the redeployment and relocation of the redundant elements of the *9.* and *10. SS-Panzer-Division*, which are designated for formation of the *17.* and *16. SS-Panzer-Grenadier-Division*.

As a result, the two *15. (Kradschützen) Kompanien* of *SS-Panzergrenadier-Regimenter 21* and *22* were assigned for the formation of *SS-Panzer-Aufklärungs-Abteilung 17*, as the *III. /SS-Panzer-Artillerie-Abteilung 10* was assigned for formation of *SS-Artillerie-Regiment 17*.

The transfer of the men was delayed, however, so that the *10. SS-Panzer-Division* – led by *SS-Brigadeführer* von Treuenfeld since November 15, 1943 – still had the following strength on December 31, 1943:

	Officers	Unterführer	Enlisted Men	Total
Actual	487	2,722	16,104	19,313
	2.5%	14.1%	83.4%	100%
Authorize	614	3,923	13,260	17,797
	3.5%	22.1%	74.4%	100%

When it was renamed, Charlemagne was to be used instead of *Karl der Große* for the planned formation of a French *SS-Freiwilligen-Regiment*.

Former *Division* member Benger remembers when *SS-Pionier-Bataillon 10* was formed:

59 Georg von Frundsberg was born September 24, 1473, at Schloss [palace] Mindelheim, near Memmingen. In 1499, he served under Emperor Maximilian I against Switzerland and was knighted in 1504. Frundsberg primarily led the troops known as the *Landsknechte* [mercenaries], and moved against Venice in 1513 and against Ullrich of Württemberg in 1519. Frundsberg died August 20, 1528, at the age of just 55.

Pionierschule [Engineering School] of the Waffen-SS in Hradischko, at the beginning of January 1943. For the first time we meet the Führer assigned for the new *SS-Pionier-Bataillon 10. SS-Hauptsturmführer* Wendler will be *Kommandeur*. We look at each other and believe that we will work together well. The *Kompanien* are set up. Service starts, weapons training, obstacle-construction service, driving school. One day, the following incident occurred: After a visit from *In 5* [Inspection Department for *Pioniere*], all Batallion Führer, except for *SS-Hauptsturmführer* Wendler, were ordered to a lecture hall. Out places were assigned as if for a written examination and we were supervised by the school Führer. There is a growing oppressive atmosphere. We were given a whole range of questions concerning our *Kommandeur* and our Führer, to answer in writing.

Finally, we were told that questions were pointless, visiting Prague off duty was not allowed, and any inquiries about Wendler were expressly prohibited.

This was a shock for us. By some means, it had become possible for me to find our good Wendler around midnight in a small psychopathic ward in Prague. These events gave us a deep mistrust.

SS-Hauptsturmführer Benz was presented as the *Kommandeur's* successor; with him, the *Bataillon* was then transferred to France in April. *SS-Hauptsturmführer* Wendler took leave of us at the train and promised to follow us soon.

We disembarked north of Angouleme and moved into local quarters on both sides of the Department of Charante. The population behaved properly – we were also not the first German soldiers here.

Combat patrol training was carried out insistently; in addition, completing our *Kompanie* training exercises with live weapons gave officers and men trust and security. Unfortunately, after we finished a *Kompanie* exercise, the *Kommandeur* made some critical remarks in front of the whole assembled *Kompanie*, which aroused conflict and internal aggression. Afterwards, when inept comments were being made even at the Führer circle's daily lunch table, there was a written complaint made to the Division; this led to the removal of *SS-Hauptsturmführer* Benz and *SS-Obersturmführer* Hermann. This whole thing weighed on the entire *Bataillon* and had a continued negative impact.

After we were detached from the command of *1. Armee* and sent to *15. Armee*, *SS-Pionier-Bataillon 10* was also redeployed to the southwest and moved into local quarters south of Pau; we moved into the western part of the Pyrenees defense sector. However, before we were able to further strengthen the places which were to be defended (railway tunnels and pass roads to Spain) with obstacles, mines, and explosives, the Division was transferred to the Mediterranean. *SS-Pionier-Bataillon-10* moved into quarters north of Aix – the new *Kommandeur* was *SS-Hauptsturmführer* Tröbinger.

In a larger sector, the troop units carried out alert and marching exercises in motorized formations, on trucks, or on foot. In the last week of October, the Division was sent back to Normandy.

One night during the transport, joking words were flying around the [train] compartment about whether, while you were playing *skat* [German card game], you hadn't forgotten to make your will... I wanted to protest about these remarks, but just then it seemed like a giant fist braked the train, the doors sprang open – as if opened by magic – the gear was ripped down, and people went flying all over the place. Then the train was jerked further forwards, again this violent braking, and then a big commotion outside and a sinister hissing. A signal squad was sent to the rear, since other trains were following us. When I went forward, the first mutilated dead of the *2. Kompanie* were brought into the *Zeltbahn* [shelter half tents]. The young *Kompanieführer* was totally frantic; he drove two older Frenchmen before him and had his MPi [*Maschinenpistole*: machine pistol] ready to fire. It was really hard for me to stop him from carrying out his intentions. The men concerned were two French railway shift workers.

The locomotive was lying half on its side. It had bored itself halfway up the boiler between the two tracks, steam poured from cracked pipes, and coals were falling out of the open firebox. The first three *G-Wagen* [*Güterwagen*: freight cars] had piled up and wedged together; on the rail tracks, our men could be recognized by their camouflage jackets. There were men still alive in other *G-Wagen*, but we could do nothing to help. I then saw that the tracks were loosened right on a bridge. A kindly fate had prevented them from shifting outwards...

The construction train, with its specialized equipment, only arrived in the morning. Our transport train was put together again and later ran on the adjacent tracks into Normandy. We disembarked in Pont Audemer and moved into quarters in the areas to the west and southwest.

In November-December 1943, the *Bataillon* was deployed laying land mines in Holland and building obstacles on the beaches. The obstacles were to be dug in very deep. Our men were hearing unpleasant things: the SS wanted to prevent any possible ways out, they were war prolongers, and the like. The condition of the field fortifications gave me a lot to think about, that life seemed more oriented to the places behind the lines.

In March 1944, as the Red Army succeeded in breaking through the *HKL* between the *4.* and *1. Panzer-Armee* in the region of Proskuroff and Tarnopol, as well as between the *1. Panzer-Armee* and *8. Armee* near Yampol, *10. SS-Panzer Division Frundsberg* was put on alert on March 26, 1944, in the sector of *II. SS-Panzer-Korps*. Transported by train, the units, travelling from the Lisieux-Bernay area by way of Nantes-Paris-Metz-Trier-Koblenz-Kassel-Hall-Cottbus-Wroclaw [German: Breslau]-Krakow, reached Podhajce on April 4, 1944.

That same day, the first elements attacked in the direction of Buczacz, over sheet ice and in heavy snowfall; their aim was, along with other German formations, to enable the encircled *1. Panzer-Armee* to escape to the west. Six days later, the entire *10. SS-Panzer-Division* got the order to attack. In heavy fighting, they were able to make contact with the *1. Panzer-Armee* and stabilize the front along the Strypa-Pilawa line. In the approximately two-week deployment, the *10. SS-Panzer-Division Frundsberg* lost a total of 2,076 men. Of these, there were:

577 killed in action
432 wounded
67 missing

On April 25, 1944, the formation marched to the area of Rohatyn-Halicz as a *Heeresgruppenreserve (4. Panzer-Armee)*. Here, three days later, *SS-Standartenführer* Harmel took over *Division* command from the tactically incompetent *SS-Brigadeführer* von Treuenfeld.

Transfer to the Eastern Front by rail. Below: ***Panzer IV Aus f. G*****.**

Versorgungsstaffel [supply detachment]. In front, a *leichter Zugkraftwagen* [light prime mover] *lt* [Italian] *(Sdr. Kfz. 10)* behind a Krupp-Protze 163.

2 cm *Flak 38* on a *Sdr.Kfz. 10* of *SS-Flak-Abteilung 10*.

Commanding General of II. *SS-Panzer-Korps*, *SS-Obergruppenführer* Hausser (center), with the *Kommandeur* of *10. SS-Panzer-Division Frundsberg*, *SS-Standartenführer* Harmel.

SS-Oberfürhrer Harmel in discussion with officers of *Sturzkampf-Geschwader 77* [wing of dive bombers].

I. Angaben
Familienname
Vornamen (Rufname unterstreichen)
Geburtstag, -monat, -jahr
2. 10. 1906
Geburtsort Verwaltungsbezirk (z. B. Kreis, Reg. Bezirk)
Staatsangehörigkeit (auch frühere)
Religion
Familienstand
Beruf (nach Berufsverzeichnis)
erlernter
ausgeübter
Eltern
Vater
(Rufname, Familienname)
Beruf (nach Berufsverzeichnis)
(wenn verstorben: † und Sterbejahr)
(Eigenhändige Unterschrift des Inhabers — Rufname, Familienname)
noch I
Dienststelle (Truppenteil usw.)
4./I SS-T. Art. Ers. Abt.

0. 5. 43	Küstenschutz an der franz.
0. 8. 43	Atlantikküste
1. 8. 43	Küstenschutz an der franz.
20.10. 43	Mittelmeer-Küste
6. 4. 44	Russland
16. 6. 44	bei Zilona u. Buczacz
26. 6. 44	Invasionsfront
3. 8. 44	Abwehrkämpfe bei Caen

am 3.8.44 verwundet
bei Ondefontaine

Emst Weinlich served from 5/30/43 in *SS-Artillerie-Regiment 10* as a driver. He was severely wounded in the head on 8/3/44 near Ondefontaine.

Harmel wrote in his first *Tagesbefehl* [order of the day]:

> Officers and men of *10. SS-Panzer-Division Frundsberg*!
>
> The *Reichsführer-SS* has charged me with command of *10. SS-Panzer-Division Frundsberg*. Today I have taken command of the Division.
>
> I am pleased to be able to lead a body of troops in whose name the glorious tradition of the *Frundsberg'schen* armies lives on. Tight discipline and relentless fighting spirit are vitally connected with this tradition. I am proud that in the recent days of fighting, this young Division has proven itself worthy of the expectations placed on it and has found full recognition.
>
> With full confidence in the spirit and stance of Führer and Enlisted Men, I expect that the Division members will worthily integrate themselves in the ranks of the old battle-tested *Divisionen* of the Waffen-SS. Your position should not be the last!
>
> Forward for Führer, *Volk* [people], and Reich!"

On May 1, 1944, the *10. SS-Panzer-Division* was given the command to march into the area of Pomorzany, where they carried out repeated operations against partisans. Four weeks later, the *Division* was placed under command of the *1. Panzer-Armee*. Even as embarkation began on June 7, 1944, at Stanislav for this move, the entire *II. SS-Panzer-Korps* was ordered to the area north of Lviv. The formation was transported by rail back to France, to combat the Allied troops which had landed in Normandy June 6, 1944.

Starting on June 20, 1944, the *10. SS-Panzer Division* transport trains, travelling by way of Jaroslaw-Opole-Wroclaw-Cottbus-Cologne-Strasbourg, reached Nancy-Bar le Duc (southwest of Metz). The same day, Hitler ordered *Oberbefehlshaber West*, with the *I.* and *II. SS-Panzer-Korps* and the *XXXXVIII. Panzer-Korps*, to split the front between the British 2nd Army and American 1st Army in the Caumont-Bayeux area, and destroy the American east flank at Balleroy. Then they were to turn against the British formations and crush them. This was an illusory order, given the Allies' materiel superiority in heavy weapons and aircraft – the ability to seize the initiative was already on the Anglo-American side.

The rapidly deteriorating situation at Caen led to a rash counterattack on June 29, 1944, by the *II. SS-Panzer-Korps* on the western flank of the advancing British troops. The *10. SS-Panzer-Division* had the following strength:

	Officers	Unterführer	Actual	Total
1st	374	2,266	10,912	13,552
	2.8%	16.7%	80.5%	100%
Authorized	614	3,923	13,260	17,797
	3.5%	22.1%	74.4%	100%

was reinforced by the *SS-Panzergrenadier-Regiment 4 Der Führer* and attacked to the right of the Villers-Bocage road. In fierce fighting, they were able to take the strategically important Hills 112 and 113, among others. Under continuous heavy naval artillery and air attacks, the units rapidly melted down. As a result, *III./SS-Panzergrenadier-Regiment 22*, after the action on Hill 122, had just 46 men on July 18, 1944! On July 16, 1944, the *Wehrmachtbericht* [Armed Forces radio report] announced:

> In the battle for Caen, the *9. SS-Panzer-Division Hohenstaufen*, led by *SS-Standartenführer* Stadler, and the *10. SS-Panzer-Division Frundsberg*, under the leadership of *SS-Oberführer* Harmel, together with *Heer* troops, have shown remarkable courage. In defense and attack, two *Divisionen* delivered heavy losses in men and materiel to the enemy. In this fighting, these *Divisionen* together destroyed 140 tanks.

After the British forces launched a major offensive on July 18, 1944, east of the Orne, the *HKL* ran in front of the *10. SS-Panzer-Division*, with its left boundary (the *277. Infanterie-Division* and parts of the *Hohenstaufen*) from Hill 113 to the west of Maltot. The *272. Infanterie-Division* was now positioned there as its right-hand neighbor; it had replaced the battered *12. SS-Panzer Division Hitlerjugend*. While there was fierce fighting east of the Orne, west of the river there were mainly localized operations on both sides. General Eisenhower, Supreme Commander of the Allied Forces, ordered the British and Canadian troops in the area of Caen to primarily hold down the German *Panzer-Divisionen* in fixed-position warfare and wear them out, and put the focus on the American forces in the west to force a breakthrough to central France.

As the Caen front was now somewhat stabilized, in late July 1944, the relief of the *II. SS-Panzer-Korps* began, so that it could be transferred as a mobile combat unit to the area of Aunay-sur-Orne (about 30 km southwest of Caen). After British troops had broken through the German front, in the boundary between the *7. Armee (II. Fallschirm-Korps)* right flank and the left flank of the *5. Panzer-Armee (LXXIV. Korps)*, and were advancing towards Vire, on August 1, 1944, the *10. SS-Panzer-Division Frundsberg* was given the mission, along with the *9. SS-* and *21. Panzer-Division*, to close the resulting gap in the front between the *7.* and *5. Panzer-Armee*

Even as the majority of the *10. SS-Panzer-Division* was on the march, an advance party arrived in the crisis area under the leadership of *SS-Sturmbannführer* Paetsch, consisting of the following:

II./SS-Panzer-Regiment 10
SS-Panzer-Aufklärungs-Abteilung 10
3./SS-Panzer-Pionier-Bataillon 10

During the night of August 2, 1944, they moved into positions west of Onderfontaine. The main body of *10. SS-Panzer-Division Fundsberg* reached the Onderfontaine assembly area the night of August 3, 1944; the thrust against the British flank was already launched the next morning. The battles for Hills 321, 301, and 248 were extremely difficult, and were fought bitterly by both sides.

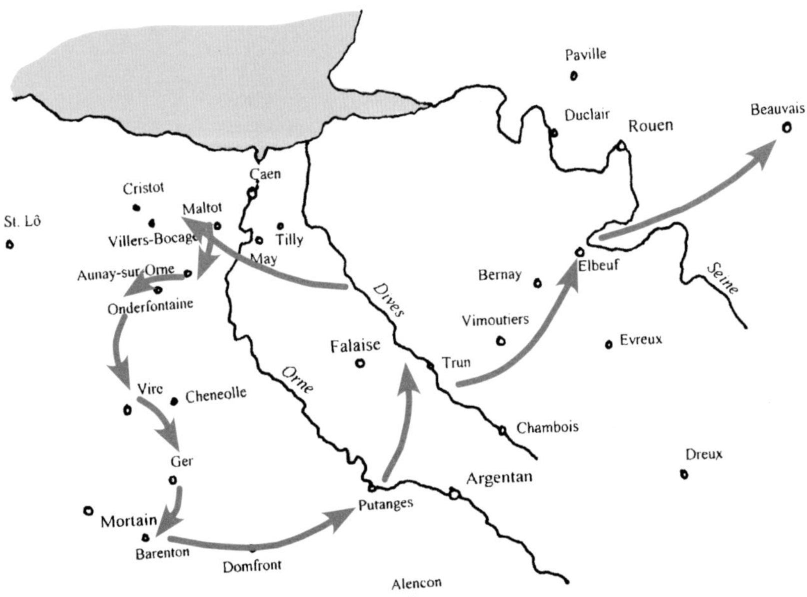

In the southwest, at the same time, British troops again succeeded in breaking through the German *HKL* and penetrating into the Burcy-Chenedolle area. While the German side was able to re-close the *HKL*, and thus briefly encircle three enemy Divisions, the Allied forces' materiel superiority denied the Germans any resounding success. Since the emaciated German troops could no longer carry out the order to straighten the front along the line northwards of Vire-Burcy-Presles-Estry with their existing forces, *10. SS-Panzer-Division Frundsberg* was again ordered, in the night of August 5, 1944, to move out from the *HKL*, and was to march to the area east of Vire.

Early in the morning the next day, the *10. SS-Panzer-Division* formed up near Chenedolle in several combat groups. After initial small successes, the counterattack was, however, soon stalled under the heavy enemy artillery and ground-attack aircraft fire. The conquest of Vire by British troops August 7, 1944, made it impossible to continue the attack – the front was pulled back to the line south of Vire-Chenedolle. The *10. SS-Panzer-Division Frundsberg* immediately received a new command to redeploy to the area of St. Clément-Ger, to be at the disposal of the German *7. Armee* offensive towards Avranches.

At Avranches, the Third U.S. Army had forced its way through the German positions and was thus able to push forward into the open French interior. Hitler ordered the *7. Armee* under *SS-Oberstgruppenführer* Hausser to make an immediate counterattack, which would again close up the front as far as the coast and annihilate the enemy forces. Given the Allied superiority, a fantastic suggestion.

Under the code name *Lüttich* [Liege], during the night of August 6-7, 1944, the German formations formed up in the region of Sourdeval-St. Clement-Barenton, and were to reach Avranches in two days. Here, the *II. SS-Panzer-Korps* was intended to form the second wave. After some initial successes, the Allied Air Forces began waves of attacks, which quickly put nearly 100 German combat vehicles out of action. *Oberbefehlshaber* West, *Generalfeldmarschall* Kluge, ordered the cessation of further attacks and retreat to the starting positions – *Unternehmen Lüttich* had realized nothing, except to further weaken the already-battered German combat units. On August 9, 1944, the U.S. Third Army launched a counterattack.

10. SS-Panzer-Division Frundsberg was placed under command of the *LVIII. Panzer-Korps* and got the order to occupy Barenton and secure the Mortain-Domfront road. Furthermore, they were to make contact with the *2. SS-Panzer-Division Das Reich* and cover its southern flank. On August 11, 1944, American troops succeeded in taking Mortain and pushing the *10. SS-Panzer-Division Frundsberg* out of the Barenton area. In the evening, the *Division* reported the following combat strength:

SS-Panzer-Grenadier-Regiment 21	**about 500 men**
SS-Panzer-Grenadier-Regiment 22	**about 250 men**
SS-Panzer-Pionier-Bataillon 10	**about 150 men**
SS-Panzer-Aufklärungs-Abteilung 10	**about 350 men**
SS-Panzer-Regiment 10	**8 *Panzer***
SS-Panzer-Flak-Abteilung 10	**9 *Flak* 8.8 cm**
SS-Panzer-Artillerie-Regiment 10	**25 *Rohre* [barrels]**

As U.S. troops also took Domfront on August 14, 1944, and occupied the hills north of the town, *SS-Oberführer* Harmel ordered a limited counterattack using *SS-Panzer-Regiment 10*'s last *Panzer*. This move would at least be able to secure the *Division*'s further withdrawal. Events came thick and fast: a command, which was to transfer the *Divisio*n to the *5. Panzer-Armee* in the area north of Argentan, where it would secure the withdrawal of the *7. Armee* as a mobile *Kampfgruppe*, was redundant, since the *Division* could no longer even reach the area – the U.S. troops were faster.

In the night of August 16-17, 1944, the *10. SS-Panzer-Division Frundsberg* marched into the area of Putanges (some 18 km west of Argentan), and there was placed under command of the *LXXXIV. Armee-Korps*. During the night, the remainder of the *Division* crossed the Orne towards the north. From there, the troops marched to Villedieu les Bailleul (about 3 km southwest of Trun).

When the 1st Polish Armoured Division succeeded in making contact with the troops of the XV U.S. Corps near Chambois on August 19, 1944, they closed the Falaise pocket. The remnants of four German *Armee-Korps*, with about 80,000 men, were encircled. In the absolute chaos, the mechanized units of various *Divisionen* were immediately formed into *Kampfgruppen*, which were to force a breakthrough out to the east.

As a result, what remained of the *SS-Panzer-Aufklärungs-Abteilung 10* and the *I./SS- Panzer-Grenadier-Regiment 21* formed *SS-Kampfgruppe Brinkmann*; this group, led by *SS-Panzer-Aufklärungs-Abteilung 10 Kommandeur SS-Sturmbannführer* Brinkmann, was ultimately placed under command of the *II. Fallschirmjäger-Korps*. The wounded *Oberbefehlshaber* of the *7. Armee, SS-Oberstgruppenführer* and *Generaloberst der Waffen-SS* Hausser, was also there.

The first elements of the *10. SS-Panzer-Division Frundsberg Kampfgruppen*, located between Trun and Chambois and extended over the Dives, were placed under command of the *2. Panzer-Division*.

By the morning of August 21, 1944, about 20,000 men were able to escape from the pocket. Like most units, *10. SS-Panzer-Division Frundsberg* had lost all their equipment and weapons, and had a head count of only about 3,000 men. A former member remembers the breakout from the pocket:

> On August 17, 1944, after my sidecar motorcycle got hopelessly wedged into the columns during the night, we felt our way forwards, looking to make contact with parts of the *LAH* [*Liebstandarte* Adolf Hitler]. But the enemy took care of all our worries – he was already marching against us on a parallel road, with tank columns and mounted infantry. When we pulled back cautiously, we were shot at by a patrol a short distance away. I was wounded and picked up by a *Sanka* (SPW, *Sanitärkraftwagen*: ambulance]. The Red Cross flag, which one wounded man was holding, was respected by the *Jabos* [*Jagdbombers*: fighter bombers]. In the evening, I got my first treatment at a Luftwaffe dressing station. At dawn, I was awakened by a young *Unterarzt* [assistant physician] with the words: "If it matters to you if you stay out of prison, you have to get away by yourself; we have orders to transfer the wounded to the enemy with San-Personal [medical personnel]."
>
> So I was off; right away, I had to dig a small hole in the slit trench; later I ended up with a *LAH Wespen-Batterie* [wasp battery; slang for German self-propelled light field howitzer]; from there, I was then taken to the *LAH* command post. Towards evening, the vehicles began to stream back again. Only with his pistol drawn was the *Ib* [2nd General Staff Officer in the supply group of a Division HQ] able to get me into a *Feldgendarmerie* [military police] car; later, I was in the Horch [car manufacturer] heavy vehicle of a General, which was attached to a *schwerer Instandsetzungsstaffelwagen* [heavy repair detachment vehicle]. The older driver told me that his General was already up front. I can hardly describe what I went through that night!
>
> Insanity, hysteria, and violence had gripped these worms of columns; the big devoured the small, meaning there were so many more victims of the incessant air strikes and heavy artillery fire of all

> calibers. At dawn, our car ran into a small column that had halted helplessly on the road; there was a long rise in the ground in front of us. Left of the road was an orchard, where paratroopers were falling back. Tank shots rumbled across. A short estimate of the situation at the "General's car." On my mark, with 80 m space, and at the utmost speed, over the hill. We got through, and were able to go a longer way and disappear into the woods. Later we travelled on in an ambulance bus. To cheer me up, the *Stabsarzt* [staff surgeon] gave me a cigar. In front of Bernay, a *Pionier* vehicle with mines was burning on a curved stretch of road. The bus stopped on the road, and the wounded got out and lay on a small slope, all wearing bandages and hardly a complete uniform. We barely paid any attention to the *Jabos* ...
>
> Then roaring engines, our bus was already burning, and in the next moment, the small hill where the wounded were was under fire from *Bordkanonen* [aircraft on-board cannons], and anything which could still move was being hunted down.
>
> Somehow I got to Rouen, and was again very moved when a French woman shyly looked around and then reached a bag of cookies to the wounded in the ambulance.

Beginning on August 24, 1944, bit by bit came the first arriving supply trains, and a little later the combat units crossed the Seine, bit by bit, and concentrated near Beauvais by the end of the month. There, the *Division* was officially attached to the *LXXXI. Armee-Korps*. Since the units had no contact with their commanding *Korps*, they placed themselves under command of the *I. SS-Panzer-Korps*. After some skirmishes, they marched to Wavre September 3, 1944. Here again, they were placed under command of the *II. SS-Panzer-Korps*, and eventually were to be refitted in the area east of Arnhem.

For this purpose, they were sent two reconstituted *Panzergrenadier-Bataillone* and an *Artillerie-Abteilung* of the *9. SS-Panzer-Division Hohenstaufen*, as well as 1,500 *Luftwaffe* members and 1,500 *Volksdeutsche* from Romania. Altogether, there were around 5,000 replacements.

Without the opportunity to actually refit the *Division*, *SS-Brigadeführer* Harmel had already sent a *Kampfgruppe* to the front September 13, 1944. British troops had established a bridgehead over the Meuse-Scheldt Canal, barely 100 km southwest of the containment area at Neerpelt. The *Regiment*-strong *SS-Kampfgruppe Heinke*, in the sector of the *LXXXVI. Armee-Korps*, tried without success to intercept the advance on Eindhoven. There were more unsuccessful battles near Veghel as part of the defense operations against the Allies' airborne Operation Market Garden, launched on September 17, 1944. On September 26, 1944, the German leadership ordered the forces stationed to the south to pull back across the Meuse, and finally across the Waal. Here, what remained of *SS-Kampfgruppe Heinke* again went under the command of the *10. SS-Panzer-Division Frundsberg*.

As the Anglo-American airborne operation emerged, other operational *Division* troop units were given the mission to move into positions along the Waal, east of Nijmegen. As the Allied forces attempted to drive forward over Lower Rhine on the bridge at Arnhem, there was heavy fighting with the British paratroopers who had already landed there. While elements of the units – as *SS-Kampfgruppe Reinhold* – moved through Pannerden to the place where they were ordered, *SS-Kampfgruppe Brinkmann* remained in Arnhem until the heavy street and house-to-house fighting ended September 26, 1944. Then, it followed the troops of the *10. SS-Panzer-Division Frundsberg*, which meanwhile had concentrated and were fighting in the area of Elst. The former *Kommandeur* of *SS-Panzer-Pioneer-Battalion 10*, *SS-Sturmbannführer* Albert Brandt, remembers:

> Before the airborne landing of the 1st British Airborne Division made it necessary to take action, we were concentrated for refitting and retraining. My *Pionier-Bataillon* now consisted of two battered *Kompanien*. By disbanding the *1. Gepanzerten Pionier-Kompanie*, *Pionierzug*, and *Stabskompanie*, I first formed an operational *Pionier-Kompanie* (mot.) under *Kompanieführer* Baumgärtel. After a further change of command, as well as getting some replacements, I set up a second *Pionier Kompanie* (mot.) under *Kompanieführer* Munski.
>
> I had to give this *Kompanie* up to a unit assigned to our right to lay mines. During the airborne alert, Baumgärtel and I were then the first, along with another *Grenadier-Bataillon*, on the bridge at Nijmegen. Baumgärtel also remained on active service there until the end, and nearly all the replacements were sent to him. A Regiment had its command post in a kind of castle with a high tower, which we often used as an observation post.
>
> I myself was often in the sector of both *Regimenter* – one of the *Regimentskommandeure* had only just joined the Division. We laid many mines, but built few field fortifications due to the terrain. The ferry [berths] took a lot of work, since we could only use the ferries shown on the map; the Lower Rhine had a walled embankment. We also had to blow up the church spires, because they set the artillery fire right under our noses, like precision fire. Baumgärtel was also awarded the *Deutsches Kreuz* in gold. He later fell at Szczecin [German: Stettin]. The *Volkssturm* [national milita] and *Todt* [Organization: militarized construction operation] had expanded a position

on the lower, but it was not used. *Kamerad* Roestel was assigned at the far right of the sector and had set up an observation post in a brick chimney, but this was constantly under artillery fire. Finally, we had to blow up the chimney anyway. We also had to create a field of fire. To do this, we blew up an old Dutch concrete bunker. We had a few 2 cm and 3.7 cm Flak at the ferry berths. We often had to repair the dikes, hit by artillery and *Jabos*.

When we were already loading up, I had to repel an attack in a wooded area with just remnants of my *Stabskompanie* and all other men available; six Panzer V Panther also took part. Later, I was replaced by a *Landesschützen-Regiment* [regional defense]. I still remember that one time a Division Special order was issued, in which my battalion and I were named.

Attempts to hit the flanks of the enemy, advancing northward from October 1, 1944, miscarried with heavy casualties. On October 7, 1944, the commanding *II. SS-Panzer-Korps* renewed the attack. The enemy eventually succeeded in pushing the German forces – except for a few positions – back across the Lower Rhine. As a result, the *Kampfgruppe/10. SS-Panzer-Division* moved into positions southeast of Arnhem up to Millingen.

After the situation in the sector quieted down and another Allied offensive developed in the Aachen area, the *10. SS-Panzer-Division* was ordered to move to Linnich in mid-November 1944. As *OKH-Reserve*, the formation reached the *5. Panzer-Armee* near Erkelenz, moving by way of Emmerich-Wesel-Krefeld-Mönchengladbach. On November 22, 1944, the mission to retake Geilenkirchen was launched in the sector of the *XXXXVII. Panzer-Korps*. In the heavy fighting, which was costly for both sides, the German forces could not carry this operation out, while beyond this, the enemy forced the *10. SS-Panzer-Division* out of their starting positions across the Ruhr, near Linnich.

After this abortive mission, the formation was redeployed on December 6, 1944, to complete its refitting, which had been started in September 1944, in the region of Blatzheim- Euskirchen-Kerpen. It had at this time:

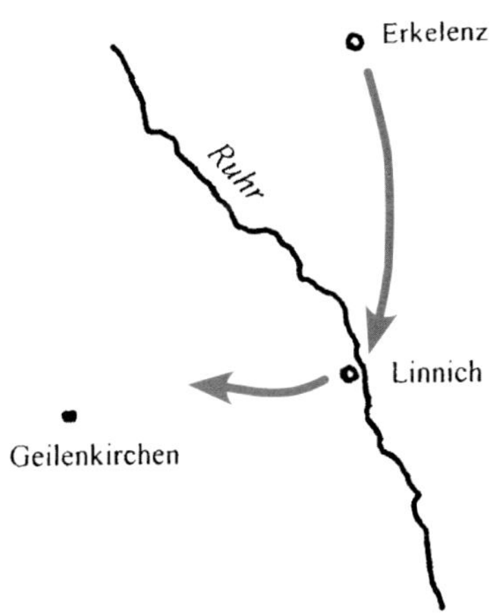

	Authorized	Actual	In delivery	Lacking	Above Quota
Panzer V	60	4	25	31	-
Panzer IV	30	10	34	-	-
Sturmgeschütze	21	11	3	7	14
schwere Pak	28	6	15	7	-
leichte Feldhaubitzen	37	37	-	-	-
schwere Feldhaubitzen	18	18	-	-	-
10 cm *Kanonen* 4	8	-	-	4	-

After some 24 months, the *10. SS Panzer-Division Frundsberg* was finally sent *I. (Panther)/SS-Panzer-Regiment 10* from the Grafenwöhr troop training ground.

For almost two years, the formation had only one *Panzer-Abteilung*, which was equipped mostly with *Sturmgeschütze*. In fact, this situation corresponded to the organization of a *Panzergrenadier-Division*.

After the German Ardennes offensive failed to achieve the desired success, on January 1, 1945, Hitler ordered the *1. Armee* to launch *Unternehmen Nordwind* [Operation North Wind] to the south in Alsace. As this offensive also got bogged down by enemy defensive operations, in mid-January 1945, the *19. Armee* was also brought in to join the offensive. For this operation, *10. SS-Panzer-Division* got a transfer order on January 7, 1945, to the *XXXIX. Panzer-Korps* in the area west of Bühl. A member of *SS-Panzer-Aufklärungs-Abteilung 10* remembers:

> We had been in action in the Arnhem bridgehead up to November 18, 1944, when we were relieved by *Fallschirmeinheiten*. After just a few days of rest and refitting, we were loaded up in Boetichen and sent to a new operational area. The trip was short, for we had already unloaded in Reydt (Rhineland). In motorized march we went to Jüchen, and from there into the battle area at Aachen. The *Aufklärungs-Abteilung* was sent to the Wels-Rurdorf sector.
>
> Early one afternoon, a young *Ordonnanzoffizier* [aide-de-camp, or special missions staff officer] came up with the order that the *Abteilung* was to re-establish the lost contact with *SS-Panzergrenadier-Regiment 22*.
>
> There was extremely heavy artillery fire over the whole battle sector; enemy fighter bombers were hounding the positions and made any movement impossible.

Since the situation was totally unclear, we proceeded in a northwesterly direction and spotted some soldiers digging in a few hundred meters away. Just as we thought we had fulfilled our mission, when we got closer, to our terror we found that the Americans were there in front of us. The low December sun had blinded us, so that we only recognized the *Amis* [German slang for Americans] very late. Barely 50 meters separated us from the enemy. Could it be that the *Amis* were thinking that we were about to defect? Well, he had made the reckoning without the host [were counting chickens before they hatched]. Our moment of fear was short, and we showed the *Amis* some clean heels. This was a really big surprise for us; we had not expected the enemy to have gotten so far. So we had to deal with this, in order to prevent further encroachment. The situation was reported to the *Abteilung*, and we asked for reinforcements. Not long, and a *Heereskompanie* was sent in. They attacked immediately, but advanced only a few meters, and remained stuck because of the casualties. The *Kompanieführer*, a *Leutnant*, now lost his head and wanted to pull back again, but we energetically stopped that. Luckily, the *Strafvollstreckungszug* [penal unit] of our Division came up and was positioned to our right. We still had no contact with Regiment 22. Unfortunately, the *Heereskompanie* was pulled out during the night, so then some of our *SS-Pioneer-Battalion 10* went into the *HKL.*

As the daylight grew the enemy artillery fire got stronger, and this showed that there would be more enemy attacks. Nothing had happened by midday, but then all hell broke loose. Bombers nosedived towards our positions, not to mention the tremendous artillery fire. Then came a smoke screen – the sign that the enemy attack was beginning. Everyone was ready for defense and tried to penetrate the smoke with their eyes. Then infantry fire began, and then finally the smoke lessened. The *Amis* had pushed through between us and Regiment 22 – the *Strafvollstreckungszug* had pulled out already!

From the left flank came bad news that we had no more contact on the left with our own *Abteilung*. Flares rising from the outskirts of Rurdorf showed us our situation. It was clear that we had to hold the position until dark, then win contact to our own forces. We asked for artillery fire to make the enemy's actions more difficult. The *Jabos* even helped us – they did not recognize the lines and dropped bombs on their own troops. As bad as that was for the *Amis*, for us, the help came just in time. Then a new disaster – the *Amis* had tanks on the Linnich-Rurdorf road in front of the village. Right in back of us. We were also being fired on from there. In the darkness, we were able to break away from the enemy unhindered. Immediately we moved into a new position for all-round defense of Rurdorf. Late that evening, a small *Stoßtrupp* [assault detachment] was put together, to get out a wounded *Rottenführer* of our *Zug* who was supposed to be in the hospital. The hospital was midway to Linnich and was occupied by the *Amis*. We were able to get the *Rottenführer* out, and he thus escaped captivity. A special fate befell *Sturmmann* Thomalla. The poor guy had fever all day, but could not get back. Now, when the evacuation was to take place, he fell under artillery fire. Thomalla had distinguished himself in Arnhem by destroying bunkers right in front of the *Abteilungskommandeur's* eyes, and received the *EK* [*Eisernes Kreuz*: Iron Cross]. The whole night there was lively artillery fire on our position, which got even worse by morning. Then, all at once, there was lots of shouting and shooting, because the *Amis* had also already broken into Rurdorf. The elements of *SS-Pioneer-Battalion 10*, which were to our left, had already been bypassed and left their positions, so we had no time to linger any longer. The *Amis* were inside Rurdorf and we were cut off again. What counted now was to get over the Rur in as much of one piece as possible.

Everything went relatively well. The *Strafvollstreckungszug* held a bridge over the Rur. At dawn, we went into prepared rear positions on the opposite bank. The footbridge was blown up. But now came a rude awakening. The rear positions should have been occupied, but we could see nothing of the sort, so we had to occupy the positions – we still had no contact, neither to the left nor to the right. What was going on? The *Amis* again started artillery fire. They seemed to believe that they could smoke us out with phosphorus grenades. The men stood in the water, holding wet handkerchiefs over their noses and mouths. Bombers provided the musical accompaniment. In the course of the day, we were able to make contact with the unit to which this sector actually belonged. In the evening, a *Zugführer* [platoon leader] tried to find the *Heer* command post with a messenger, to clarify the situation. After an initial disagreement and unwillingness to understand, the matter was then rectified quickly.

By command of *SS-Panzer-Aufklärungs-Abteilung 10*, we were to concentrate in Hottorf. As quickly as possible, we were relieved and sent back to Hottorf. Midway, two SPW came up to us to take up the men who were in really bad shape. While the entire *Abteilung*, from the *Kommandeur* down to the last man, had swum over the Rur, we were spared that by the footbridge!

On January 17, 1945, the *Division* formed up for an attack on Brumath from the Rhine bridgehead at Gambsheim. This operation was also bogged down by enemy defensive fire and Air Force attacks. After regrouping forces, a new attack was launched on January 24, 1945 – this time from the area of Schirrheim to Haguenau. When that failed, the entire *Unternehmen Nordwind* was finally abandoned.

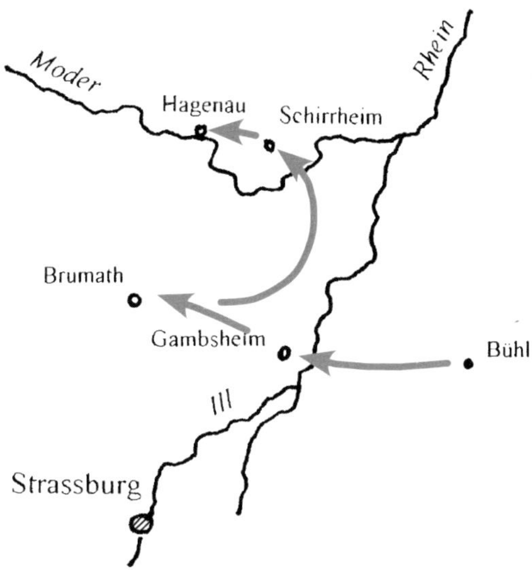

On February 3, 1945, the *10. SS-Panzer-Division Frundsberg*, in the *XXXIX. Panzer-Korps* sector, began to be pulled out, this time for redeployment to Pomerania. Two days later, the first transports reached the Szczecin [Stettin] area. On February 15, 1945, the units marched through Altdamm to Stargard, and the next day took part in *Unternehmen Sonnenwende* [Operation Solstice]. Placed under command of the *11. Armee*, the troops were supposed to attack the flanks of the Red Army, which had already reached the Oder river.

The *10. SS-Panzer-Division* attack – with the aim of crossing the Schönings canal and occupying Pyrzyce [German: Pyritz] – remained stuck, like the other *XXXIX. Panzer-Korps* formations, in the swampy terrain and the fierce Soviet defenses. After the offensive was abandoned by February 20, 1945, the *10. SS-Panzer-Division* had to pull back to its initial positions across the Ina river.

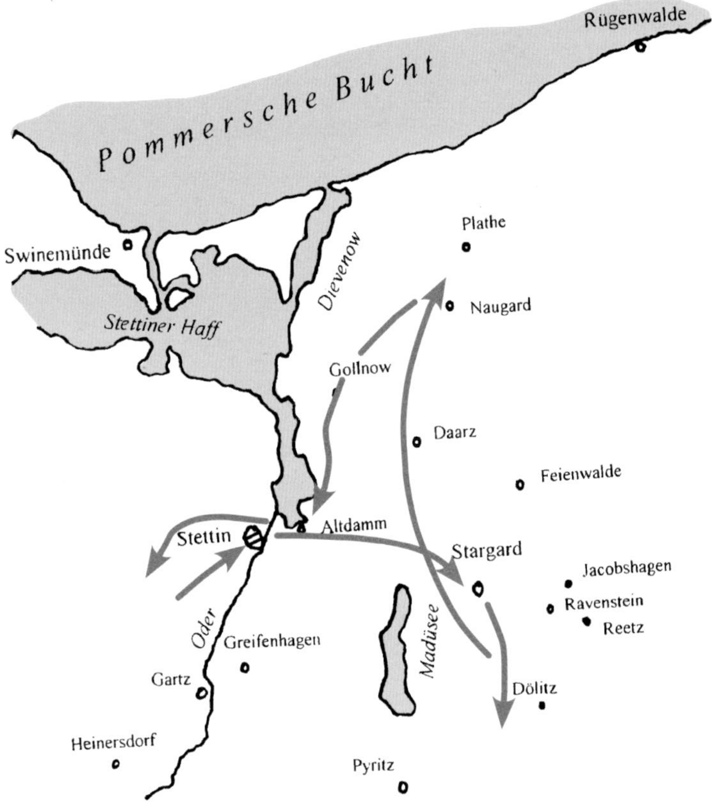

Although the *10. SS-Panzer-Division* was initially going to be taken out of active service, the *Division* was swept up into the Soviet offensive which was launched on March 1, 1945, to destroy the Soviet bridgehead at Fürstenwalde in the *9. Armee* sector. To prevent the Soviets from rolling up the front, the formation was ordered to the area of Plathe up to south of Naugard. By March 8, 1945, in heavy defensive fighting, the units drew back to the Oder bridgehead at Altdamm.

Here, the Red Army launched a major offensive on March 15, 1945. Fighting defensively in a very confined space, *10. SS-Panzer-Division* suffered extremely high casualties, like all the forces in the bridgehead. To prevent the threatened loss of their heavy weapons and equipment, Hitler approved the evacuation of the bridgehead on the night of March 19-20, 1945.

7.5 cm Pak 40 on the bridge at Nijmegen.

The bridge at Arnhem.

Positions on the Arnhem-Millingen line.

Panzer III (above) and Panzer IV with side skirts.

The last battles in the Lausitz [Lusatia region].

The *10. SS-Panzer-Division* then marched into the area southwest of Szczecin, and there was ordered by the *Generalinspekteur der Panzertruppen* [Inspector General of Armored Troops] to reorganize as a *Panzer-Division 45* [Type 1945]. For this purpose, on March 25, 1945, the formation reported a strength of:

	Officers	Unterführer	Enlisted Men	Total
Actual	369	2,570	12,028	14,967
	2.4%	17.2%	80.4%	100%

WEAPONS AND EQUIPMENT ON HAND:
35 Panzer IV *(II. /SS-Panzer-Regiment 10)*
47 Panzer V *(I. /SS-Panzer-Regiment 10)*
10 Panzer Sherman *(5. /SS-Panzer-Regiment 10)*
12 Panzerjäger IV *(I. /SS-Panzer-Regiment 10)*
6 Panzerjäger V *(2. /SS-Panzerjäger-Abteilung 10)*
8 Flak-Panzer IV *(3. /SS-Panzerjäger-Abteilung 10)*
4 Berge-Panzer V
16 Panzerspähwagen
138 Schützenpanzerwagen
8 Panzer-Befehlswagen III, IV,* and *V
8 Artillerie-Beobachtungspanzer III* and *IV
21 leichte Feldhaubitzen *(I. and II. /SS-Pz. Art. Rgt. 10)*
12 schwere Feldhaubitzen *(III. /SS-Pz. Art. Rgt. 10)*
10 Kanonen 10 cm *(III. /SS-Pz. Art. Rgt. 10)*
10 8.8 cm Flak
12 Flak 3.7 cm
27 Flak 2 cm
***8 Flak 2 cm* four-barreled**
***4 Flak* three-barreled**
8 schwere Pak 7.5 cm
9 K.W.K. 7.5 cm [Kampfwagenkanone:* armored vehicle gun*]

Compared to other formations, or a *Panzer-Division 45*, the *10. SS-Panzer-Division* was unusually well-equipped. The *Division* represented a special strategic reserve, although its potential operational capability was extremely limited due to the lack of fuel.

While providing mobile, operational reserves for defense against the expected Soviet offensive between Seelow and Luban [German: Lauban], the formation was ordered to redeploy to *Heeresgruppe Mitte* in Lower Silesia. Positioned at the boundary between the *4. Panzer-* and *17. Armee*, east of Görlitz to south of Luban (command post: Heidersdorf), the troop units again had the opportunity to refit.

As the Red Army launched its Berlin Operation across the Oder and Neisse rivers on April 16, 1945, the next day the *Oberbefehlshaber* of *Heeresgruppe Mitte* ordered the *OKH-Reserve* to be transferred to the *4. Panzer-Armee* in the Bautzen area. Due to the lack of fuel, the combat units could only get as far as Sprembert, while the *Nachschubtruppen* were left behind in Bautzen. Engaged in heavy offensive and defensive fighting, *10. SS-Panzer-Division*, along with other formations, was encircled at Spremberg on April 20, 1945. Against Hitler's order to push northward to the *V. Armee-Korps*, the troops broke out towards Senftenberg, suffering very high casualties and losses of materiel.

For Hitler's birthday, a delegation was ordered to go to Berlin: Artur Axmann remembers this event in his book *Das kann doch nicht das Ende sein* [*This cannot be the end*]:

> On the afternoon of April 20th, I was present as part of our delegation in the *Reichskanzlei* [Reich Chancellery] garden. There was a unit of the *Kurland-Armee* [Army Group Courland] and one from *SS-Division Frundsberg* there. Our delegation took its place between them. Hitler came out of the bunker with Dr. Goebbels, Heinrich Himmler, Albert Speer, and Martin Bormann. Hermann Göring was not there, but had been with Hitler earlier. I delivered our message to the Führer. Then he walked with me in front of the delegation. He walked slightly bent over, holding his trembling hands clasped behind his back. He made a short speech. [...] What was amazing, was the force of will and determination this man still displayed. All were under his spell, myself included.

As the formation marched into the region north of Radebeul, the troop units which had been previously stranded near Bautzen also reached this assembly area. Here, *SS-Brigadeführer* Harmel was relieved of his command for failing to comply with Hitler's orders and replaced by the *Kommandeur* of *SS-Panzerjäger-Abteilung 10*, *SS-Obersturmbannführer* Roestel.

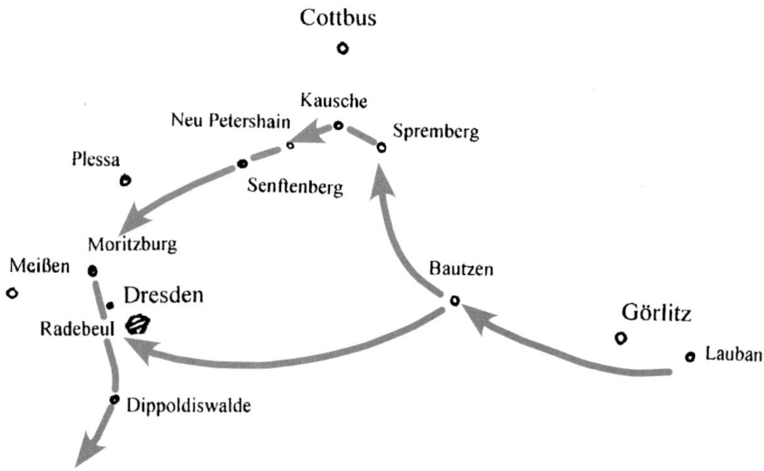

After the last skirmishes on May 3, 1945, at Moritzburg, in the general retreat two days later, the remnants of the *Division* marched to the *4. Panzer-Armee* through Grampitz-Dippoldiswalde to Teplice [German: Teplitz-Schönau], which they reached May 8-9, 1945. After the capitulation, the *Division*, unlike many other formations, did not go into captivity as prisoners of war, but mostly broke up into smaller groups that tried independently to reach home. This made it possible for most members to evade Soviet imprisonment. Some elements were imprisoned by the Americans; of these, most were released by 1948.

In the 28 months of its existence, the formation had taken part in many major missions. Based on the principle for strategic use of a *Panzer-Division*, it was always deployed at the *Schwerpunkt* [point of main effort] in (offensive) operations. Because, in the transition to fixed-position warfare, *Infanterie* formations took over the *HKL*, *10. SS-Panzer-Division Frundsberg* usually remained in a front sector only briefly. The fact that it was fully outfitted during the last phase of the war shows that the German command had high confidence in the *Führung* and the *Division*. It is interesting that the *Kommandeur* of *10. SS-Panzer-Division Frundsberg*, *SS-Brigadeführer* Harmel, disappointed Hitler precisely in April 1945, when he did not carry out the command for a thrust on Berlin.

12.

SS-PANZER-DIVISION HITLERJUGEND

The SS-Panzergrenadier-Division Hitlerjugend

In January 1943, the *Reichsjugendführer* [Reich Youth Leader], influenced by the tragedy of Stalingrad, offered to raise a *Division* of *Hitlerjugend* members, of the age group born in 1926. This meant that the members of this *Division*, unlike those of the *9.* and *10. SS-Panzergrenadier-Divisionen*, would be youth who had not yet fulfilled their *Reichsarbeitsdienst*.

The formation was to be established with the help of the *SS-Panzergrenadier-Division Leibstandarte SS Adolf Hitler*; together they would constitute the *I. SS-Panzer-Korps*. In this respect also, the contradiction became evident between the recruitment potential for *Mannschaften* and the lack of *Führer* and *Unterführer*. Temporary attachments from fellow formations could only be realized in a limited way, because of their active service. Therefore, the cadre of about 300 *Führer* and 3,500 *Unterführer* had to be trained specifically in order to form the new *Division*.

In February 1943, Heinrich Himmler, who often pursued naive ideas, proposed training 4,000 *HJ-Führer* from the age group born in 1925 to become *Unterführer*; they were to get a four-month course immediately after the end of their basic training. In addition, some 500 former *HJ-Führer* already serving in the *Waffen-SS* were also to get four months training to become *Reserveführer*.

Since there was no staff available – especially in the *Panzergrenadiere* – to carry out this training, the youth were to be trained and prepared, both physically and mentally, in *Hitlerjungend* military training camps for four weeks, initially without weapons.

While the *SS-Panzergrenadier-Division Leibstandarte SS Adolf Hitler* was preparing for its redeployment to Italy, on July 26, 1943, Hitler finally ordered the establishment of *SS-Panzergrenadier-Division Hitlerjugend.*[60] Under the command of *SS-Standartenführer* Witt, it was to be formed on the Beverloo troop training grounds (about 25 km southwest of Neerpelt) in Belgium, with the following organization, and be operational by April 1944:

DIVISIONSSTAB
SS-Panzergrenadier-Regiment 1 (I.-III. Bataillon)
SS-Panzergrenadier-Regiment 2 (I.-III. (gp.) Bataillon)
SS-Panzer-Artillerie-Regiment[61]
SS-Panzer-Flak-Abteilung
SS-Panzer-Regiment
SS-Panzer-Nachrichten-Abteilung
SS-Panzer-Aufklärungs-Abteilung
SS-Panzerjäger-Abteilung
SS-Panzer-Pionier-Bataillon
SS-Wirtschafts-Bataillon
***SS-Feldersatz-Bataillon* [Field Replacement]**
SS-Sanitäts-Abteilung

During July-August 1943, initially some 10,000 young men arrived in Belgium; another approximately 10,000 recruits followed by September 1943. The bottlenecks in supplying materiel meant that at first, they would only be given formal training; they often did not even have *Waffen-SS* uniforms. When the still-lacking numbers of recruits arrived, nominal formation of the troop units was completed in September 1943.

60 Propaganda Minister Dr. Goebbels considered the new *Division*'s name unwise, because it would show the world that Germany already had to take children away from their school desks.

61 Beginning October 30, 1943, after it was re-designated a *Panzer-Division*, the term *Panzer* was added to the unit designations.

The 12. SS-Panzer-Division Hitlerjugend

After Hitler commanded on October 21, 1943, that the *I. SS-Panzer-Korps* was to consist of two *Panzer-Divisionen*, on October 30, 1943, the formation was re-designated a *Panzer-Division*. Since the *Division* already practically had *Panzer-Division* structure, only the formation's name was changed. In the simultaneous serialization of the *Waffen-SS* formations, the *Division* received the number ***12*** and the two *SS-Panzergrenadier-Regimenter* the numbers ***25*** and ***26***.

Tactically part of the *15. Armee*, for training purposes, the *Division* was subordinate to the *General* of *Panzertruppen West*, *General der Panzertruppen* Geyr von Schweppenburg. Initially only four *Panzer V Panther* and four *Panzer IV* were available for training the crews of this *Panzer-Regiment* on the training grounds at Mailly-le-Camp. The *Panzer-Artillerie-Regiment* was trained using *leichte Feldhaubitze*. The formation became 80% mobile when it acquired Italian vehicles. Then-*SS-Untersturmführer* Otto Berke remembers the sub-standard captured vehicles:

> Our 7.5 cm Pak was successful in armored combat, but the captured Italian vehicles – Spa [Italian Fiat make] *Radschlepper* [wheeled tractors] – were totally inadequate as prime movers. Big as barn doors, they consumed 50 liters per 100 km! Already by the first days of the invasion, we were able to capture a Canadian *Karette* [transporter] and use it as a prime mover with good success. It was even ideal this way, since the grain fields were higher than the *Karette*....

After individual training was completed, in early 1944, *Division* training as a formation began. On December 31, 1943, it reported the following strength:

Officers	Unterführer	Enlisted Men	Total
406	1,767	19,309	21,482
1.9%	8.2%	89.9%	100%

Reichsjugendführer Axmann with the *Kommandeur* of *12. SS-Panzergrenadier-Division Hitlerjugend*. *SS-Oberführer* Witt. Witt fell on June 12, 1944, at Caen.

17-year-old recruits of the *12. SS-Panzergrenadier-Division Hitlerjugend* in Belgium.

Young *Panzergrenadiere* of the *12. SS-Panzergrenadier-Division Hitlerjugend*.

Driver's training on a *Panzer IV*.

Because this active service unit still lacked about 2,600 *Führer* and *Unterführer*, it definitely could not de deployed as a *Division*. Some steps were taken to compensate for the still-missing officers through attachments from the *1. SS-Panzer-Division Leibstandarte SS Adolf Hitler*,[62] by taking former *HJ-Führer* from the *Wehrmacht*, and by returning the *Mannschafts-dienstgrade* [enlisted ranks] who had been ordered to *SS-Unterführerschulen* [non-commissioned officers' training] at the *SS-Unterführerschule*.[63]

In any case, when *Oberbefehlshaber West Generalfeldmarschall* von Rundstedt had made his final inspection, the process of organizing the *Division* was considered completed. In April 1944, *12. SS-Panzer-Division Hitlerjugend* was transferred to the area between the Dives and the Seine, in the Bernay-Evreux-Chambois-Trun region, to place it at the *OKW*'s disposal for the expected invasion. Here, on April 2, 1944, there was an attempted attack on a transport train at Ascq (near Lille). As a result, *Transportführer SS-Obersturmführer* Hauck had 70 men from the surrounding homes and 16 men from the village shot.[64]

In addition to their on-going training in battalion or regimental formations (especially night attack exercises and night motorized marches),[65] the units were also assigned to carry out operations against the French Resistance. As was noted in the *KTB* [War Diary] of *I./SS Panzergrenadier Regiment 25* on May 3, 1944:

> I c [Chief Intelligence Officer] – Report to the Regiment about incidents in Chambois. Based on a report by French *V-Enlisted Men* [*Verbindungsperson* or *Vertrauensperson*. i.e., informants] of the SD [*Sicherheitsdienst*: SS Security Service], suspected persons could be named as terrorists. In the early morning, the place was surrounded and house searches started. Ten people and a lot of weapons, ammunition, and political propaganda material were secured and turned over to the Alencon SD. One man was shot while trying to escape by *Kompaniechef Oberleutnant* Fuchs.[66]

62 A military court convened after the war in Lille initially sentenced all the accused to death, and finally to prison. Walter Hauck was released in 1957.

63 The German leadership was aware that, due to the enemy's materiel superiority – especially air superiority – their own operations should or must be primarily carried out at night.

64 This involved a former *HJ-Führer* in the *Wehrmacht*, ordered to join the *Waffen-SS*.

65 The German leadership was aware that, due to the enemy's materiel superiority–especially air superiority–their own operations should or must be primarily carried out at night.

66 This involved a former *HJ-Führer* in the *Wehrmacht*, ordered to join the *Waffen-SS*.

During the invasion launched on June 6, 1944, Canadian troops succeeded in building a 10-km-deep bridgehead west of the Orne. The *I./SS-Panzergrenadier-Regiment 25 KTB* reported: "3:00 Alert. Enemy landings northwest of Caen and on both sides of the mouth of the Seine."

Alerted, the *Division* was ordered, through the *I. SS-Panzer-Korps*, to move to the area northwest of Caen up to Cristot, to stand ready for a counterattack. For this mission, *SS-Panzergrenadier Regiment 25* was reinforced by *II./SS-Panzer-Abteilung-12*, and *SS-Panzergrenadier Regiment 26* was reinforced by *I./SS-Panzer-Abteilung*. Due to the continuous fighter-bomber attacks, they suffered their first casualties and materiel losses when they were still on the march.

On June 7, 1944, *SS-Panzergrenadier Regiment 25* reached Caen, along with more than 50 *Panzer IV*. In this, it was demonstrated that the *Panzer IV* were inferior to the enemy tanks. When *SS-Panzergrenadier-Regiment 26* and *I./SS-Panzer- Regiment 12* remained stuck still 30 km east of the Orne due to lack of fuel, initially the reinforced *SS-Panzergrenadier Regiment 25* formed up for defense against the Canadian armored spearheads north of Caen. Because there was no continuous *HKL*, however, the attack was then called off, because the German forces were unable to cover the flanks.

On June 8, 1944, the German forces violated the laws of war when 35 Canadian prisoners of war were shot by members of *II./SS-Panzergrenadier Regiment 26* at Le Mesnil. Two Canadians were able to escape and were taken prisoner by other German units. At the same time, about 40 other Canadian prisoners of war were shot by *SS-Panzergrenadier Regiment 25* soldiers near Authie and Baron. At Chateau d'Audrieu, members of *SS-Panzer-Aufklärungs-Abteilung 12* shot 26 Canadian prisoners of war the same day.[67]

When the enemy ceased its attack on the *Division*'s right flank at Caen, because of its tenacious holding power, the reinforced *SS-Panzergrenadier-Regiment 26* went on the offensive at Fontenay-Villers-Bocage, starting June 21, 1944. On June 26, 1944, the far superior enemy forces succeeded in breaching their positions and advancing on Caen from the southwest. Elements of *I./SS-Panzer- Regiment 12* formed up immediately with parts of the newly brought up *10. SS-Panzer-Division Frundsberg*, to carry out the successful recapture of the strategically important Hill. Four days later, the Division reported a strength of:

67 *SS-Oberführer* Kurt Meyer was sentenced to death by a Canadian court-martial for this on December 27, 1945. In January 1946, the sentence was changed to life imprisonment. Imprisoned first in Canada and then in Germany, Meyer was released September 7, 1957.

	Officers	Unterführer	Enlisted Men	Total
Actual	461	2,281	15,116	17,858
	2.6%	12.8%	84.6%	100%
Authorized	655	4,177	14,246	19,078
	3.4%	21.9%	74.7%	100%

Massive artillery fire, constant fighter-bomber attacks, and extremely heavy offensive and defensive fighting had inflicted total casualties during the past three weeks of nearly 4,000 men killed, wounded, and missing! The biggest impact was due to the loss of *Führer* and *Unterführer*.

On July 7, 1944, the Anglo-American bomber formations turned the northern outskirts of Caen into a desert of rubble. While the *12. SS-Panzer-Division* held their positions, the *16. Luftwaffe-Feld-Division*, positioned on its northwest side, was decimated. To cover their own right flank, *II./SS-Panzer- Regiment 12* moved towards Cabaret. On July 9, 1944, the *Division* crossed the Orne in the southern district of Caen. Two days later, the *272. Infanterie-Division* took over the sector of the *12. SS-Panzer-Division*, which was transferred to the area of Potigny (north of Falaise). Due to the very high casualties, the remnants of the two *SS-Panzergrenader-Regimenter* were reconstituted into two battalion-strength *Kampfgruppe* and put in reserve. *SS-Panzer-Regiment 12* had suffered around 50% casualties and still had about 50 *Panzer IV* and *V*. Other *Division* units, such as *SS-Panzer-Aufklärungs-Abteilung 12*, were moved to the Evreus area for refitting. By July 17, 1944, a *Kampfgruppe* was again alerted when the enemy succeeded in breaking through the *272.-Infanterie-Division* positions west of the Orne, near Maltot. The other *Kampfgruppe* was moved to the east the next day, near Vimont, on the left wing of the *21. Panzer-Division.*

Because almost all German *Panzer* forces in the sector of the *XXXXVII.* and *II. SS-Panzer-Korps* were given the mission of retaking Avranches (southwest of Caen) in *Unternehmen Lüttich*, set to begin August 7, 1944, the enemy was planning to encircle those German troops west of Falaise in a pincer movement. In addition to what remained of the *89. Infanterie-Division*, the task fell to the *Regiment*-strong *12. SS-Panzer-Division* to prevent the II Canadian Corps from advancing southwards, starting August 8, 1944. The German *Panzer* succeeded in inflicting heavy losses on the hesitant enemy forces. An erroneous Anglo-American bomber attack on the Canadian formations made it impossible for them to exploit their own superiority. On August 12, 1944, the deployed elements of the *12. SS-Panzer-Division* transferred the positions at Potigny to the newly brought up *85. Infanterie-Division* and moved into a prepared rear position from north of Falaise up to Dives. On August 13, 1944, *Kampfgruppe/12. SS-Panzer-Division* (strength: about 2,000 men) had the following:

500 *Panzergrenadiere*
20 *Panzer IV* and *V*
3 *Schützenpanzer*
4 *Flak* 8.8 cm
8 *Flak* 3.7 cm
12 *Flak* 2 cm
8 *Feldhaubitzen* 10.5 cm and 15 cm
3 *Kanonen* 10 cm

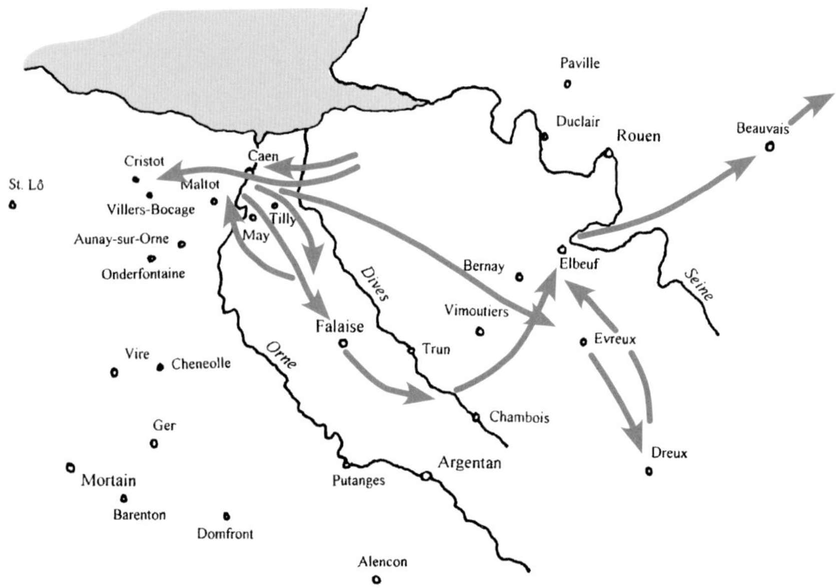

The next day, the II Canadian Corps, strongly reinforced with materiel, broke through the *85. Infanterie-Division* positions and initially succeeded in taking ground forward of the *Kampfgruppe/12. SS-Panzer-Division* positions. This force eventually drew back across the Aute river. When elements of the II Canadian Corps were able to meet up with the U.S. XV Corps forces that were fighting their way towards them from the southwest near Tran, on the Dives, on August 17th, the remnants of the battle-weary *12. SS-Panzer-Division*, together with some 80,000 other German soldiers, were encircled.

While the *1. SS-Panzer-Division*, together with the *3. Fallschirmjäger-Division*, was given the mission of forcing a breakthrough to the east on August 20, 1944, the *12. SS-Panzer-Division* was assigned to hold the northern front of the pocket at Falaise. The breakout was an inferno. Crowded together in a small area, the soldiers were *en masse* victims of enemy artillery, tanks, and fighter planes. A former member remembers:

> At the beginning of the invasion, *SS-Panzerjäger-Abteilung 12* was stationed with its headquarters in Nogent le Roi, *1. Kompanie* in Villiers le Noiharnes, *2. Kompanie* at Castle Chaudon, and *3. Kompanie* in Villemeu.
>
> We had already gotten some of the new *Jagdpanzer* ["hunting tank"/mobile self-propelled tank destroyers] in Chaudon. Here we familiarized ourselves with them daily and made practice runs on little-travelled country roads. It turned out, I had received a piece of junk. On a test drive, I got stuck right in the middle of the St. Martin village street. Then came *Jabos* [fighter-bombers]. The civilians were afraid of an attack, and I made it clear to them we had a malfunction. There was a stack of wood stored in a barn there. We packed the entire *Panzer* in it, to make it look like it was a farmer's wooden sledge. The people helped. The *Jabos* didn't recognize the *Panzer* and moved away after several low-altitude flights. In the gearbox, the cardan coupling was broken. After getting it repaired by the *1-Staffel* [Echelon], we got back to our quarters at night. Two days later, the engine was broken. The *1-Staffel* men worked all night in the Nogent le Hoi repair garage and installed a new engine.

Our *Kompanie* drove to the front for active duty. I followed in the day's march, camouflaged with a lot of green branches. When, after a few kilometers, the battery went on strike, I was sure getting worried bit by bit, and my enthusiasm for the new *Panzerjäger-Typ* was sinking very fast. Finally, everything seemed to be going fine. We passed Dreux on the right side, drove over fields of stubble, and climbed a slope up to the road to Nonancourt. The *Jabos* barely hindered us. We always found shelter under the trees along the roads. The sun was burning hot, and our *Panzer* marched along on the smooth asphalt at 50 km/h in some places. We drove towards Verneuil, where I was stationed in 1942 with the *LAH*.

Behind Verneuil, the *Kompanie* took a rest in some woods. We arrived there in the late afternoon. Quickly fill the tank, check the treads, and get some sleep. Then the *Kompanie* moved on in a night march. The next morning, we reached a large wooded area and parked the *Panzer* and supply vehicles far apart. In the evening, we went to the assembly area. In the early dawn, my *Panzer*, after a stop driving uphill, suddenly turned to the left and stopped, stuck in the entrance to a large pasture bordered on the road side by a thick hedge and trees. The road took a bend to the left, and the *Panzer's* rear lay right in the curve and stuck out into the roadway. The *Panzer* was really a piece of junk, because now it turned out that the left intermediate gear was broken. We had to get a new one from Sens, near Paris. I thought that would take at least a week. We re-camouflaged the *Panzer* every morning.

Finally, the waiting was over. Late one afternoon, the *1-Staffel* took out the gear and installed a new one. After the tread was back on, we continued on to the front in the twilight. It wasn't far away. During all these days, we kept hearing the rumble of the guns. That same day, all hell broke loose. The area was plowed up by bombs. In the afternoon that "blessing" lightened up a bit, and I was piloted to a position. An attack was expected there the next morning; I was in a wooded area.

The next morning, all hell broke loose: *Jabos*, artillery, and tanks on the opposite slope, moving towards us. They were driving up packed close in the glare of the sun and kept stopping. The distance was too great. I fired twice, but no success. That let the enemy locate me, and I came under artillery fire. Around noon, the situation became untenable. I decided to make a break for it. We drove back at full throttle; after a slight bump we turned and crossed the open field, and got behind a small hill to save ourselves. There we met three *Panzer* from our *Kompanie* and four *SS-Panzer-Regiment 12 Panzer IV*.

> So we fought for several days as a small *Kampfgruppe* in what was becoming the Falaise pocket. Every night we shifted position. On August 17, 1944, I had to blow up my *Panzer*. I had been towing a *Panzer IV* for two days, and it ruined my engine. We then broke out of the pocket at Trun and fled across fields and hedges, away from the road, away from the *Jabos*, to the Seine, which we crossed near Rouen. Going through Fleury, we got further eastwards, and in the forest of Compiegne we met our *Kompanietroß* [company supply train].

At the same time, the units which had been sent to the Evreux area for refitting on July 11, 1944, moved into positions near Dreux and delayed the advance of American armored units. This made it possible for some 20,000 German soldiers who had gotten out of the Falaise pocket to pull out across the Seine. By way of Le Neubourg, the *Divisionsstab* reached Louviers and again took over leadership of the amalgamated units. By August 21, 1944, the *12. SS-Panzer-Division* thus again had a fighting strength of about 2,500 men (of whom only about 300 were *Panzergrenadiere*) and ten *Panzer*. *SS-Panzer-Artillery-Regiment 12*, like most other units, had lost all their equipment.

In the period up to August 26, 1944, the remainder of the *Division* moved back across the Seine at Elbeuf. After the last battles, it was transferred first to the roughly 75 km distant Beauvais, and from there another 150 km further to the French-Belgian border near Hirson by August 29, 1944. While the *Versorgungstruppen*, the non-operational combat units, and combat support units were moved across the Meuse, the troops still fit for action pulled back, carrying out delaying actions against the American forces and fighting until September 2, 1944, 35 km to the north, towards Hirson. Here they crossed the Belgian border.

From there, they retreated to Florennes on September 4, 1944, and crossed the Meuse at Yvoir. Finally, they were to move into positions near Godinne. Since U.S. forces then succeeded in crossing the Meuse, the next move was to retreat through Spontin-Durbuy across the Ourthe river. This led to heavy fighting with American tank units, as well as combat with Belgian partisans. During the retreat, on September 6, 1944, *Divisionsführer SS-Oberführer* Kurt Meyer was taken prisoner. The *1. Generalstabsoffizier*, *SS-Obersturmbannführer* Hubert Meyer, took over command.

In mid-September 1944, the formation was taken out of active service and transferred to the Sauerland, 200 km away. Here the *Division* was assembled and refitted. In the last three months of almost daily combat operations the formation lost overall:

	Officers	Unterführer	Enlisted Men	Total
Killed in Action	55	229	1,548	1,832
Wounded	128	613	3,684	4,425
Missing	56	182	2,012	2,250
Deceased	7	16	96	119

The *12. SS-Panzer-Division Hitlerjugend* had lost half of its membership, with about 9,000 killed in action, wounded, missing, and taken prisoner of war. The number of vehicles was only about 25% of the authorized amount; it scarcely had any more heavy weapons. In October 1944, *12. SS-Panzer-Division Hitlerjugend* was sent to the area west of Nienburg/Weser, to be available in case of an Allied landing on the East Frisian coast.

With attachments of about 10,000 members of the *Luftwaffe* and *Kriegsmarine*, as well as convalescents and newly-trained recruits from the *SS-Panzergrenadier-Ausbildungs- und Ersatz-Bataillon 12*, the *Division* had again attained its nominal strength of 19,657 men by December 1944. The *schwere Heeres-Panzerjäger-Abteilung 560* formed the *II./SS-Panzer-Regiment 12*.

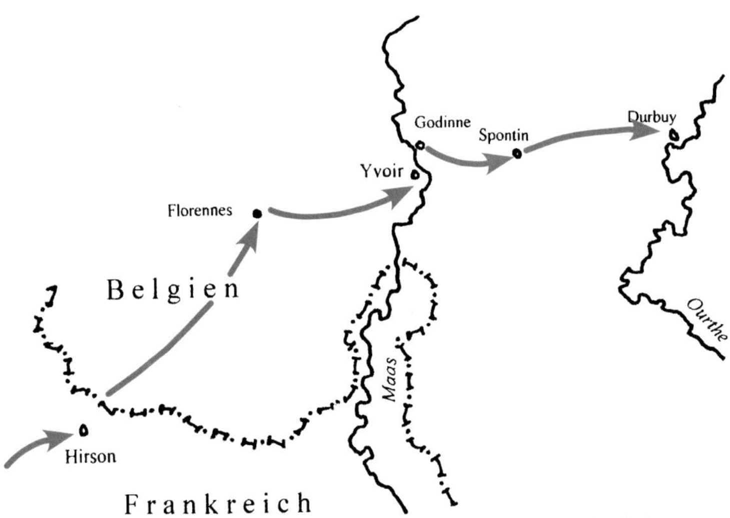

10.5 cm *Feldhaubitze 18/2* on the chassis of a Panzer II (Sf.) *(Sdr.Krz 124)* *Wespe* [wasp].

7.5 cm Pak 40.

The last *Kommandeur* of *12. SS-Panzer-Division Hitlerjugend*, Hugo Krass, here still as an *SS-Standartenführer*.

SS-Oberführer Kurt Meyer, here as an *SS-Standartenführer,* was given command of *12. SS-Panzer-Division Hitlerjugend* after the death of *SS-Brigadeführer* Witt. He was taken as an Allied prisoner of war September 6, 1944.

After about 12 weeks refitting, starting December 13, 1944, the formation marched into the Blankenheimer Forest for the upcoming Ardennes Offensive. At this time, the *Division* reported:

	Authorized	Actual
Panzer IV	34	42
Panzer V Panther	34	41
Sturmgeschütze	21	22
schwere 7.5 cm Pak	28	25
leichte Feldhaubitzen	-	36
schwere Feldhaubitzen	-	12
10 cm Kanonen	-	4

The *Division* shifted its main point of effort to Büllingen on December 20, 1944; this town had already been captured by the *1. SS-Panzer-Division.* This led to fighting with the remaining U.S. forces. The next day, the formation began its unsuccessful attack on Bütgenbach. After ceasing the attack, the Division concentrated near Amel, and on December 26, 1944, was placed under command of *II. SS-Panzer-Korps*, stationed about 40 km to the southwest, north of Laroche. Two days later followed the equally unsuccessful attack to form a bridgehead over the Ourthe.

SS-Soldbuch
zugleich Personalausweis
Nr. 19
für
den SS-Hauptsturmführer (Dienstgrad)
ab (Datum) (neuer Dienstgrad)
ab
ab
Hermann Lütgert (Vor- und Zuname)
Beschriftung und Nummer der Erkennungsmarke Stab II./SS-T.I.R. – 1217 –
Blutgruppe 0 (Null)
Gasmaskengröße 2
Wehrnummer Bielefeld 15/69 Halle/W.
K 167 SS-Vordruckverlag W. F. Mayr, Miesbach 16881

geb. am 1.1.1915 in Halle/Westfalen (Ort, Kreis, Verw.-Bezirk)
Stand, Beruf SS-Führer
Religion ggl.
Personalbeschreibung:
Größe 1,80 Gestalt schlank
Gesicht oval Haar blond
Bart ohne Augen blau
Besondere Kennzeichen (z. B. Brillenträger):
Schuhzeuglänge 44 Schuhzeugweite
Hermann Lütgert (Vor- u. Zuname, eigenhändige Unterschrift des Inhabers)
Die Richtigkeit der nicht umrandeten Angaben auf Seite 1 und 2 und der eigenhändigen Unterschrift des Inhabers bescheinigt
Rgt.Gef.Std., den 10. März 1944
SS-Pz.Rgt. 12 / 12.SS-Pz.Div. „Hitlerjugend" (Ausfertigende Truppenteil, Dienststelle)
(Dienststempel)
SS-Hauptsturmführer u. Rgts.-Adjutant
(Eigenh. Unterschrift, Dienstgrad u. Dienststellg. d. Vorgesetzten)
2

Bescheinigungen über die Richtigkeit der Zusätze und Berichtigungen auf Seiten 1 und 2

Lfd. Nr.	Art der Änderung	auf Seite	Datum	Truppenteil	Unterschrift	Dienstgrad und Dienststellung

Hermann Lütgert initially served in the *SS-Totenkopf-Division* and was later transferred to *SS-Panzer-Regiment 12*. What was unusual, was his assignment in 1945 to the *Waffen-SS Gebirgsjägerschule* [Mountain Infantry School.

Interesting here is the signature of the son of the German Reich *saußenminister* [Foreign Minister], *SS-Obersturmführer* [First Lieutenant] Rippentrop.

...über ausgezahlte Gebührnisbeträge ... fremder Zahlmeisterei mit Unter-
Zugleich Mitteilung (Vordruck) an zuständige Zahlmeisterei nach A.

am	für (Zeit)	Erläuterungen	RM	Rpf
	Auszeichnungen.			
25.4.42	KVK. 2.Kl. m. Schwertern			
15.9.42	Ostmedaille 41/42			
	Sudeten-Erinnerungsmedaille			
	i.V. ... SS-Hauptsturmführer u. Rgts.-Adjutant			
1.9.44	KVK I m. Schw.	... SS-Ostuf + Div. Adj.		

28

Beurlaubungen über fünf Tage

1. Vom 8.4. bis 25.4.43 nach München
Grund: Erholungsurlaub
den 7. April 1943
gez. Unterschrift
SS-Hauptsturmführer
(Dienststempel) (Unterschrift des Komp.-, Truppenführers usw.)

2. Vom 21.11.44 bis 6.12.44 nach Halle/Westf.
14 Tg + 2 Tg.
Grund: Einsatzurlaub
den 20. November 1944
SS-Sturmbannführer
(Dienststempel) (Unterschrift des Komp.-, Truppenführers usw.)

3. Mit Wirkung vom 7.5.45 aus dem Wehrdienst entlassen.
7.5.1945.
(Dienststempel) (Unterschrift des Komp.-, Truppenführers usw.)

4. Vom .... bis .... nach
Grund:
den
(Dienststempel) (Unterschrift des Komp.-, Truppenführers usw.)

31

This above-average actual strength was, however, only relative due to the lack of fuel reserves, as well as the unfavorable operating area for armored units. The plan stipulated that the *272. Volksgrenadier-Division* would break through the American positions first, then the *12. SS-Panzer-Division Hitlerjugend* was to overtake them and push through to the Meuse.

Because the *272. Volksgrenadier-Division* failed to break into the American lines December 16, 1944, the next day, *SS-Panzer-Grenadier-Regiment 25* and *SS-Panzerjäger-Abteilung 12* were sent into battle. December 18, 1944, the entire *12. SS-Panzer-Division* formed up for a breakthrough at Krinkelt. Because of the strong defense, the attack group shifted its main point of effort to Büllingen December 20, 1944; this town had already been captured by the *1. SS-Panzer-Division*. This led to fighting with the remaining U.S. forces. The next day, the formation began its unsuccessful attack on Bütgenbach. After ceasing the attack, the Division concentrated near Amel, and on December 26, 1944, was placed under command of the *II. SS-Panzer-Korps*, stationed about 40 km to the southwest, north of Laroche. Two days later followed the equally unsuccessful attack to form a bridgehead over the Ourthe.

Redeployed further south and placed under command of the *5. Panzer-Armee*, the formation was engaged in heavy fighting to the north

of Bastogne starting January 1, 1945. After the enemy dismissed the offer for negotiations, the Ardennes Offensive was abandoned at the beginning of January 1945. *12. SS-Panzer-Division* was pulled out of active service and moved to the region west of Cologne by January 10, 1945. There, it had another short period of rest and reinforcement, until the beginning of February 1945. Starting February 2, 1945, the formation was redeployed to the *6. SS-Panzer-Armee* sector on the Eastern Front.

A former member remembers:

> On January 6, 1945, the *2. /SS-Pionier-Bataillon 12*, after a mission in the early evening, moved into quarters in Steinbach, where other *Bataillon* units had also taken quarters. With my *Kompanietrupp* [Company HQ personnel] I found a place to stay in a house, where the *Bataillongefechtsstand* [command post] was set up. Around midnight, *Bataillonskommandeur SS-Hauptsturmführer* Taubert got the order by telephone from *Divission I* [*1. Generalstabsoffizier*: 1st General Staff Officer] *SS-Obersturmbannführer* Meyer, to assign a *Kompanie* for an *Infanterie* mission and have the responsible *Kompanieführer* report to him.
>
> The *2.* and *4. Kompanie* were available for this. Possibly for the sake of expediency – there I was at the command post – *2. Kompanie* was given the mission. The next morning, the *Kompanie* went on the march. After two vehicles (Mercedes diesel) broke down, the *4. (schwere) Zug* stayed behind. After a *Horizontschleicher* [advance skirting enemy lines] of about 15 km, we reached the Division command post. *SS-Hauptsturmführer* Taubert, who was also on hand with the *Stabszug* [staff platoon], and I reported to the *Ia. Divisionskommandeur*, and *SS-Brigadeführer* Kraas arrived and briefed us on the situation:
>
> On orders of the *Heeresgruppe*, Hill 510 west of Mageret, from where you could see to Bastogne, was to be attacked and occupied. This was almost one of the last missions of *Division Hitlerjugend*, which was to be relieved by a *Volksgrenadier-Division* and sent to the Eastern Front.
>
> The attack was to begin at 17 hours. To prepare and support the attack, *SS-Panzer-Artillery-Regiment 12* and *Korps* artillery were available.
>
> After occupying Hill 510, *2. Kompanie* was to be pulled out and replaced by a unit of the *Volksgrenadier-Division*.

The *Divisionskommandeur* insisted on personally briefing *SS-Hauptsturmführer* Taubert and myself on the terrain. We boarded a *SPW* [*Schützenpanzerwagen*; armored personnel carrier] and – as best as we could – made ourselves familiar with the terrain. It had been snowing; the weather was misty and visibility was poor. During the exploratory trip, we came across some Panzer of the *Kompanie* von Ribbentrop, which were securing the way to Bizory. The *Kommandanten* shared their observations with us.

We returned to the Division command post, and the *Divisionskommandeur* gave the order to get snowsuits, to give the attackers some camouflage. Around noon, *2. Kompanie* reached Mageret. The vehicles were parked in front of the village and camouflaged. We made the necessary preparations, such as making concentrated and elongated charges, readying the flame throwers, and so on.

The *Bataillon* command post was in a building next to the church. There the *Batallion* doctor, *Stabsarzt* Zöbelein, had set up the aid station in a cellar. Prior to the attack, my command post was located in a house on the western outskirts of Mageret, which was directly on a road leading to Bizory. Also in this house, a *Fernsprech-Trupp* [telephone squad] of *SS-Nachrichten-Abteilung 12* had already set up, so there was a telephone connection to the *Division* command post.

The *SS-Divisions-Begleit-Kompanie* [escort company], under the command of *SS-Obersturmführer* Stier, was providing cover to the south. We made contact with the *Führer* of the *Volksgrenadier-Division* unit which was to replace *2. Kompanie* after Hill 510 was taken. He was a *Hauptmann* [captain] who was already in Mageret.

2. Kompanie was made ready for the attack after the camouflage clothing was brought in on time. We had just 80 men. By 17 hours, our own artillery barrage began on Hill 510, which lasted about five minutes. The enemy returned fire, and hit mainly the western outskirts of Mageret. Several houses were set on fire.

At 17.05 hours, the *Kompanie* attacked. We overpowered the enemy pockets of resistance; some tanks that were dug in were put out of action with sapper equipment and flamethrowers. It also turned out that our *Artillerie* had done a good job . By around 19 hours, the Hill was in our hands. I told the *Ia* by telephone that the *Kompanie's* casualites were substantial, and it would not be possible to hold the Hill if there were a counterattack. He told me that it would be immediately arranged for the *Volksgrenadier-Division* unit be moved up and *2. Kompanie* reinforced or relieved. Unfortunately there was

Panzer VI
Tiger I
Ausf. E.

Panzer IV Ausf. H.

Sturmgeschütz III Ausf. G.

Transport and deployment of Sturmgeschütz III and Panzer IV and VI in Hungary, 1945.

Panzer V Panther Ausf. A.

Panzer VI
Tiger I.

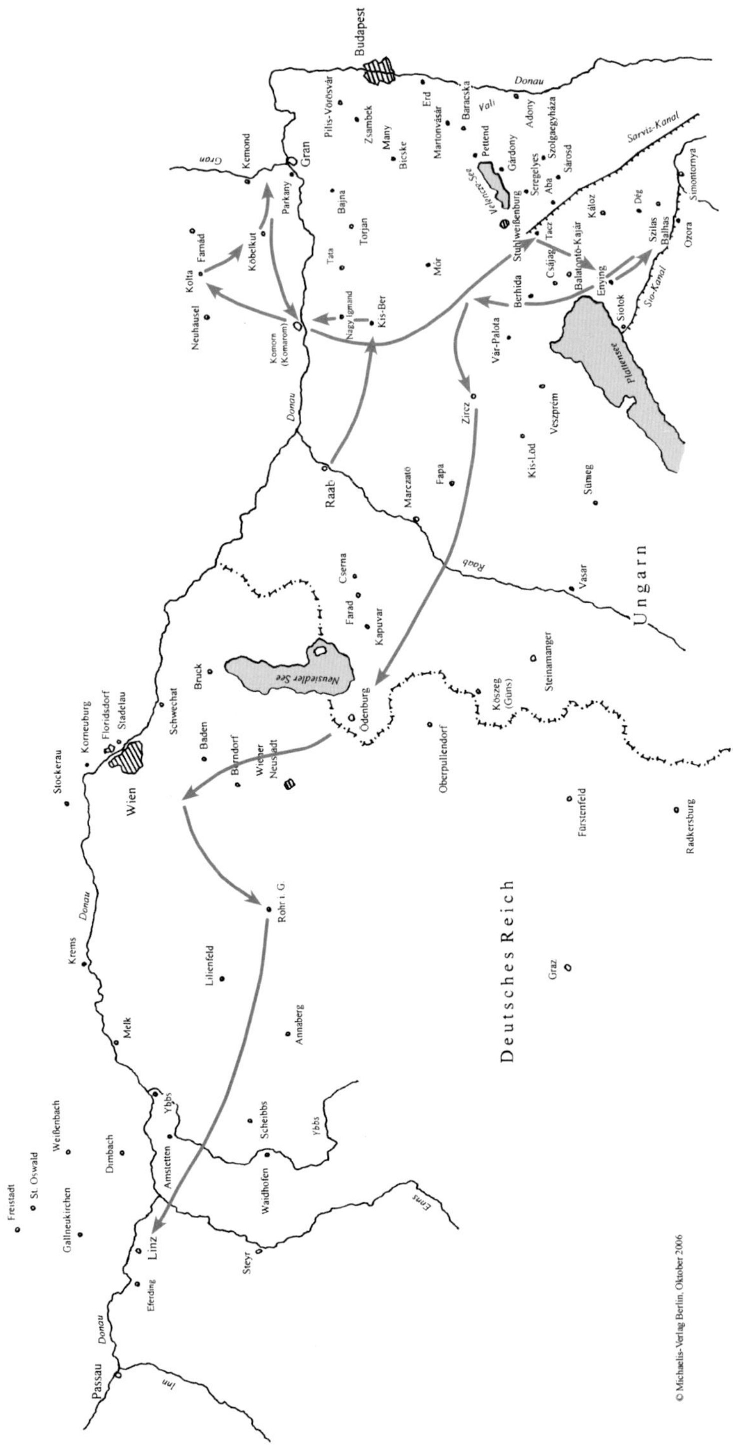
Budapest
Donau
Gran
Kemond
Parkany
Pilis-Vörösvár
Zsambek
Many
Bicske
Erd
Martonvásár
Baracska
Vali
Adony
Pettend
Gárdony
Velencze-See
Seregelyes
Szolgaegyháza
Aba
Sárosd
Sarviz-Kanal
Simontornya
Dég
Káloz
Stuhlweißenburg
Tacz
Csájág
Balatonfo-Kajár
Enying
Szilas
Balhas
Ozora
Sio-Kanal
Siotok
Plattensee
Berhida
Vár-Palota
Veszprem
Zircz
Mór
Kis-Ber
Nagy Igmand
Tata
Bajna
Torjan
Kobelkut
Kolta
Farnád
Neuhäusel
Komorn (Komarom)
Raab
Marczato
Papa
Kis-Lod
Sümeg
Csema
Farad
Kapuvar
Vasar
Ungarn
Neusiedler See
Bruck
Ödenburg
Köszeg (Guns)
Steinamanger
Oberpullendorf
Schwechat
Stadelau
Floridsdorf
Korneuburg
Stockerau
Wien
Baden
Berndorf
Wiener Neustadt
Fürstenfeld
Radkersburg
Deutsches Reich
Graz
Rohr i. G
Lilienfeld
Annaberg
Krems
Melk
Ybbs
Scheibbs
Amstetten
Waidhofen
Weißenbach
Dimbach
St. Oswald
Freistadt
Gallneukirchen
Linz
Steyr
Eferding
Passau
Inn
Enns
© Michaelis-Verlag Berlin, Oktober 2006

> a longer delay, because this unit was not under command of the *12. SS-Panzer-Division Hitlerjugend.* Meanwhile, the enemy made a counter-strike with tanks from Bizory and Harzy. The heavy casualties, the loss of most *Gruppenführer*, and the lack of *Panzerfäusten* made it impossible to hold the Hill. The *Kompanie* was forced to make a fighting withdrawal to Mageret. The *Zug* casualty report showed that about 35 *Unterführer* and *Enlisted Men* had been killed, wounded, or were missing. So the mission had brought nothing except new deaths and some badly wounded!

To camouflage the *Division* for the upcoming *Plattenseeoffensive*, it was designated as the *Ersatz-Staffel* [replacement echelon] *Wiking* – that is, as replacements for the *5. SS-Panzer-Division Wiking,* which was already in the region. The initial deployment, however, was northwards across the Danube, to attack the Soviet Gran bridgehead. Concentrated by mid-February 1945 near Raab, the formation moved via Kisbér- Komárom to the Koltra assembly area on February 14, 1945. From there, the units first attacked Köbölkut on Febrary 17, 1945. In heavy fighting, the soldiers succeeded in reaching Beny, on the Gran river, on February 24, 1945, where they put pressure on the enemy bridgehead. By the next day, *Ersatz-Staffel Wiking*, with a strength of about 17,423 men, marched through Komorn to the area of Tac, south of Székesfehérvár.

By March 6, 1945, the attack – now from the Kisláng area southwards – got bogged down in the exceptionally difficult terrain one kilometer north of *Psz.* [manor] Fekete and in the hills south of Kislang. The next day, the units were stranded before the extensive and heavily occupied enemy positions. On March 8, 1945, the soldiers reached the area southeast of Enying, where they were stopped by a minefield. After clearing it, *Ersatz-Staffel Wiking* pushed on to Szilas-Balhas and reached the Sio Canal March 10, 1945. That day, *12. SS- Panzer-Division Hitlerjugend* had:

5 strong and 1 average *Grenadier-Bataillonen*
12 *schwere Panzerabwehrkanonen* 7.5 cm
6 *Jagdpanzer IV*
6 *Panzer IV* and 9 *Panzer V*
12 *Sturmgeschütze*
16 *leichte Feldhaubitzen* 10.5 cm
6 *schwere Feldhaubitzen* 15 cm
3 *Feldkanonen* 10 cm
8 *Nebelwerfer* [smoke mortars]

In contrast to the some 100 *Panzer* and *Sturmgeschütze* it had before the Ardennes Offensive, now only 33 were still operational. Despite this, the formation was rated "provisionally fit for attack operations."

On March 12, 1945, it succeeded in building a small bridgehead across the Sio Canal. As the enemy, making stronger counter-attacks, succeeded in forming a bridgehead at Ozora, *Ersatz-Staffel Wiking* was also moved against this on March 17, 1945.

After the Red Army breakthrough north of Székesfehérvár, the troops – from March 18, 1945, again designated as the *12. SS-Panzer-Division* – were redeployed from the Falubattyan area to the *Margarethe-Stellung* [Margaret position] at Zircz (some 30 km southwest of Mör). With no possibility of establishing a continuous front, the units moved back across the Raab on March 27, 1945, to the area of Sopron. *Heeresgruppe Süd KTB* stated the next day:

> Among the very young age groups (*Div. Hitlerjugend*) there is fear of artillery fire because of the experience in the West. With lack of energetic *Führer*, the soldiers halt already when artillery fire starts.

***SS-Panzer-Regiment-12* had operational on April 1, 1945:**
Panzer IV
***Panzer IV* long**
12 *Panzer V Panther*

This was approximately *Batallion* strength. Since the Red Army had already reached Sopron ahead of them, intense fighting started there. Marching initially north to the area of Baden, and engaging in heavy fighting at the Schöpfl mountain at St. Corona, the *Division* pulled back, moving through Rohr, on the Schwarzau river, another 100 km in the direction of Linz, to the line of demarcation on the Enns. A former member remembers the last days of the war:

> In early April 1945, we had neither a fuel nor a munition depot to guard for the *Nachschub-Kompanie*, nor was there much for the *Fahrkompanie* [transport company] to transport. There was no fuel, like everywhere else. What was more obvious, than stick us in a *Kampfgruppe*! So there came the order that the *Nachschub-Kompanie*

must release all non-essential people to the *Kampfgruppe*. We members of the *SS-Nachschub-Bataillon 12* assembled at the *1. Fahr-Kompanie* in Hainfeld. There we got some real hot food (the first since a very long time), as well as cold rations. *1. Fahr-Kompanie* vehicles then drove us to the village of Kaumberg. We stayed there the first night; the next day, a very thin skirmish line was formed, and we moved through forest and meadow towards St. Corona. No one knew where the Russians were. East of St. Corona, on the road to Klausenleopoldsdorf, we took up a position. Left of the road was a Luftwaffe unit, armed with rifles and machine guns taken from the aircraft. Right of the road was our *Kampfgruppe*. When the Russians attacked the Luftwaffe unit, they took off fast. To take over those positions, every other man had get out of our line and fill in over there. To the right of our *Kampfgruppe*, there was no contact with any other military unit. The fighting was very costly for us, since we had no infantry experience and no entrenching tools.

Our cover was either sawn logs or just a depression in the forest floor. In just a short time, Russian snipers shot three of our *MG Schütze 1* in the head and killed them. Since the pressure from the Russians kept getting heavier, we had to clear out of the position and built a new position on the southwest outskirts of the village. That night, I was in an outpost with a comrade with a MG, about 200 m from the edge of the village. Although we had warned the women of the place to hide somewhere safe, they didn't believe us. The women's screams went on throughout the night and pierced us to the core. Sometimes we could even see, lit by the fires, the Russians chasing after the women. At dawn, we took our MG back into the new position. The rapidly built up line was reinforced by comrades from *SS-Panzer-Regiment-12*. Where they suddenly came from, I don't know.

The Russians now tried to set their attacks on our positions from outside the village. They got bloody heads for this, because we were on the edge of a forest on a hill and already saw them coming across the meadows from the outskirts of the village. When one day a stronger Russian assault detachment was able to break through some young saplings into our position, we fought in close combat, in which the Russians came off worse and had to pull back. There were dead and wounded on both sides. We took our wounded *Kameraden* to the St. Corona-Kaumberg road, from where they would be taken away. We left the dead *Kameraden* where they had fallen, hoping to be able to bury them later. On one of the next days, when the Russians launched especially strong attacks on our positions, we almost faltered; a *Schützenpanzerwagen* came with mounted four-barrel Flak to help us. That gave us some breathing space.

The next day, when the four-barrelled Flak was gone, they strafed us with artillery and mortar fire, and in the next attack we had to give way, and take flight over mountain and forest. We were going towards Kaumberg. We could stay only a short time on the Araburg [castle ruins]. There, we also came upon some from our *SS-PanzergGrenadier-Regiment 26*. I would like to mention that we were designated *SS-Kampfgruppe von Reitzenstein* (he was *Kdr.* [*Kommandeur*] of *SS-Panzer-Aufklärungs-Abteilung 12*).

The fighting around St. Corona on *Schöpfl* [mountain] was very bloody for us, which is also shown by the mass grave in the village cemetery of St. Corona. Because of the unfortunate circumstances, almost all of our *Kamaraden* lost their ID tags, so that when the remains were taken to Blumau for reburial, as many as 80% were buried as unknown.

From mid-February to May 8, 1945, the formation had a total of 7,500 killed in action, wounded, and missing, with at least some of those in the latter considered as taken prisoner of war. On May 8, 1945, the formation consisted of the following:

	Officers	**Unterführer**	**Enlisted Men**	**Total**
Actual	328	1,698	7,844	9,870
	3.3%	17.2%	79.5%	100%
Authorized	655	4,177	14,246	19,078
	3.4%	21.9%	74.7%	100%

crossed the demarcation line and went into American captivity. This ended the history of the *12. SS-Panzer-Division Hitlerjugend*. When the *Division* was thrown into a key focus point on the invasion front, most of the soldiers were only 17 or 18 years old, and they held their positions against a far superior enemy. As the war came to an end a year later, very few of those who had formed its ranks when it was first established were still there as members of the *Division*.

APPENDICES

Feldpostnummern
[Field Post Numbers]
and
Divisionskommandeure

1. SS-Panzer-Division Leibstandarte-SS Adolf Hitler

Feldpostnummern:

Divisionsstab	21 825
SS-Panzergrenadier-Regiment 1	00 933
I. Bataillon	29 707
II. Bataillon	11 150
III. Bataillon	09 842
SS-Panzergrenadier-Regiment 2	04 124
I. Bataillon	09 088
II. Bataillon	14 103
III. Bataillon	08 280
SS-Panzer-Aufklärungs-Abteilung 1	01 893
SS-Panzer-Artillerie-Regiment 1	03 903
I. Abteilung	02 924
II. Abteilung	11 808
III. Abteilung	04 539
IV. Abteilung	41 805
SS-Panzerjäger-Abteilung 1	12 611
SS-Panzer-Regiment 1	48 020
I. Abteilung	48 477
II. Abteilung	28 129
SS-Sturmgeschütz-Abteilung 1	08 917
SS-Flak-Abteilung 1	05 583
SS-Panzer-Pionier-Bataillon 1	05 113
SS-Panzer-Nachrichten-Abteilung 1	08 259
SS-Nachschubdienste 1	08 661

Kommandeure:

03/1933-07/1933-1943	SS-Obergruppenführer Dietrich
07/1943-08/1944	SS-Brigadeführer Wisch
08/1944-02/1945	SS-Oberführer Mohnke
02/1945-05/1945	SS-Brigadeführer Kumm

2. SS-Panzer-Division Das Reich

Divisionsstab	200	092
SS-Panzergrenadier-Rgt. 3 Deutschland	21	867
I. Bataillon	27	064
II. Bataillon	01	602062
III. Bataillon	28	688
SS-Panzergrenadier-Rgt. 4 Der Führer	03	669
I. Bataillon	15	807
II. Bataillon	11	707
III. Bataillon	05	452
SS-Panzer-Aufklärungs-Abteilung 2	41	940
SS-Panzer-Artillerie-Regiment 2	005	992
I. Abteilung	12	626
II. Abteilung	10	074
III. Abteilung	15	982
IV. Abteilung	03	504
SS-Panzerjäger-Abteilung 2	48	963
SS-Panzer-Regiment 2	48	800
I. Abteilung	27	310
II. Abteilung	20	973
SS-Sturmgeschütz-Abteilung 2	08	917
SS-Flak-Abteilung 2	23	223
SS-Panzer-Pionier-Bataillon 2	14	179
SS-Panzer-Nachrichten-Abteilung 2	06	146
SS-Nachschubdienste 2	25	089

Kommandeure:

10/1939-10/1941	SS-Obergruppenführer Hauser
10/1941-12/1941	SS-Brigadeführer Bittrich
01/1942-04/1942	SS-Brigadeführer Kleinheisterkamp
04/1942-03/1943	SS-Gruppenführer Keppler
04/1943-11/1943	SS-Gruppenführer W. Krüger
12/1943-07/1944	SS-Brigadeführer Lammerding
07/1944-12/1944	SS-Standartenführer Baum
01/1945-02/1945	SS-Standartenführer Kreutz
02/1945-03/1945	SS-Gruppenführer Ostendorff
03/1945-04/1945	SS-Standartenführer Lehmann
04/1945-05/1945	SS-Standartenführer Kreutz

3. SS-Panzer-Division Totenkopf

Feldpostnummern:

Divisionsstab	17 492
SS-Panzergrenadier-Rgt. 5 Totenkopf	00 746
I. Bataillon	31 256
II. Bataillon	18 249
III. Bataillon	33 501
SS-Panzergrenadier-Rgt. 6 Theodor Eicke	13 203
I. Bataillon	07 526
II. Bataillon	39 153
III. Bataillon	22 135
SS-Panzer-Artillerie-Regiment 3	36 883
I. Abteilung	39 245
II. Abteilung	36 053
III. Abteilung	08 014
IV. Abteilung	11 020
SS-Panzer-Flak-Abteilung 3	34 963
SS-Panzer-Regiment 3	48 550
I. Abteilung	32 238
II. Abteilung	48 279
SS-Sturmgeschütz-Abteilung 3	10 003
SS-Panzer-Nachrichten-Abteilung 3	16 224
SS-Panzer-Aufklärungs-Abteilung 3	34 404
SS-Panzerjäger-Abteilung 3	01 475
SS-Panzer-Pionier-Bataillon 3	16 192
SS-Wirtschafts-Bataillon 3	22 404
SS-Sanitäts-Abteilung 3	29 199

Kommandeure:

10/1939-02/1943	SS-Gruppenführer Eicke
02/1943-04/1943	SS-Brigadeführer Simon
04/1943-07/1944	SS-Brigadeführer Priess
07/1944-05/1945	SS-Brigadeführer Becker

5. SS-Panzer-Division Wiking

Feldpostnummern:

Divisionsstab	16 284
SS-Panzergrenadier-Rgt. 9 Germania	30 003
I. Bataillon	33 576
II. Bataillon	30 629
III. Bataillon	34 002
SS-Panzergrenadier-Rgt. 10 Westland	25 854
I. Bataillon	26 907
II. Bataillon	27 026
III. Bataillon	28 109
SS-Panzer-Artillerie-Regiment 5	20 060
I. Abteilung	21 432
II. Abteilung	22 855
III. Abteilung	23 604
IV. Abteilung	24 976
SS-Panzer-Flak-Abteilung 5	40 017
SS-Panzer-Regiment 5	58 040
I. Abteilung	08 158
II. Abteilung	57 084
SS-Sturmgeschütz-Abteilung 5	02 131
SS-Panzer-Nachrichten-Abteilung 5	33 631
SS-Panzer-Aufklärungs-Abteilung 5	39 688
SS-Panzerjäger-Abteilung 5	45 750
SS-Panzer-Pionier-Bataillon 5	44 189
SS-Feldersatz-Bataillon 5	19 637

Kommandeure:

12/1940-10/1942	SS-Brigadeführer Steiner
10/1942-08/1944	SS-Brigadeführer Gille
08/1944-10/1944	SS-Standartenführer Mühlenkamp
10/1944—5/1945	*SS-Standartenführer* Ulrich

9. SS-Panzer-Division Hohenstaufen

Divisionsstab	20 046
SS-Panzergrenadier-Regiment 19	21 770
I. Bataillon	23 295
II. Bataillon	23 940
III. Bataillon	24 111
SS-Panzergrenadier-Regiment 20	20 340
I. Bataillon	25 120
II. Bataillon	25 405
III. (gp.) Bataillon	23 474
SS-Panzer-Regiment 9	21 118
I. Abteilung	21 815
II. Abteilung	22 336
SS-Panzerjäger-Abteilung 9	21 144
SS-Sturmgeschütz-Abteilung 9	23 565
SS-Panzer-Artillerie-Regiment 9	24 537
I. Abtcilung	20 488
II. Abteilung	21 339
III. Abteilung	22 728
IV. Abteilung	21 419
SS-Flak-Abteilung 9	20 565
SS-Panzer-Pionier-Bataillon 9	21 649
SS-Panzer-Nachrichten-Abteilung 9	24 742
SS-Feldersatz-Bataillon 9	56 136

Kommandeure:

02/1943-07/1944	SS-Brigadeführer Bittrich
07/1944-07/1944	SS-Oberführer Stadler
08/1944-10/1944	SS-Oberführer Bock
07/1944-05/1945	SS-Brigadeführer Stadler

10. SS-Panzer-Division Frundsberg

Feldpostnummern:

Divisionsstab	21 003
SS-Panzer-Grenadier-Regiment 21	27 001
I. Btl. (SPW)	25 685
II. Btl.	26 966
III. Btl.	28 227
SS-Panzer-Grenadier-Regiment 22	25 685
I. Btl.	29 638
II. Btl.	28 588
III. Btl.	28 383
SS-Panzer-Regiment 10	25 520
I. Abt. (Panther)	27 732
II. Abt. (Pz. IV, Sturmgeschütze)	26 006
SS-Panzerjäger-Abteilung 10	29 343
SS-Panzer-Aufklärungs-Abteilung 10	29 022
SS-Panzer-Artillerie-Regiment 10	26 606
I. Abt.	27 311
II. Abt.	25 836
III. Abt.	22 513
SS-Flak-Abteilung 10	27 480
SS-Panzer-Pionier-Bataillon 10	28 028
SS-Panzer-Nachrichten-Abteilung 10	45 215
SS-Sanitäts-Abteilung 10	15 407
SS-Wirtschafts-Bataillon 10	27 654
SS-Divisions-Nachschubtruppen 10	27 654
SS-Feld-Ersatz-Bataillon 10	57 815

Kommandeure:

01/1943-11/1943	SS-Gruppenführer Debes
11/1943-04/1944	SS-Brigadeführer von Treuenfeld
04/1944-04/1945	SS-Brigadeführer Harmel
04/1945-05/1945	SS-Obersturmbannführer Roestel

12. SS-Panzer-Division Hitlerjugend

Feldpostnummern:

Divisionsstab	59 900
SS-Panzergrenadier-Regiment 25	56 840
I. Bataillon	58 048
II. Bataillon	56 377
III. Bataillon	59 601
SS-Panzergrenadier-Regiment 26	58 077
I. Bataillon	57 403
II. Bataillon	59 760
III. Bataillon	56 804
SS-Panzer-Artillerie-Regiment 12	59 611
I. Abteilungen	56 762
II. Abteilung	58 343
III. Abteilung	57 766
SS-Panzer-Flak-Abteilung 12	59 572
SS-Panzer-Regiment 12	59 230
I. Abteilung	59 043
II. Abteilung	58 696
SS-Panzer-Nachrichten-Abteilung 12	57 824
SS-Panzer-Aufklärungs-Abteilung 12	58 286
SS-Panzerjäger-Abteilung 12	59 805
SS-Panzer-Pionier-Bataillon 12	58 497
SS-Feldersatz-Bataillon 12	59 805
SS-Werfer-Abteilung 12	10 443

Kommandeure:

06/1943-06/1944	*SS-Brigadeführer* Witt
06/1944-09/1944	*SS-Oberführer* Kurt Meyer
10/1944-11/1944	*SS-Brigadeführer* Kraemer
11/1944-05/1945	*SS-Oberführer* Kraas

Comparison of Ranks

German rank	Rank of foreign members**	Heer	
SS-Grenadier [SS-Infantry rifleman]	*Waffen-Grenadier*	*Grenadier*	Infantryman
SS-Sturmmann [SS-Stormtrooper private first class]	*Waffen-Sturmmann*	*Gefreiter*	Acting Corporal or Private
SS-Rottenführer [SS-Corporal]	*Waffen-Rottenführer*	*Obergefreiter*	Corporal
SS-Unterscharführer [Junior Squad Leader/Sergeant]	*Waffen-Unterscharführer*	*Unteroffizier*	Sergeant
SS-Scharführer [SS-Squad Leader/rank between Sergeant and Corporal]	*Waffen-Scharführer*	*Unterfeldwebel*	Staff Sergeant
SS-Oberscharführer [SS-First Sergeant]	*Waffen-Oberscharführer*	*Feldwebel*	Technical Sergeant
SS-Hauptscharführer [SS-Master Sergeant]	*Waffen-Hauptscharführer*	*Oberfeldwebel*	Master Sergeant
SS-Untersturmführer [SS-Second Lieutenant]	*Waffen-Untersturmführer*	*Leutnant*	Second Lieutenant
SS-Obersturmführer [SS-First Lieutenant]	*Waffen-Obersturmführer*	*Oberleutnant*	First Lieutenant
SS-Hauptsturmführer [SS-Captain]	*Waffen-Hauptsturmführer*	*Hauptmann*	Captain
SS-Sturmbannführer [SS-Major]	*Waffen-Sturmbannführer*	*Major*	Major
SS-Obersturmbannführer [SS-Lieutenant Colonel]	*Waffen-Obersturmbannführe*	*Oberstleutnant*	Lieutenant Colonel
SS-Standartenführer [SS-Colonel]	*Waffen-Standartenführer*	*Oberst*	Colonel
SS-Oberführer [SS-"Senior Colonel"]	*Waffen-Oberführer*	No comparable rank	
SS-Brigadeführer [SS-Brigadier General]	*Waffen-Brigadeführer*	*Generalmajor*	Brigadier General
SS-Gruppenführer [SS-Major General]	*Waffen-Gruppenführer*	*Generalleutnant*	Major General
SS-Obergruppenführer [SS-Lieutenant General]	*Waffen-Obergruppenführer*	*General*	Lieutenant General
SS-Oberstgruppenführer [SS-General]		*Generaloberst*	Full General

** "Waffen" was substituted for "SS" before the rank.

Order of Battle
Panzer-Division 43

Authorized strength: approx. 14,000 men
Divisionsstab
2 Panzergrenadier-Regimenter (of which one armored Bataillon)
Bataillon (1.-3. Panzergrenadier- and 4. (schwere) Kompanie)
Bataillon (5.-7. Panzergrenadier- and 8. (schwere) Kompanie)
Bataillon (9.-11. Panzergrenadier- and 12. (schwere) Kompanie) Panzer-Regiment
Abteilung (1.- 4. Kompanie (a 22 Panzer V Panther)) XXX check ‚a 22‘
Abteilung (5.-6. Kompanie (a 22 Panzer IV)) Panzer-Artillerie-Regiment (mot.)
Abteilung (1.-2. Batterie mit Feldhaubitzen 10,5 cm (Sf.) Wespe u.
Batterie mit Feldhaubitzen 15 cm (Sf.) Hummel)
Abteilung (4.-5. Batterie mit Feldhaubitzen 15 cm mot. Z.)
Abteilung (6.-7. Batterie mit Feldhaubitzen 15 cm (mot. Z.) und
Batterie mit Feldkanonen 10 cm) Panzer-Aufklarungs-Abteilung
1 Panzerspähwagen-Kompanien 3 Kompanien (Kräder und Volkswagen)
1 schwere (Schützenpanzerwagen) Kompanie Panzerjäger-Abteilung (Sfl.) mit 3 Kompanien (a14 Pak 7,5 cm)
Flak-Abteilung (mot. Z.)
1 Batterie (12 Flak 2 cm)
1 Batterie (9 Flak 3,7 cm)
Batterie (4 Flak 8,8 cm)
Panzer-Pionier-Bataillon
Kompanien (mot.)
1 Kompanie (gepanzert)
Panzer-Nachrichten-Abteilung
1 Kompanie (Fernsprecher)
Kompanie (Funker)
Feldersatz-Bataillon mit 5 Kompanien Nachschubtruppen (mot.)
Werkstatt-Kompanie
Nachschub-Kompanie
Kraftfahr-Kompanien
große Kraftwagen-Kolonnen
Betriebsstoff-Kolonnen Verwaltungstruppe
1 Verwaltungs-Kompanie
Bäckerei-Kompanie
Schlächterei-Kompanie Sanitäts-Abteilung (mot.)
Sanitäts-Kompanien
Krankenkraftwagen-Züge

Panzer-Division 44

Based on the new guidelines of the OKH, on June 2, 1944, the SS-FHA announced new organization for Panzer-Divisionen 44. Compared to Panzer Division 43, the number of Panzerjäger-Kompanie was reduced from 22 to 17. This meant, on the one hand, a savings of 40 Panzer – on the other side, of course, a serious weakening of the fighting strength of a Panzer-Division. Furthermore, the Panzergrenadier-Regimenter were reduced to two Bataillonen each. The Panzerjäger-Abteilungen were to consist of two companies of assault guns and a company of 7.5 cm Pak (Sf.) Fahrgestell XX.

Panzer-Division 45

Authorized strength: approx. 10,000 men
Overall, the authorization for a Panzer Division 45 provided:
54 Panzer IV or V Panther
Jagdpanzer Hetzer
90 Schützenpanzer
Divisionsstab
2 Grenadier-Regimenter
Bataillon (1.-3. Schützen- and 4. (schwere) Kompanie)
Bataillon (5.-7. Schützen- and 8. (schwere) Kompanie) combined Panzer-Regiment
(Panzer-) Abteilung with
1.-4. Kompanie (Panzer IV or V Panther)
Kompanie (Flak 3.7 cm and 2 cm four-barrelled)
(Panzergrenadier-) Bataillon with
1-3 Panzergrenadier- and 4 (schwere) Kompanie
Panzer-Artillerie-Regiment (mot.)
Abteilung (Sf.XX Selbstfahrlafette self-propelled chassis) with 1.- 2. Batterie Feldhaubitzen 10,5 cm (Sf.) Wespe Selbstfahrlafette
Batterie Feldhaubitzen 15 cm (Sf.) Hummel
Abteilung (mot. Z.) mit 4.-5. Batterie Feldhaubitzen 15 cm
Abteilung (mot. Z.) mit 6.-7. Batterie Feldhaubitzen 15 cm
Batterie Feldkanone 10 cm
Panzer-Aufklärungs-Abteilung
1 Panzerspähwagen-Kompanien
Kompanien (Kräder und Volkswagen)
1 schwere (Schützenpanzerwagen) Kompanie Panzerjäger-Abteilung (Sf.) mit 3 Kompanien (a 14 Pak 7,5 cm)
Flak-Abteilung (mot. Z.)
1 Batterie (12 Flak 2 cm)
1 Batterie (9 Flak 3,7 cm)
Batterie (4 Flak 8,8 cm)
Panzer-Pionier-Bataillon mit 2 Kompanien (mot.) und 1 Kompanie (gepanzert)
Panzer-Nachrichten-Abteilung
Panzer-Aufklärungs-Abteilung
Panzerspäh-Kompanien 1 Volkswagen-Kompanie
schwere Kompanie gemischte Panzerjäger-Abteilung
Kompanien Jagdpanzer Hetzer
1 Kompanie (Schützenpanzerwagen)
Flak-Abteilung (mot. Z.)
1 Batterie (12 Flak 2 cm)
1 Batterie (9 Flak 3,7 cm)

1 Batterie (4 Flak 8,8 cm)
Panzer-Pionier-Bataillon mit 1 Kompanie (mot.) und 1 Kompanie (gepanzert) Panzer-Nachrichten-Abteilung
1 Kompanie (Fernsprecher)
1 Kompanie (Funker)
Feldersatz-Bataillon mit 5 Kompanien Nachschubtruppen (mot.)
1 Kraftfahr-Kompanie
kleine Nachschub-Kolonnen Kraftfahrparktruppen mit 2 Werkstatt-Kompanien (mot.)
Verwaltungstruppe mit 1 Verwaltungs-Kompanie
Sanitätstruppe (mot.) mit 1 Sanitäts- und 1 Krankenkraftwagen-Kompanie

Selected Sources and Literature

Bundesarchiv Berlin: Bundesarchiv/
Militärarchiv Freiburg: Bundesarchiv Koblenz:
Zentrale Stelle der Landesjustizverwaltungen Ludwigsburg:
various personal records
Files of the army groups and armies
Aktenbestand Reichsführer-SS File collection Reichsführer-SSAktenbestand
Various investigations and case files
Forschungsstelle für Zeitgeschichte (Hrsg.): Der Dienstkalender Heinrich HimmlersResearch Centre for Contemporary History (ed.): The service calendar Heinrich Himmler
1941/42, Hamburg 1999 Frießner, Hans: Verlorene Schlachten, Hamburg 1956 Hausser, Paul: Soldaten wie andere auch, Osnabrück 1966
Krätschmer, Emst-Günther: Die Ritterkreuzträger der Waffen-SS, Pr. Oldendorf 1982
Manstein von, Erich: Verlorene Siege, München 1979
Michaelis, Rolf: Die Waffen-SS-Mythos und Wirklichkeit, Berlin 2006
Preradovich von, Nikolaus: Die Generale der Waffen-SS, Berg 1985
Reitlinger, Gerald: Die SS-Tragödie einer deutschen Epoche, München 1957
Schramm, Percy (Hrsg.): Kriegstagebuch des OKW, München 1982
Stein, Georg: Geschichte der Waffen-SS, Düsseldorf 1967
Wegner, Bernd: Hitlers politische Soldaten, Paderborn 1982
ohne: Die Wehrmachtberichte 1939-1945, München 1985